JAMES

A Bible Commentary in the Wesleyan Tradition

J. MICHAEL WALTERS

General Publisher: Nathan Birky
General Director: Ray E. Barnwell
Managing Editor: Russell Gunsalus
Senior Editor: David Higle
Editor: Kelly Trennepohl
Editorial Assistant: Gail Whitmire

CONTENTS

EDITOR'S PREFACE

This book is part of a series of commentaries seeking to interpret the books of the Bible from a Wesleyan perspective. It is designed primarily for lay people, especially teachers of Sunday school and leaders of Bible studies. Pastors will also find this series very helpful. In addition, this series is also for people who want to read and study on their own for spiritual edification.

Each book of the Bible will be explained paragraph by paragraph. This "wide-angle lens" approach helps the reader to follow the primary flow of thought in each passage. This, in turn, will help the reader to avoid "missing the forest because of the trees," a problem many people encounter when reading commentaries.

At the same time, the authors slow down often to examine particular details and concepts that are important for understanding the bigger picture. Where there are alternative understandings of key passages, the authors acknowledge these so the reader will experience a broader knowledge of the various theological traditions and how the Wesleyan perspective relates to them.

These commentaries follow the New International Version and are intended to be read with your Bible open. With this in mind, the biblical text is not reproduced in full, but appears in bold type throughout the discussion of each passage. Greater insight will be gained by reading along in your Bible as you read the commentaries.

These volumes do not replace the valuable technical commentaries that offer in-depth grammatical and textual analysis. What they do offer is an interpretation of the Bible that we hope will lead to a greater understanding of what the Bible says, its significance for our lives today, and further transformation into the image of Christ.

David A. Higle
Senior Editor

AUTHOR'S PREFACE

Soft commitment!" That was how a group of two dozen pastors responded when I asked them to tell me the biggest problems they face in pastoral ministry. Pressing them to define what they meant, they used words like "halfhearted," "shallow spirituality" and "lack of submission." They spoke of the desperate need to take people beyond the surface-level spirituality of popular religious culture into the deeper waters of total surrender. They spoke of the need for integrity and authenticity in the daily lives of professing Christians. Over the past several months of intensive study in the book of James, I have thought often of those faithful pastors and have realized anew the absolute relevance of James's epistle.

In an "image is everything" world, James's message is for Christians to "get real!" The virtual spirituality that plagues much of the North American church is not capable of sustaining vital religion in an increasingly hostile culture. James's call to authentic faith—what I have termed "true religion" throughout this commentary—is a call to arms for every pastor, teacher and disciple of our day. As one who has spent nearly twenty years in pastoral ministry, I have found a new ally in the call to total surrender to God, and his name is James, the servant and half brother of Jesus.

Truth be told, the book of James never would have been my first choice about which to write a commentary. Like many others, I viewed James as a loosely structured letter, filled with wise counsel, but difficult to grasp because of the lack of unity and an overall purpose. But the last few months have changed my perspective on this epistle. I have gone from viewing it as a somewhat disjointed group of random sayings to seeing it as the impassioned cry of a real pastor's heart. Like all good pastors, James knows his sheep, and he lovingly but firmly calls them back to the place of vital spirituality. Here is an epistle that makes the Wesleyan call to full surrender and a holy life, filled with the fruits of righteousness, shine like a laser, piercing the darkness of space.

My approach to the interpretation and application of this letter is primarily from pastoral concerns and a shepherd's interest in the growth of believers and the unity of the church. I have attempted to portray the Epistle of James as a unified treatise written by a pastor-leader worried about the problems that threaten to divide and undermine the Jewish-Christian communities he so loves. I have tried to emphasize several noteworthy characteristics of James's writing.

First, James uses colorful words in the Greek language to express himself. Many of those words are found nowhere else in the New Testament. I have attempted to cite the richness of those terms where helpful, without bogging readers down with linguistic details.

Second, I wanted to portray the "Jewishness" of the Epistle of James. It is certainly the most Jewish book of the New Testament, with the possible exception of Matthew's gospel. I have allowed that to come through, particularly in regard to the author's use of the Old Testament. He is steeped in the Torah and the Wisdom writings of his spiritual forebears, and his own letter is the richer for it.

Third, I have given much attention to James's usage of the teachings of Jesus, his half brother. The sayings of Jesus, particularly from the book of Matthew, would seem to underlie much of the teachings of this letter. This sets James's epistle apart from other New Testament books in ways which are addressed in this commentary.

Finally, I have attempted to place James's words within the broader context of New Testament teaching in general. Historically, this epistle often has been treated as something of a "black sheep" among the New Testament books. I have taken the opportunity to show how similar James's teachings are to those of other New Testament writers—notably Paul, Peter and John.

As one schooled primarily in the tasks and disciplines of parish ministry, I cannot claim scholarly insight or novel interpretations likely to spawn deep study by students of the New Testament. But I have worked with people as their pastor, spiritual guide and mentor, and I have found in James a pastor's heart of great conviction and deep compassion. His single-minded approach to practical faith is something I can recommend to all who seek the ways of authenticity. But beware the quick fix!

The journey to true religion is the journey of a lifetime. James cautions us against trying to find shortcuts. God's ways are the ways of endurance, obedience, and even brokenness. Working with the words of this short letter has been a powerful tool in God's hands to further the progress of my own spiritual journey. As I endeavor to become that real person God desires all of us to be, James's call to practical holiness has been imminently personal and transforming. It is through the reminders of Abraham's genuine faith, Job's patient trust, and Elijah's powerful and righteous prayers that James would call all of us onward in our daily quest to become authentic.

Special thanks to The Wesleyan Church for undertaking this series. To be part of a church body that genuinely cares about authenticity in spiritual life and putting God's Word into the hands of its people is a privilege. Thanks also to Dave Higle for his patient editorial assistance and encouragement through this project. Thanks to my beloved wife, daughter, and son—Nancy, Jennifer, and Joshua—who supported me through many hours of absence from them so that this work could be finished. And thanks most of all to the God and Father of our Lord Jesus Christ, who poured His Spirit into men like James so that all of us might be encouraged in the ways of wisdom and true religion.

J. Michael Walters
Houghton, New York
Lent, 1996

INTRODUCTION

The world of religious faith is a world filled with possibilities for good and evil. On one hand, authentic religious faith is considered by its adherents to be the most important element in their lives. It serves as an anchor of stability within the rapidly changing scenes of life.

On the other hand, few aspects of human experience are as prone to being counterfeit and downright phony as is religious faith. If people so desire, they can adopt certain marks of religion and be thought righteous by many around them without experiencing any of the moral transformation that is normally associated with religious practice. In such a case, the real aim of authentic faith has been supplanted by a kind of surface-level "religiosity"—an outward "faith"—that never accomplishes its inner, transforming purpose.

This was the kind of world to which the letter of James was written. The people of James's day had become satisfied with certain outward marks of religion that failed to penetrate the ultimate target of Christian faith—their hearts. The result of such religiosity is a fractured, fragile Christian community confronted with a multitude of issues that threaten to disrupt and destroy. The only hope for such people is a recovery of authenticity in their faith practices and the total commitment of their hearts to God. That is the fundamental intent of this short letter. James means to call his readers home. They need to turn away from the popular forms of shallow faith and return to the ways of "true religion."

The Epistle of James is a commentary on our times. We live in a day where religion is approved—but only up to a point. There is a certain amount of affirmation given to people who profess to believe specific truths or tenets of the faith. It is culturally acceptable to be involved in religion, as long as one doesn't go too far. Large percentages of the North American public indicate their continued belief in God, in prayer, even in the importance of being "born again." However, there is an ever-widening gap between religious profession and religious practice.

This has resulted in a situation very similar to the days in which James wrote his epistle. We see widespread profession of religion with little

11

corresponding practice of religion. We are living in the days of "virtual Christianity."

Christianity for many is simply a matter of believing certain things quite apart from any real or lasting effect on the rest of life. Our shallow approach to faith has led to the ironic state where more people than ever are professing religion while the culture around us becomes less hospitable to religion all the time. James's words are a needed antidote to the spiritual malaise of our own day. He champions the cause of true religion as opposed to the empty hype of pretend religion. His words call the believer back to the practice of wholehearted spirituality that has characterized the authentic people of God from the beginning.

James has gained a well-deserved reputation across the years for presenting a no-nonsense approach to Christianity. He has little patience with the posturing and pretense of shallow faith. He minces no words as he calls his readers (and all of us as well) back to the foundations of an authentic, biblical faith—something he calls "pure" religion (Jas. 1:27).

This commentary is written from the viewpoint that pure religion, or what is termed in these pages "true religion," is the major focus of the epistle. The following comments are designed to acquaint the reader with author, text, and circumstances of writing so that the letter itself can be read with understanding and appreciation.

AUTHORSHIP OF THE EPISTLE OF JAMES

While the author of the epistle identifies himself in the first verse as James, it remains to be seen just who this James really is. For there are three men named James mentioned in Scripture who could have authored the letter.

Most initial attention would obviously center on James the son of Zebedee and brother of John the Beloved Apostle. This James, along with his brother and Peter, comprised the inner circle of Jesus' disciples and thus would have been intimately acquainted with the teachings of the Lord. That fits well with the Epistle of James since it leans so heavily on the teachings of Jesus. But the problem with assigning authorship to this James is that the son of Zebedee is commonly thought to have died somewhere between A.D. 41 to 44— executed by Herod Agrippa I (see Acts 12:1-2). This would necessitate dating the epistle earlier than even the first missionary journey of Paul, a theory which has little, if any, support. This dating problem would eliminate the well-known disciple of Jesus as the author.

But Jesus had another disciple named James. He was James, son of Alphaeus. The problem with ascribing the authorship of the epistle to this man is that he is such an anonymous member of the disciples. The opening verse of the letter says simply, "James, a servant of God and of the Lord Jesus Christ, To the twelve tribes scattered among the nations: Greetings." A nearly anonymous apostle could never get away with an introduction that brief.

That leaves one other James from the New Testament, and all signs point to James the half brother of Jesus as being the author of this letter. Besides the interest in James's relationship with Jesus, the epistle's authorship is all the more intriguing because the New Testament portrays Jesus' own family as fairly skeptical of Him (see John 7:1-5). We're not told whether they were present for His miracles or not, but we can say that it was more difficult for them to come to faith in Him than for many of the others. Anyone who has had a "famous" relative would likely understand why.

At some point, this situation obviously changed, although we're not told under what circumstances it happened. It is possible that just as Mary—Jesus' mother—was present for the Crucifixion, so also the siblings of Jesus, including James, were somewhere in the vicinity. That powerful scene at Calvary may have been the turning point in James's faith. But at least one New Testament scholar suggests that the turning point is to be found in Paul's assertion in 1 Corinthians 15:7 of the resurrected Jesus' appearing to James.[1]

We can only wonder what such an encounter between the risen Christ and His unbelieving half brother might have involved, but if James's conversion took place at that point, it's not hard to imagine why. We know from Acts 1:14 that the brothers of Jesus were among those who were gathered in the Upper Room prior to Pentecost, so James was certainly part of the group of believers by that time.[2]

Some have argued that the style and language of the letter are far beyond the capabilities of an unlearned peasant. But that argument is countered by the presence of some obviously awkward uses of language.[3] A person with great linguistic skill surely would have smoothed over such lapses. Further, a look at the social milieu of first-century Jerusalem is enough to explain how James became acquainted with the Greek language and its ideas. Others have cited the absence of emphasis upon Jewish ritual and legalism as evidence that someone other than the brother of Jesus wrote this letter. But there is no evidence to suggest that James the Just was ever characterized by the legalism that was so common among the Jews in general.

THE ROLE OF JAMES IN THE LIFE OF THE CHURCH

The combination of James's blood relationship to Jesus, along with the apparent depth of his conversion, enabled him to rise quickly to a place of prominence in the early church. One commentator even suggests that James may have had something more going for him in terms of physically resembling the earthly Jesus.[4] While this is mere speculation, it is beyond question that something led to James's rapid ascent into leadership.

Some of the writings of the early church fathers suggest that Jesus himself may have designated James as a leader. For example, the Gospel of Thomas, a second-century work, contains the following verse: "The disciples said to Jesus, 'We know that you will leave us. Who is he who will be great over us?' Jesus said to them, 'In the place to which you come, you will go to James the Just, for whose sake heaven and earth were made.'"[5] Jewish tradition held that heaven and earth were made for the sake of righteous Israelites. Even given the fact that the Gospel of Thomas is not part of the Bible, it still represents an early source testifying to the elevation of James as a leader.

Clement of Alexandria, a second-century church leader, wrote, "Peter and James and John, after the Savior's ascension, though preeminently honored by the Lord, did not contend for glory, but made James the Just Bishop of Jerusalem."[6] The name "James the Just" seems to be an acknowledgment of the deep righteousness that characterized this man and likely contributed greatly to his stature as a leader. Another early church historian reported of James that his knees became "hard like those of a camel because of his continuance in prayer."[7]

Several verses in the book of Acts demonstrate James's standing with the church. Acts 12:17, which tells of Peter's release from prison, says, "Peter motioned with his hand for them to be quiet and described how the Lord had brought him out of prison. 'Tell James and the brothers about this,' he said, and then he left for another place." James's leadership role at the crucial council in Jerusalem in Acts 15 underscores his position as the leader of the church. And Acts 21:18-19 demonstrates Paul's sense of James's standing: "The next day Paul and the rest of us went to see James, and all the elders were present. Paul greeted them and reported in detail what God had done among the Gentiles through his ministry."

Actually, Paul bore an even earlier witness to James's leadership in his letter to the Galatians, where Paul spoke of having gone "to Jerusalem to get acquainted with Peter and stayed with him fifteen days. I saw none of the other apostles—only James, the Lord's brother" (Gal. 1:18-19). Galatians is likely an earlier book than Acts, so this places James's leadership well within the time frame necessary to have him as the author of the epistle bearing the same name.

Perhaps more significant is the inference from this passage that James was considered an apostle! Peter, who himself was the "rock" upon whom some believed Jesus would build His church, is not the first acclaimed leader of the early church—it is James. He who had not even been a disciple of Jesus during His earthly ministry was soon the unquestioned leader of the church in Jerusalem.

Tradition has it that unlike the other disciples who had itinerant ministries, James stayed put in Jerusalem, which doubtless increased his leadership profile. The fact that James's authority was widely recognized is borne out by the introduction of the epistle that has no authoritarian appeal whatsoever. Even Paul felt the need to assert his apostolic status in his letters. James did not.

However it came about, James was the unquestioned leader of the church in Jerusalem, remaining there until the late 50s of the first century. What happened to him next is mostly conjecture. James is variously described by different sources to have been beheaded or stoned or thrown from the Temple and then stoned, then beaten to death with a club, all around the period of A.D. 62 to 63. Josephus, the Jewish historian of the first century, contends that James's death was primarily at the instigation of Ananus the High Priest.[8]

According to this account, Ananus was a member of the Sadducees, the wealthy upper class of Judaism.[9] He and his fellow Sadducees in the Sanhedrin were angry over James's public support for the poor, along with his willingness to criticize the wealthy (see comments on James 5:1-6). The decade of the 50s was particularly difficult for the region around Jerusalem. There appear to have been a number of small uprisings by the dissatisfied peasants against the wealthy (see comments on 5:7-11).

With James's public outcry against the rich and his emphasis on the judgment coming to those who exploit the poor, it's clear that James made himself some powerful enemies. The widely held belief that he was martyred for his stand, regardless of the debate over the exact method, is virtually indisputable. Tradition has it that a brother of Jesus named Symeon was chosen to succeed James, but the Jerusalem church fled the Roman armies in A.D. 66 and never again had the prominence it had under James's leadership.[10]

DATE OF WRITING

Dating the book of James depends upon one's view of authorship. For those who consider this the work of James the Just, an early date—perhaps as early as the late 40s—must be assigned much of the material. For one thing, the kinds of problems cited in the church by James certainly could have appeared in Jerusalem and elsewhere by this time. That there is no hint of early divisions between Christians and Jews also argues for an early date of writing.[11] Although some would argue that this epistle is the first actual book of the New Testament to appear in writing, assigning it a date of around A.D. 45, little can be said with certainty about the date. It is best to consider the letter to have been written somewhere between the late 40s and James's martyrdom in A.D. 62.

BACKGROUND AND THEMES OF THE EPISTLE OF JAMES

To discover the background of any writing, one needs to answer the question, "Why was this written?" That can be a difficult task under the best of circumstances, but with the Epistle of James it is particularly complex. James is grouped with those New Testament books known as General Epistles.[12]

Determining the reason behind James's letter then becomes extremely difficult. For example, in the Corinthian letters, we can examine other pieces of data from the history, geography and literature of Corinth. But with James we have no such luxury. Thus there has been much debate about the exact circumstances that surrounded this writing.

Taking seriously James's position as leader of the Jewish-Christian community and the different indications in the letter that he is writing to Jewish believers, it is possible to construct something of the circumstances that prompted this epistle. Certainly the overall "Jewishness" of the letter is striking and has to be considered in any interpretation of it. James talks to his readers as to people who would know the Old Testament and the teachings of Jesus. He assumes they have that kind of knowledge. In the classic Jewish way of emphasizing the practicalities of faith, James's letter can be viewed essentially as ethical teaching or practical instruction on how to live as Christians. The author is greatly concerned by the kinds of problems facing the Christian community—problems that appear to indicate a fairly shallow approach to the practice of religion.

Specifically, James was confronted with a situation that centered around increasing tensions between the rich and poor. On one hand, there were the poor (along with the messianic priests) who comprised the majority of the church members. On the other hand, there were members of the aristocratic classes, particularly people who came into the church as members of the Jewish party, known as the Sadducees. The Sadducees were traditionally the wealthy and socially elite of the Jewish faith. There also may have been present within these churches members of the Jewish party of Zealots. These people agitated rebellion against the Romans and, significantly, had a long history of hatred toward the richer Jewish classes. The combination of Zealots and Sadducees was a most volatile mixture.

In addition, the appeal of Christianity to the poor, the morally unacceptable, and other social outcasts made some form of social conflict with the upper classes virtually inevitable. James was thus faced with the task of speaking to the issues of rich versus poor in a way that promoted peace and understanding rather than violence and class warfare.

It is not clear whether James was speaking to the situation in the Jerusalem area churches or to churches scattered more extensively throughout Palestine and even Syria. Both views have their proponents, but either would support the essential purpose outlined above. We know that the Jerusalem church was affected by extreme poverty. Paul's letters and the book of Acts refer to an offering being collected in the Gentile churches to help the poor saints in Jerusalem. The city of Jerusalem itself had experienced bad times, the decade of the 40s producing a series of famines.

Following the death of Herod Agrippa I in A.D. 44, Palestine suffered from a string of inept Roman leaders. This led to general unrest among the populace and brought about several "mini-rebellions" by the Jews. At this time, the Christian church was viewed by the Romans as just another party within Judaism, so the pressure of Roman disapproval combined with the overall dire economic outlook made for difficult times.[13]

The church at this point had become primarily a community of the poor. And, as we know, poverty has a way of making problems involving wealth seem bigger than they are. In addition, it appears from the epistle (see 2:1-13) that there was some discrimination against the poor within the churches. James is clearly aiming at this form of pandering to the wealthy in the letter, denouncing it as a form of compromise with the world. To fail in basic Christian charity toward one another is to undermine any profession of faith. So James warns against the temptation on the part of the poor to try to attain wealth, either through

17

compromise or taking matters into their own hands in rebellion. Instead, James counsels the believers to put away their double-minded approach to religion and to wholeheartedly trust God, who will make things right in His own way and in His own time.

The Epistle of James is written to address the needs of the community more than those of individual believers. Certainly much of what James writes has individual applications, but the letter must be read as the attempt of this concerned apostle to preserve the unity and harmony of his churches. The problems addressed in the letter are the kinds of problems that make communities disintegrate. James's primary concern is to prevent that from happening. He offers the everyday practice of true religion as the best means of preventing such destruction.

James concerns himself with the practicalities of righteousness. He stresses authenticity in matters of faith and practice. As Jesus said in the Sermon on the Mount, appearances do not count for much. James urges his readers to actually *be* what they claim to be. This is accomplished by doing what God commands. While James's emphasis on "deeds" has caused him some difficulty with theologians across the years, his words serve as a most relevant antidote to today's hypocritical culture. He stresses the truth that God, who has given us birth through the Word, actually expects our lives to mirror that reality. James believes in holiness of life and heart.

He explodes the myth of so-called "success theology" which equates the blessing of God with material plenty.[14] He teaches us that authentic faith is likely to be greeted with poverty, suffering and severe trials in the present world. But James doesn't leave us in the present world. His letter is filled with the hope of the coming Judge. With only one other exception (the book of 1 Enoch, a nonbiblical Jewish writing), Jesus and James alone pronounce woe on the rich.[15] The present circumstances are part of the test of our faith to determine its authenticity and to enable us to mature and grow in Christ.

So we look at this letter as a writing addressed to the believing communities, the majority of whom are suffering from grinding poverty and hostile environments. We see James as a Jewish-Christian leader caught in a delicate position. He has firmly allied himself with the poor, declaring his and God's sympathy for their plight. He wants the wealthy to soberly consider the eternal implications of materialism. On the other hand, James is adamantly opposed to actions which would pit the rich against the poor in some kind of class warfare. He thus warns against trying to do God's work for Him and counsels patient trust on the part of the churches.

James is against favoritism of any sort, condemning it in the lives of the wealthy and in the courts. But he is equally opposed to double-mindedness, which typically involves failure to trust God and instead takes matters into one's own hands. James's hopes are firmly resting in the coming of the Righteous Judge.

The Epistle of James is written against the backdrop of extremely sensitive social issues that plague the modern church in every case. That's one of the great appeals of this small letter. James represents a socially sensitive conscience that parallels that of John Wesley (see later comments in the introduction).

Like Wesley in his day, James champions the cause of the economically disadvantaged who are victimized by oppression and injustice. He speaks up for the widows and orphans, who have no legal voice of their own. He presses the claims of biblical justice against the rich and unconcerned. He calls the bluff of any who claim the mantle of religious faith but whose lives fall short in living it out. James fearlessly confronts the hypocrisy and pretense of his own day, and in so doing confronts those of the modern church as well.

CHARACTERISTICS OF THE EPISTLE OF JAMES

Although one of the shorter books of the New Testament (with 108 verses), James's epistle has several noteworthy characteristics.[16]

First, this epistle has a clear, authoritative tone. From beginning to end, the author expects to be taken seriously. One scholar has calculated the presence of over fifty imperatives or commands in this short letter.[17] This indicates a person who knows he is speaking with great authority and who also demonstrates a good deal of pastoral concern.

Second, the epistle is noteworthy for the absence of Christian doctrine. This is what troubled Luther and other figures in church history. For example, there is nothing in the epistle about the death and resurrection of Jesus. James seems content to assume that his readers already know the teachings of the church but need to assimilate and practice those teachings in their lives.

Third, James is exceptionally practical in his approach. Practical religion is what James is best known for among Christians. He seems disinterested in the theoretical aspects of religion, but he is passionate about what works—about what is genuine. He wants to present the faith to his readers as a good way to live. This is why James emphasizes the importance of obedience—of being a doer of the Word and not a hearer only.

Fourth, the Epistle of James is notably impersonal. There are no personal names used in the letter—no indications given that would help to identify the original readers in any way. Yet, the author knows these people well enough to call them "brothers" throughout the letter, and to reveal himself simply as "James, a servant of God and of the Lord Jesus Christ."

Fifth, there is a high appreciation of nature in the book. James uses illustrations from agriculture, the weather, the oceans and other natural settings. As a result, the epistle is often linked with the Wisdom Literature of the Old Testament, which is noteworthy for its emphasis on the wonders of creation as signs of God's majesty and greatness.[18]

Sixth, the teachings of James bear a marked similarity to the teachings of Jesus, particularly those of the Sermon on the Mount. This characteristic is significant enough to merit special treatment (see additional notes on James and the New Testament at the end of chapter 6 of the commentary), but a remark by D. A. Hayes summarizes well this important characteristic of James's writing: "James says less about the Master than any other writer in the New Testament, but his speech is more like that of the Master than the speech of any one of them."[19]

Seventh, James's writing bears marked similarities to the Wisdom writings of Old Testament Israel, as noted above. James shares certain characteristics with these Old Testament books, including Proverbs, Job, Ecclesiastes, and Song of Songs. These common characteristics will be discussed in more detail.

Finally, the epistle was written in the Greek language in a style that represents some of the highest quality Greek in the New Testament. As was stated earlier, this often has been used to cast doubt on the authorship of James, the half brother of Jesus. But such criticisms often represent our own cultural biases as much as any genuine evidence supporting such views.

The cosmopolitan, world-class atmosphere of the city of Jerusalem, considered along with the fact that Greek was the language of the marketplace in first-century Palestine, can explain most, if not all, of the questions dealing with style. In addition, some believe that like Paul, James may have employed the use of a secretary to write down what he dictated. The use of a secretary—known as an amanuensis—to write the manuscript could also explain the high quality of the letter.

STRUCTURE OF THE EPISTLE OF JAMES

For centuries, the conventional approach to the book of James was to view it as a loosely structured collection of ethical sayings. The epistle was often spoken of as a kind of New Testament edition of Proverbs. In the same way that Proverbs seems to move from topic to topic without any necessary correlation to that which precedes, so James was viewed as an effort by its author to share wisdom with his readers over a wide range of topics. The technical term for this kind of literature is "paraenesis," and James was considered a classic example of ethical maxims and exhortations that were without any single unifying theme. That approach to James left readers to interpret the letter according to the individual sayings or groups of sayings apart from any larger purpose on the part of the author.

Happily, that conventional wisdom has been challenged repeatedly over the past several years by notable New Testament authorities.[20] Rather than viewing James as a mere collection of ethical sayings, the letter has more recently been interpreted from the standpoint of the circumstances confronting the leader of the Jewish-Christian communities—the danger of splitting apart into class warfare. This "unified" case for James swings on the hinge of verses 26 and 27 of chapter 1: "If anyone considers himself religious and yet does not keep a tight rein on his tongue, he deceives himself and his religion is worthless. Religion that God our Father accepts as pure and faultless is this: to look after orphans and widows in their distress and to keep oneself from being polluted by the world." In this approach to the epistle, these verses would be viewed as a summary of James's essential message.[21]

The approach of this commentary is to affirm these verses as key to the letter. They identify what is described throughout as "true religion," the unifying theme of James. Specifically, James presents the consistent practice of true religion as the means of experiencing God's blessings, which are not related to material well-being. On the other side, failure to obey and practice the tenets of true religion is to subject oneself—and the Christian community—to the curse of disobedience and, ultimately, to the judgment of God.[22]

Closely related to James's focus on true religion is his concern with the causes that gave rise to this unauthentic religious faith in the first place. The term he uses to describe this condition is "double-minded"—literally, "two-souled." The combination of a halfhearted commitment to God with the presence of human desire—so easily exploited—makes this problem the essential issue to solve in the letter. James 4:1-10 addresses this issue. This commentary views that portion as the climactic point of the entire letter. As long as the double-minded approach to religion is practiced, all other "solutions" to the symptoms of this problem are mere Band-Aids. James seeks to solve the problem by appealing to God's abundant grace and therein provides the theological center of the epistle.

JAMES AND JOHN (WESLEY)

This commentary is part of a series written in the Wesleyan tradition. The message of this book is intended not for promoting sectarian diversity within the church, but for encouraging harmony among all believers. So in that respect, James is in fact a "general epistle."[23] But, at the same time, there are some clear points of identification that this epistle makes with the broader Wesleyan tradition that show James to be a book of significant interest to the sons and daughters of John Wesley.

For one thing, James is the supreme illustration of practical righteousness in the New Testament. The author has no patience for professions of faith that are not backed up by solid lives. This has always been a fundamental concern of the followers of Wesley. John Wesley was most impatient with a "faith" that had no outward manifestations. He was a most practical kind of theologian. It was his practical approach to religion that has made his message so powerful and appealing. "The lure of Wesley is not primarily his theology. That was traditional enough. The contribution of Wesley is in his ability to put theology into Flesh and Blood. . . . Wesley's concern was the relating of God's grace to human experience, theology to religion, logic to life, the church to society."[24]

This practical approach to religion brought charges of "works-righteousness" against Wesley, even as the words of James have sparked similar charges throughout history. Wesley was even accused, on occasion, of being a Roman Catholic because he steadfastly believed in the necessity of good works. He adamantly believed—like James—that religion of the heart was continually demonstrated in one's life. He refused to separate the "fact of faith" from the "fruit of faith." One of his sermons on the subject shows his conviction on this issue.

It has been often objected that religion does not lie in the outward things, but in the heart, the inmost soul; That is in the union of the soul with God, the life of God in the soul of man; that outside religion is nothing worth; seeing God delighteth not in burnt offerings, in outward services, but a pure and holy heart is the sacrifice he will not despise.

I answer, it is most true that the root of religion lies in the heart, in the inmost soul; that this is the union of the life of God in the soul of man. But if this root be really in the heart, it cannot but put forth branches. And these are the several instances of the outward obedience, which partakes of the same nurture with the root; and, consequently, are not only marks or signs, but substantial parts of religion.[25]

These words sound strangely familiar to anyone who has digested the message of James. One of Wesley's clearest and most concise summaries is given under the heading of "true religion" which admittedly influenced the use of those terms in this commentary as the key concept in James's epistle. These words of Wesley wonderfully demonstrate his commitment to a kind of religion that has both the vertical dimensions of one's fellowship with God and the horizontal dimensions of one's fellowship with other human beings:

> True religion is right tempers [we would say "attitudes" or "affections"] towards God and man. It is in two words, gratitude and benevolence; gratitude to our Creator and supreme Benefactor, and benevolence to our fellow-creatures. In other words, it is the loving God with all our heart, and our neighbors as ourselves. It is in consequence of knowing God loves us that we love him, and love our neighbor as ourselves. Gratitude towards our Creator cannot but produce benevolence to our fellow-creatures. The love of Christ constrains us, not only to be "zealous of good works"; "as we have time, to do good unto all men"; "and to be patterns of all true genuine morality; of justice, mercy, and truth." This is religion, and this is happiness; the happiness for which we were made.[26]

It would not be difficult at all to hear James the Just giving a loud and hearty "Amen!" to Wesley's definition of true religion.

Another place of close identification between James's epistle and the Wesleyan tradition would be found in James's social concern, particularly manifested by his identification with the poor. One of the things that made Wesley and his followers controversial was a tendency to get themselves involved in issues often thought to be too controversial for "religious" people. Wesley's support for the poor of his day parallels the support James voices for those oppressed by poverty in his epistle. James's unwillingness to sanction any form of favoritism that discriminated against common people was echoed in Wesley's influential efforts to end slavery in the British Empire and to raise the dignity of the poor all around him. The Wesleyan Church was born in the abolitionist conscience of the early nineteenth century which viewed slavery as an offense to God and a scandal to authentic Christian profession.

The Wesleyan heritage is one of viewing religion to be as wide as human life itself. Therefore, nothing that involves the lives and interests of humankind is off limits to the claims of true religion. James rightly calls our attention to the prophetic aspects of the Christian faith, rooted in the Old Testament notions of justice and mercy. All Christians—and Wesleyans in particular, since it is part of our heritage—need to pay strict attention to the social conscience that James portrays as indispensable to true religion (Jas. 1:27).

Wesley's followers must understand that his struggle, and thus our struggle, was between two equally affirmed theological truths. On one hand, he stood solidly in the line of the Protestant Reformation thinking of justification by faith alone.[27] On the other hand, he was insistent that the righteousness of faith is designed by God to promote actual righteousness in Christian living. Wesley would never, therefore, allow emphasis on justification by faith to weaken his stress on human responsibility in living and acting as recipients of God's amazing grace. That is the conviction of James as well. We are saved for a purpose—a life of righteousness, according to James 1:20—and God's grace is meant to make a difference in the way we treat others. God's people are responsible for making society a better place.

In our current world, Christians are increasingly being told to "keep their religion to themselves." Both James and Wesley would laugh at the utter folly of such an idea. Private religion was as unthinkable to James and to Wesley as "holy adultery." That kind of faith is a contradiction in terms.

Finally, James's epistle is significant for those in the Wesleyan tradition because of his convictions surrounding heart purity. James was convinced that until the divided heart of a person is made whole— "purified," as he puts it in chapter 4 of his epistle—true religion will remain only a theoretical concept and not a powerful reality. Fundamental to the Wesleyan tradition is the belief that God desires all of us, our total selves, to be in surrender to Him. Wesleyans believe that apart from such full surrender, our sinful hearts will continue to divide our loyalties and affections for God. This kind of "religion" can easily become a game one plays on Sundays and at other times when it is convenient. This church is built on Wesley's call to love God "perfectly," that is, with all our heart, soul, mind, and strength.

In portraying the ultimate problem of his readers as one of being double-minded, James helps us to grasp the significance of the Wesleyan emphasis upon full surrender and cleansing of our lives from the power of inbred sin. It might be an exaggeration to say that James makes this case better than any other New Testament writer, but it is not an exaggeration to say that James makes this case very strongly.

So is James the most "Wesleyan" book in the New Testament? The question is not one of significance; Wesley himself was known as a "man of one book." He would never differentiate between the books of Scripture in that way, and neither can we. But in this Epistle of James we find encouragement, reinforcement, and needed corrections in our pursuit as Wesleyans in the call to true religion.

ENDNOTES

[1] F. F. Bruce, *Peter, Stephen, James and John: Studies in Non-Pauline Christianity* (Grand Rapids, Michigan: Wm. B. Eerdmans Publishing Co., 1979), p. 87.

[2] In the New Testament, Pentecost primarily referred to the event when the Holy Spirit was given to the church; this occurred on the Day of Pentecost. The Greek term which *Pentecost* comes from means "fiftieth" or "the fiftieth day," and is literally the fiftieth day after the end of the Passover. It is also known as the Jewish Feast of Weeks. This day is part of the Jewish observances, and was the beginning of the offering of first fruits.

[3] Peter Davids, *James,* New International Bible Commentary (Peabody, Massachusetts: Hendrickson Publishers, Inc., 1983), p. 7.

[4] Stephen Paine, *Studies in the Book of James* (Old Tappan, New Jersey: Fleming H. Revell Co., 1955), p. 14.

[5] Cited in Ralph Martin, *James,* Word Biblical Commentary (Waco, Texas: Word Books, Publisher, 1988), p. xliv.

[6] Cited in Paine, p. 12.

[7] Ibid., pp. 14–15.

[8] Cited in Martin, p. lxiv.

[9] Judaism is the belief and cultural system of the Jewish people, referring to the Jews' way of life as those in a covenant relationship with God, rather than just to their religious doctrine. Judaism in Jesus' day differed according to different sects, and there are still various branches of Judaism today, but the underlying theme among them has been a belief in one God and a recognition of the Law of God. Law here refers to the Pentateuch (the first five books of the Old Testament: Genesis, Exodus, Leviticus, Numbers, and Deuteronomy).

[10]Davids, p. 3.

[11]Simon Kistemaker, *Exposition of the Epistle of James and the Epistles of John* (Grand Rapids, Michigan: Baker Books, 1986), pp. 18–19.

[12]The General Epistles are the books of James; 1 and 2 Peter; 1, 2, and 3 John; and Jude. They are called General Epistles because they are books or letters written to broad groups of people, rather than being addressed to specific individuals or churches the way that, say, Paul's letters to the Corinthians were.

[13]See endnote 9.

[14]Blessings and curses refer to the response of God to His people in accordance with their obedience to Him (blessings) or their disobedience (curses). In the Old Testament, God's power was invoked through power-laden words (blessings and curses) often spoken in prayer form. Through these blessings or curses, God's people would call upon Him to provide or care for them by affecting them in a positive way or those around them in a positive or negative way. In Judaism (see endnote 9), some blessings were reserved for the priests, but others were a regular part of the synagogue services. Curses were much less prominent and were forbidden. In the New Testament, the ultimate blessing came from God to mankind in Jesus Christ, and blessings accompanied righteousness. Curses accompanied sin.

[15]Davids, p. 21.

[16]Much of this material is taken from Everett F. Harrison, *Introduction to the New Testament* (Grand Rapids, Michigan: Wm. B. Eerdmans Publishing Co., 1971), pp. 383–84.

[17]Kistemaker, p. 5.

[18]The Wisdom Literature includes the books of Job, Proverbs, Ecclesiastes, and Song of Songs (Song of Solomon). Also known as the Books of Poetry. These writings are collections of statements of wisdom, often dealing with the great issues of life, such as the problem of suffering, practical ethics and morality, and the meaning of life and love.

[19]Cited in Harrison, p. 384.

[20]See, for example, Davids, Kistemaker and Martin, listed above.

[21]F. O. Francis, "The Form and Function of the Opening and Closing Paragraphs of James and 1 John," cited in Martin, p. xi.

[22]See endnote 14.

[23]See endnote 12.

[24]Mildred Bangs Wynkoop, cited in J. Michael Walters, "The Social Consciousness of John Wesley" (Unpublished Master's Thesis, St. Mary's University, 1979), p. 5.

[25]Cited in Walters, pp. 10–11.

[26]John Wesley, *The Works of John Wesley*, vol. VII (Grand Rapids, Michigan: Zondervan Publishing Co., 1958), p. 269.

[27]The Reformation was a religious movement in the sixteenth century establishing the Protestant church which "protested" against religious abuses at that time. Also called the Protestant Reformation. The beginning of this movement is marked by Martin Luther's nailing of the "Ninety-Five Theses" to the church door at Wittenburg, Germany. This movement rejected or sought to modify some of the practices and doctrine of the Roman Catholic Church.

JAMES OUTLINE

I. THE CALL TO TRUE RELIGION (1:1-27)
  A. Greeting (1:1)
  B. Trials and True Religion (1:2-12)
    1. 1:2-4   Blessing in Trial
    2. 1:5-8   The Problem of Double-Mindedness
    3. 1:9-11   Prosperity and True Religion
    4. 1:12   The Blessing of Perseverance
  C. A Dangerous Deception (1:13-18)
  D. The Nature of True Religion (1:19-27)
    1. 1:19-21 The Goal of True Religion
    2. 1:22-25 The Practice of True Religion
    3. 1:26-27 The Touchstone of True Religion

II. BARRIERS TO TRUE RELIGION (2:1-26)
  A. The Barrier of Favoritism (2:1-13)
  B. The Barrier of Easy Faith (2:14-26)

III. TEACHERS AND TRUE RELIGION (3:1-18)
  A. The Tongue and True Religion (3:1-12)
  B. True Wisdom and True Religion (3:13-18)

IV. THE GREATEST BARRIER TO TRUE RELIGION (4:1-10)
  A. The Problem of Double-Minded Desires (4:1-5)
  B. The Solution to Double-Minded Desires (4:6-10)

V. MORE BARRIERS TO TRUE RELIGION (4:11–5:12)
  A. The Barrier of Judging Others (4:11-12)
  B. The Barrier of Presumption (4:13-17)
  C. The Barrier of Materialism (5:1-6)
    1. 5:1-3   The Foolishness of Materialism
    2. 5:4-6   The Injustice of Materialism
  D. The Barrier of Impatience (5:7-11)
  E. The Barrier of Impiety (5:12)

VI. THE DISPOSITIONS OF TRUE RELIGION (5:13-20)
  A. The Disposition of Authentic Spirituality (5:13-16a)
  B. The Disposition of Righteous Prayer (5:16b-18)
  C. The Disposition of Caring Community (5:19-20)

Part One

THE CALL TO TRUE RELIGION

James 1:1-27

Times were tough in the Christian communities comprised of Jewish believers. The realities of life seemed to run counter to popular religious ideas that promised blessing in the form of material prosperity as well as escape from many of life's challenges. Beyond the trials of everyday life, there was a broad-based shallowness in many of the Christian lives inhabiting these communities. Profession of faith was common, but conscientious obedience to the Word was becoming alarmingly rare. Religious faith was degenerating into a mere social convention rather than a transforming way of life. It was increasingly difficult to see any real difference between those who professed to follow Jesus and those who didn't.

Perhaps most sobering, though, was a growing rift within the Jewish-Christian community itself. The distance between the rich and poor was increasing, and the effects of divisions on the basis of social class, so commonly observed outside the church, were beginning to emerge inside the church as well. Talk was carelessly and slanderously creating divisions within the church body, and a judgmental spirit was at work. In short, authenticity within the Christian community was an endangered species. Shallow thinking, shallow talk and shallow living threatened to engulf the Jewish churches, the founding churches of the Christian religion.

It is to such struggling communities that the Epistle of James is directed. James, the uncontested leader of Jewish Christianity, writes a no-nonsense letter admonishing the Hebrew believers to give themselves wholeheartedly to the practice of true religion. By "true religion," he means a religious life that is firmly based on the historic Scriptures and is lived out in obedient faith. James has no patience with hollow claims of faith that make no difference in a person's life. Here he calls the Jewish-Christian community back to the roots of *real* religion, a religion born within the covenant community of Old Testament Israel, and renewed and reaffirmed in the teachings of Jesus the Messiah.[1]

James appeals to the Old Testament roots of Christianity, for there the Jewish people learned firsthand the blessing of obedient faith and the curse of halfhearted religiosity. Adopting the language of blessing and curse, God's approval and God's condemnation, and reward and judgment, James urges the Christians under his leadership to submit themselves wholeheartedly to the practice of true religion.[2]

Perhaps more so than any other New Testament author, James also utilizes the teachings of Jesus. He is particularly drawn to the Lord's words in the Sermon on the Mount (see Matthew 5–7). These teachings of Jesus serve to underscore the connection between the blessing of hearing and doing the Word, and the condemnation inherent in failing to practice obedience. Though the person of Jesus is seldom directly invoked in this short letter, His teachings underlie every theme that James employs in calling his readers to authenticity in their faith.

Here are the words of a true pastor's heart, written with burning concern to communities wavering between real faith and the disastrous consequences of pretend religion. James reminds all Christians—those directly in his mind as he writes, and all believers since—of the blessedness of true religion.

ENDNOTES

[1] A covenant is a solemn promise made binding by a pledge or vow, which may be either a verbal formula or a symbolic action. A covenant often referred to a legal obligation in ancient times. In Old Testament terms, the word was often used in describing the relationship between God and His chosen people, in which their sacrifices of blood afforded them His atonement for sin, and in which their fulfillment of a promise to live in obedience to God was rewarded by His blessings. In New Testament terms, this relationship (the new covenant) was now made possible on a personal basis through Jesus Christ and His sacrifice of His own blood.

[2] Blessings and curses refer to the response of God to His people in accordance with their obedience to Him (blessings) or their disobedience (curses). In the Old Testament, God's power was invoked through power-laden words (blessings and curses) often spoken in prayer form. Through these

blessings or curses, God's people would call upon Him to provide or care for them by affecting them in a positive way or those around them in a positive or negative way. In Judaism (the belief and cultural system of the Jewish people), some blessings were reserved for the priests, but others were a regular part of the synagogue services. Curses were much less prominent and were forbidden. In the New Testament, the ultimate blessing came from God to mankind in Jesus Christ, and blessings accompanied righteousness. Curses accompanied sin.

GREETING

James 1:1

The first chapter of the Epistle of James is doubtless the key to grasping the rest of the letter. It is both the longest and most complex chapter in the epistle. The chapter revolves around James's exhortations to his readers related to the practice of real faith or true religion. Beyond the brief introduction, the chapter has three major sections which all relate to James's concern for authenticity in the lives of his readers. Whether urging his fellow Jewish Christians to persevere through trials, or admonishing them to practice the Word they claim to have heard, James always aims toward the same target—true religion.

Perhaps nothing reveals the character of a person more than what he says about himself. Reading James's introduction to his epistle helps us to understand something of the self-perception of this man. **James, a servant of God** (Jas. 1:1), isn't much of an introduction, especially in comparison with other literature of the day, and yet it speaks volumes about the author. The word **servant** literally means "slave." James viewed himself as the property of God. His self-understanding was born from the deep conviction that life is intended to be defined in relationship to God and to His purposes. Even as Israel was the servant of Yahweh (the Hebrew name for God), so James, as a latter-day Israelite, viewed himself in those same terms.

Further, we have to take into account what James *doesn't* say in his introduction. We surely could imagine him using his relationship to the Lord Jesus, his half brother, to his advantage. It could go a long way in garnering authority and influence for his writing. But in reference to Jesus, he simply added, **And of the Lord Jesus Christ**—Christ being another One who deserved his servitude. Were James a man typical of our times, he would doubtless remind us of his advanced standing in the Jerusalem church. He would engage in a bit of divine "name-dropping"—for example, "James, the brother of the Lord Jesus Christ."

He might even fall back on the name that had been given to him because of his reputation in the church: "James the Just."

But the fact that this man felt no compelling need to underscore either his apostolic authority in the Jerusalem church or his blood kinship to Jesus himself tells us what we really need to know. Here was a man secure in who he was and satisfied to be known simply as God's servant. In opting for such a humble introduction, James set the tone for the important teachings to follow that would urge humility as an important evidence of possessing true wisdom.

The use of the title **Lord** (Jas. 1:1) is noteworthy because although Jesus is mentioned only here and one other place in the epistle (see also 2:1), the attitude and perspective of this letter is charged through and through with the concept of Jesus as Lord. Jesus' lordship was commonly associated in the early Jewish church with the idea of His exaltation and triumphant return to this world. Christ's return to the earth as judge was of particular concern to James; thus this picture of Jesus as Lord dominates the rest of the epistle. So, even though references to Christ in this letter are rare, Christ's lordship over history provided the perspective from which James wrote.

The words **To the twelve tribes scattered among the nations: Greetings** make James's introduction among the briefest in the New Testament. This general, nonspecific introduction places James among the General Epistles.[1] But, given James's Jewish roots and the broadly accepted notion that he was writing to Jewish or Hebrew Christians, this brief word of greeting takes on added significance.

The Greek term translated here as **scattered** more technically refers to "dispersion." Originally, the "dispersion" was a historical event associated with Jewish people living outside of Palestine after the Babylonian captivity in the sixth century B.C. Through the years the term came to refer to Jews who were dispersed geographically throughout the known world. Since this letter is addressed to Christians, the usage is obviously figurative, but given James's concern with living in obedience to the Word, the words of Moses in Deuteronomy 30 may have been in the back of his mind.

Moses had urged the gathered tribes of Israel, on the verge of entering the Promised Land, to remember his words to them (the text of Deuteronomy), especially when times were tough: "When all these blessings and curses I have set before you come upon you and you take them to heart wherever the LORD your God disperses you among the nations . . ." (Deut. 30:1). James is about to remind his readers, dispersed as they are, to remember the tenets of true religion and to put them into practice. He will call them to consider how obedience brings blessing and how forgetfulness and disobedience bring curses.[2] Thus, his greeting may be an intentional link to the theology of covenant keeping and obedience that Moses presented in Deuteronomy.[3]

Beyond such a possible link, the word of greeting combines the unity of God's people with the circumstances of their being scattered here and there throughout the world. All good Israelites knew that no matter where they found themselves on the earth, they remained a called people. Whatever the circumstances of their lives, there was still one abiding reality that pertained—they were Israel. And they were expected to live like it, circumstances notwithstanding.

James is reminding his readers that the church is a distinct gathering of people, the *ecclesia,* the "called-out assembly." Wherever God's people are, they are to be distinct and recognizable as such. Even when the church often finds itself "scattered" in the world—a minority of faith in the midst of accommodating unbelief—there remains one abiding reality: they are part of God's people. Circumstances are never valid reasons for losing one's essential spiritual identity.

Whatever the specific circumstances that may underlie such a greeting by James, the reality is that the **twelve tribes** are neither large nor powerful. Their confidence cannot be in any of the factors that typically appeal to nations or peoples. Their confidence is owing to one thing alone—they belong to God. So this greeting, short as it is, reminds readers that this is the word of God's servant to a servant people who are scattered literally and figuratively in a world which may not take notice of them.

ENDNOTES

[1]The General Epistles are the books of James; 1 and 2 Peter; 1, 2, and 3 John; and Jude. They are called General Epistles because they are books or letters written to broad groups of people, rather than being addressed to specific individuals or churches the way that, say, Paul's letters to the Corinthians were.

[2]Blessings and curses refer to the response of God to His people in accordance with their obedience to Him (blessings) or their disobedience (curses). In the Old Testament, God's power was invoked through power-laden words (blessings and curses) often spoken in prayer form. Through these blessings or curses, God's people would call upon Him to provide or care for them by affecting them in a positive way or those around them in a positive or negative way. In Judaism (the belief and cultural system of the Jewish people),

some blessings were reserved for the priests, but others were a regular part of the synagogue services. Curses were much less prominent and were forbidden. In the New Testament, the ultimate blessing came from God to mankind in Jesus Christ, and blessings accompanied righteousness. Curses accompanied sin.

[3]A covenant is a solemn promise made binding by a pledge or vow, which may be either a verbal formula or a symbolic action. A covenant often referred to a legal obligation in ancient times. In Old Testament terms, the word was often used in describing the relationship between God and His chosen people, in which their sacrifices of blood afforded them His atonement for sin, and in which their fulfillment of a promise to live in obedience to God was rewarded by His blessings. In New Testament terms, this relationship (the new covenant) was now made possible on a personal basis through Jesus Christ and His sacrifice of His own blood.

2

TRIALS AND TRUE RELIGION

James 1:2-12

G iven the strong probability of difficult times confronting the readers of the Epistle of James, both from within the church and from outside the church (in society), the epistle's writer launches immediately into a fundamental teaching: the appropriate response of Christians to trials.

1. BLESSING IN TRIAL 1:2-4

Consider it pure joy, my brothers, whenever you face trials of many kinds (Jas. 1:2). James uses the term **brothers** often in this letter. It typically indicates major emphases in the text. His use of the term also shows the kind of relationship he has with his readers. While we don't know for certain to whom James is writing, it is obvious he knows his readers well. The term also demonstrates the warmth of his feelings for them. To call someone "brother" in the early Christian community was a way of showing affection and concern. Finally, the term shows James's sense of being one with them. James writes with the pastoral concern of a fellow sojourner.

Rather than beginning his letter by expressing sympathy or by offering a bit of pastoral understanding for some of the problems that plague the Christian community, James brings his readers face-to-face with a revolutionary approach to adversity. His suggested response to times of trial flies in the face of the conventional wisdom of his day and ours. He urges them to consider their diverse trials and troubles as an occasion to rejoice.

The word **consider** (1:2) is an accounting term in the sense of "count" or "deem." It speaks of a conclusion reached after conscious reflection. When viewed from the vantage point of authentic Christian faith, trials are an occasion for joy. The thinking here is that while one cannot prevent such trials, the ability to determine one's attitude and perspective in the midst of trials is a powerful possibility.

Further, the use of **whenever** (1:2) underscores the likelihood of such occasions. It is not a question of *if* trials should come, but *when*. And when they do, writes James, this is the proper attitude of true religion, namely to **consider it pure joy.** The original Greek word used for **trials** here is a word used in Acts 27:41 to describe a ship running into a reef; in other words, these are not mere inconveniences that one faces, but *real obstacles.*

James wants to inform his readers about the realities of life and to undermine any thinking that those who follow Jesus Christ are somehow exempted from such harsh realities. Jesus himself went out of His way to remind His followers that they would experience adversity, but that in the midst of it they should be filled with His peace (see John 16:33). In the Sermon on the Mount (see Matthew 5:10-11) He taught that persecution and suffering for one's faith was a reason for happiness or blessing.[1]

Surely one of the most distressing marks of modern Christian practice has been the association of true Christian faith with the absence of trials and troubles of any kind. Such so-called "success theology" counters the clear teachings of both Jesus and James, as well as the experiences of most believers in history. The facts of life in Christ are that life is hard, that it can be filled with adversity of many kinds. But in the midst of it all, believers have the option of choosing in a significant way the effect of such times upon them.

This is not mere "pie in the sky" thinking—grit your teeth now in hopes of a better future in heaven—nor is it what psychologists might call denial. We are not to pretend that trials aren't really happening. Nor is our attitude to be borne as some fatalistic notion that we all must suffer for our past sins, or any number of other ideas that have been proposed historically by well-intentioned people. James wants his readers to understand that there is a point behind trials, and thus there is good reason to consider such times as joy—**because you know that the testing of your faith develops perseverance** (Jas. 1:3).

We are to consider times of trial as occasions for joy because in such moments we realize that our faith is being developed. There is purpose in trials. Instead of "success theology" that *exempts* us from trials, James teaches about a faith that is successful *in the midst* of trials. When trials are viewed as the means by which our faith develops perseverance, then we come to understand that whatever life brings our way, God can use to accomplish His purposes (see Romans 8:28).

The critical implication for us is that except for times of trial and adversity, we would not develop perseverance; we would have no occasion to truly put our faith into practice and test it in the marketplace of human experience. Difficult times are to be accepted, if not welcomed, as necessary to developing the perseverance called for in true discipleship. The concept of overcoming adversity or resistance is part and parcel of the growth process itself.

Everyone knows that athletes desiring to get stronger must increase the resistance on the weight lifting bar. Without it, there is no growth, no increase, no perseverance. Spiritually, James tells us that the same is true regarding the development of Christian character and steadfastness. The Greek word used here for **perseverance** (Jas. 1:3) initially meant to "press to the limit," to "try one's ultimate resources."[2] Human existence reveals that our beliefs, convictions and aspirations will be put to the test to see if they can persevere in the course of our life journey. God desires that we develop the virtue of perseverance in the face of adversity, because this is how we grow.

Perseverance is not a passive virtue. Rather it is the positive development of the character of one's commitment to Christ. God desires us to become steadfast persons who can endure and overcome the temptation to give up in the midst of difficult times. Paul spoke of perseverance in Romans 5 in much the same way as James: "Not only so, but we also rejoice in our sufferings, because we know that suffering produces perseverance; perseverance, character; and character, hope. And hope does not disappoint us, because God has poured out his love into our hearts by the Holy Spirit, whom he has given us" (Rom. 5:3-5). The "character" mentioned here is developed precisely by going through times of testing. It seems risky, and it surely can be, but it is the only way to grow stronger.

Just as parents understand that in order for their children to grow and mature into whole persons, those little ones must learn to overcome adversity, God knows that unless we develop perseverance, we will never become the kind of people He wants us to be—whole and complete. What loving parent has not agonized over the temptation to step in and ease a child through a difficult or painful experience, only to refrain, knowing that the child must learn to deal with such experiences? Does this mean the parent does not love? Of course not. The parent is demonstrating the farsighted love that seeks not simply the immediate cessation of pain and anxiety, but the long-term well-being of the child. Certainly the God who loves us does not enjoy seeing us confronted with the testings of life, but being the all-loving Father He is, He rejoices when we endure triumphantly.

The key to triumphant endurance lies in the ability of humans to overcome the temptation to focus only on the immediate, and instead consider the end result. This assumes genuine faith in God and obedience to Him, two very significant issues in James. In his opening paragraph, James goes directly to the realism that characterizes his short epistle. He assumes that trials, testings and the like are part of the normal Christian experience. For James, the Christian life is "uphill all the way." Rather than become despondent over difficult circumstances, we are to remember that such testings are indispensable to our development in Christ.

Unfortunately, fewer and fewer North American Christians seem to understand this foundational teaching of Scripture. Whether it is televangelists proclaiming that "God wants us all healthy and rich," or our increasingly comfortable lifestyles that lull us into thinking that life is supposed to be easy, many contemporary believers struggle with the adversities of human life. Rather than embracing such times as necessary to help us gauge the strength and vitality of our faith, we seek ways of escaping them at almost any cost.

More than once it has been observed that "Christians in North America pray for God to deliver them from trials, while Christians in developing nations pray for grace to persevere." A walk through any bookstore, secular or Christian, convincingly proves the huge market that exists for helping people to cope with the realities of life. People are typically perplexed as to why things happen and how they can deal with such times of trouble and testing. Although the first-century church didn't have recourse to the bookstores that dot our landscape, they did share the common human experiences of finding the life of faith a tough walk indeed.

That's what makes the Epistle of James so relevant to our day. James is not suggesting the "stiff upper lip" approach to bad times. What he is saying is that life is hard—it's always been that way—but if we choose to, we can endure it with the joy that comes from knowing that such times serve a purpose. James asks his readers to consider a transformed perspective toward testings so that the testings themselves are viewed as the source of victory over them.

Once the goal of such times—when placed in God's hands—is realized, those enduring the trials can **consider it pure joy** (Jas. 1:2). That goal, says James, is maturity and completeness. Perseverance is not an end in itself, but a means to accomplishing the ultimate point behind the endurance of trials: **Perseverance must finish its work so that you may be mature and complete, not lacking anything** (1:4).

What is the point of the Christian life? Is it simply a kind of legal transaction that takes place in the heavenly courts to qualify us for heaven? Not according to James. And that is what makes persevering through times of testing so crucial. The point behind life, especially the difficulties of life, is to bring us to a point of maturity and completion, not lacking anything. The word James used here for **complete** refers to the end product. God has something in mind in redeeming our lives. He has a goal or purpose in saving us. There is something about the nature of human life that enables that goal to be reached when we submit to the processes of God and His grace.

Perseverance is not something that happens instantly or even over a period of weeks and months—it is a lifelong process. Unfortunately, this understanding of the Christian life is most foreign to the typical Western believer who lives in a culture of immediacy. We are taught the gospel of immediate gratification in everything from gaining possessions to expressing our sexuality or becoming spiritually mature persons. This instant gratification mentality is why the idea of viewing trials as an occasion for joy is so foreign. In our "instant everything" culture, we have no framework from which to deal with the lifelong process of making saints.

James insists that this process of molding our character must be allowed to have its total effect. But the constant temptation is to cut short the process, to find easy ways to spiritual vitality. Unfortunately, those same bookstores filled with books on how to cope are also filled with racks of books telling us the secret to becoming spiritual giants. Often, these shortcuts to spiritual maturity are nothing more than snake oil with spiritual sounding labels. This "cut the corners" approach to spirituality currently litters the landscape of North American Christianity. Any pastor can vouch for the countless number of people who have opted for the "easy way" to sainthood, only to live their lives in the throes of "virtual Christianity."

James's use of the terms **complete** ("perfect" [KJV]) and **not lacking anything** (1:4) brings more than a little uneasiness to the many Christians who know, all too well, their own imperfections. But **complete** refers to the finished product God has in mind. James wants us to grasp that by becoming steadfast in authentic Christian faith, we can become what God intended us to be when He created us. That's the goal of redemption: to make us like the perfect man, Jesus; to conform us to the image of God's Son (see Romans 8:29). God wants us to be whole people, mature people, just like Jesus.

The redemptive aim of God since the Garden of Eden has been restorative in the sense of bringing humankind back to that place of fellowship with Him and harmony with one another. In Jesus, we have been given a glimpse of what a "mature, complete, not lacking in anything" human being looks like. And we like what we see! And that's what the life of perseverance is meant to produce. To grasp the blessedness of true religion is to view trials through the lens of God's redemptive purposes.

This is one example of how James interfaces wonderfully with John Wesley's emphasis on living out the sanctified life. Although in the Wesleyan tradition we often speak of a second work of grace, we also (at least we should, if we follow Wesley's guidance) stress the progressive, lifelong aspects of discipleship. Former Asbury College president Dennis Kinlaw used to talk about "entire sanctification" as dealing with the sanctification of *our hearts,* and "progressive sanctification" as dealing with the sanctification of *the rest of our lives.* What God seeks to accomplish in our lives (see 1 Thessalonians 5:23) is accomplished via life itself when we commit ourselves wholeheartedly to Him.

James begins here, because the essence of true religion necessarily involves the commitment of one's life for a lifetime. And circumstances need not hinder that walk; indeed they are intended to strengthen it. In an instant gratification society that shuns the hard work of discipleship, this blue-collar approach to spirituality isn't likely to be applauded, but it is the essence of true religion.

The goal of bringing us to maturity and completion underscores the lifetime aspect of the process. In light of this, consider Tom Eisenman's words: "A good chef knows what a long soak in a fine marinade will do for a tough piece of meat. There is no way to slap on a glaze at the last second and get the same fine result. This is God's way with us. We soak in the marinade of his grace for a lifetime, and there is simply no way to rush the process without ruining the meat."[3]

2. THE PROBLEM OF DOUBLE-MINDEDNESS 1:5-8

The vision of a restored human personhood is compelling, but it also can be discouraging when we compare ourselves to the whole person of Christ. Our lacks are much too obvious. Those lacks have a way of manifesting themselves, especially during times of trial.

Lest James's readers grow too discouraged, the writer is quick to add a note to assure them that they are not left to themselves in this lifelong redemptive task: **If any of you lacks wisdom, he should ask God, who gives generously to all without finding fault, and it will be given to him** (Jas. 1:5). The crucial link between this request and successfully persevering through trials is **wisdom.** James is claiming that the inability to remain steadfast in times of testing is best offset by the addition of wisdom. By "wisdom" James means both the understanding of God's ways and the approach to life that comes through such understanding. (For a fuller treatment of James's use of wisdom, see additional notes on James and the Old Testament at the end of chapter 4 of the commentary.)

What we lack in our understanding of this discipling, maturing process can be gained by asking God for it. The lack spoken of here is the lack of knowledge of the ways of God in bringing us to completion. Wisdom is the ability to understand the ways of life and how God utilizes them for our redemptive good.

The assurance here is that God is more than willing to impart such a gift to those who ask for it. He is generous in imparting wisdom, and when we ask, He gives without making us feel "condescended to" (Jas. 1:5, The Message). God is the One "who gives generously to all men without making them feel guilty" (J. B. Phillips). This latter phrase demonstrates a fundamental element of James's view of God. God is the loving Father of His children, who desires to help and to provide them with everything they lack.

Some New Testament scholars have suggested that this lack in our lives is supplied by the gift of God's Spirit. They cite numerous references in the New Testament, particularly the teachings of Jesus regarding the Holy Spirit, as evidence that James is referring here to the Spirit as God's provision for us. For example, Jesus' portrayal of the Spirit as the "paraclete"—literally, the One who "comes alongside," or the "helper"—fits wonderfully into the picture of God's providing what we lack to assist us in our maturation and spiritual completion. Certainly the picture from Luke's gospel of the Father willingly giving good gifts to His needy children is paralleled here in James's words ("If you then, though you are evil, know how to give good gifts to your children, how much more will your Father in heaven give the Holy Spirit to those who ask him!" [Luke 11:13]).

But while some scholars are willing to make this connection (and it admittedly has a certain appeal, in light of James's further teachings on this subject in chapter 3 of his epistle), it is difficult to see how equating wisdom with the person of the Holy Spirit can be argued convincingly. Such thinking would advance the equation of the Holy Spirit with wisdom in a measure far beyond what the New Testament seems to teach on this subject. Thus, even though the idea of God imparting His own Spirit has a certain appeal and is certainly attested to in other ways and in other texts, it is probably best to think of wisdom here as an all-encompassing understanding of God's ways in life that enable one to persevere in the midst of testings. We are probably safe in claiming that while wisdom itself (in this passage) may not equate with the gift of the Holy Spirit, any wisdom we receive from God as His children will come via the ministry of the Holy Spirit (". . . he will guide you into all truth" [John 16:13]).

Knowing the ways of God as He is at work in us through life is more than adequate to make sense of this text. But, having acknowledged the resources that are available to the one who senses his or her lack, James proceeds to add a critical word of caution: **But when he asks, he must believe and not doubt** (Jas. 1:6a; literally, "but let him ask in faith, nothing doubting"). The request has one overriding condition attached— the necessity of faith.

Such a request as this—asking God to supply what is lacking in our ability to withstand testing—cannot be made in a state of wavering unbelief. J. B. Phillips renders this phrase helpfully, "But he must ask in sincere faith without secret doubts" (1:6a). James adds graphically the reason for such caution: **He who doubts is like a wave of the sea, blown and tossed by the wind. That man should not think he will receive anything from the Lord; he is a double-minded man, unstable in all he does** (1:6b-8).

In the context of seeking God's wisdom for standing firm in testing, James introduces a key concern of this epistle: double-mindedness. The picture this word brings to mind is of one who never can fully make up his or her mind. Instead of steadfastness, there is vacillation. Rather than predictable responses flowing from a steadfast character, there is erratic indecision. James himself portrays the meaning of double-mindedness through a simple image familiar to his readers: **a wave of the sea** (James is noted for his "natural" illustrations).

Waves are not predictable. Anyone who has spent much time in the surf has doubtlessly learned that lesson the hard way. The unpredictability of waves is the result of their being subject to external influences, such as the winds. Waves are not in control of their destiny because of powerful external forces. Again, note the contrast. This kind of unpredictability and instability is the direct opposite of steadfastness and permanence, which the author claims are the outcome of successfully enduring trials.

James says that **doubts** (1:6), which are the product of double-mindedness, reduce us to those who are subject to external forces. The Greek word used for "doubt" here also means "to hesitate" or "to debate." The construction of the word for "double-minded" in the Greek language is in what is known as the middle voice, which indicates a verb acting back upon the subject. In other words, double-minded is an *inward debate*. The **double-minded** person (1:8) is arguing with himself! He wonders whether or not God can really provide what he asks for in prayer. Beyond that, he isn't certain whether he truly wants God's help. That is the essence of double-mindedness—literally, being two-souled.

But there is more. This inward divisiveness is extensive. This is a person with divided loyalties and divided affections, one who desires to "keep their options open." A person torn between faith in God, especially in times of testing, and an inward debate as to whether or not God is really up to granting a request for help is not a likely candidate for God's assistance.

Many of the Old Testament kings of Judah illustrate this concept of double-mindedness. These kings were prone to turn to God in times of great need, while at the same time seeking alliances with other nations, just in case God wasn't up to the task of delivering His people. On other occasions we read, as in 2 Chronicles, of kings who "did right in the sight of the LORD, yet not with a whole heart" (2 Chron. 25:2 NASB).

This is the double-minded person: one who wants God, yet not wholeheartedly. This kind of faith is, according to James, the antithesis of true religion. The essence of genuine faith is believing that God can and will respond to those who earnestly seek after Him (see Hebrews 11:6). Such double-minded instability undermines the request for God's assistance and ironically demonstrates the ongoing need for steadfastness in one's spiritual life.

The tendency to be two-souled, or of two minds in our commitment to God, is a most vexing problem in modern Christianity. "Soft commitment" is a term pastors and other spiritual leaders use to describe the halting, wishy-washy religious lives of so many within the confines of the church. These people are indeed like the waves, blown about by external forces of culture which seem to appear with regularity and devastating effect. There is no steadfastness to their character. They are absolutely unpredictable in how they may respond in times of spiritual crisis. They truly are **unstable in all [they do]** (Jas. 1:8b).

True religion is James's passion. But true religion is undermined at every turn by a doubting, timid commitment. In a way that likely makes us uncomfortable, James removes the middle ground of religious commitment. It's wholehearted or nothing. Until we launch out into the deep waters of faith, and trust God totally, we are not viable candidates for true religion. And the result of our double-minded religion will be all too predictable—we will be unstable in all we do.

Now it is necessary to differentiate here between what James is condemning and the common doubt that all humans experience from time to time. The mere existence of doubts about life and about God does not make us double-minded people. What James is talking about here is doubt that is produced by halfheartedness or divided affections. The failure to fully commit ourselves to God and to His way for our lives is to choose a life of instability, ups and downs—not unlike the waves of the sea.

Everyone experiences the pangs of doubt from time to time, especially in times of perplexity and trouble. But the doubt that condemns us to failure as believers is that which arises because of our divided hearts. Double-minded religion is false, not true religion. Such faith is not blessed—it is doomed to fail.

3. PROSPERITY AND TRUE RELIGION 1:9-11

At first glance, James 1:9-11 seems to be one of those disjointed sayings that the writer has been noted for by those who view the Epistle of James as structurally similar to Proverbs (see introduction). But remember James's concern for encouraging his readers to stand firm in times of trial. This passage is necessary to eliminate one serious misconception about testings—that they have to do with one's personal prosperity. The rift between the rich and the poor is a major subplot within this epistle. James addresses that subplot here in terms of how it connects with the issue of trials.

The idea that the wealthy are somehow exempt from the ups and downs of life has been with humankind throughout history and cuts across religious traditions. There has always been the temptation to gauge spiritual progress and one's acceptance by God according to one's material well-being. Given the problems of this sort that seem to plague the Christian communities to which he writes, James intends to strike a blow at such thinking early on in his letter.

Whatever else the cause of testings and trials, poverty is no sign of God's disapproval, and wealth is no reason to think that we are exempt from trouble: **The brother in humble circumstances ought to take pride in his high position** (Jas. 1:9). Rendered literally, this verse says to let the humble brother boast "in the height of him." The idea is that **humble circumstances** are akin to the humility which God himself exalts (4:6, 10). However much poverty might contribute to the trials of life, we must never assume that this has anything to do with how we are valued by God as persons. In fact, James will argue later that the poor are especially prized by God (see 2:5).

James seems particularly committed to squelching any connection between "health and wealth" and genuinely possessing the blessing of true religion.[4] Beyond that, James wants to assure the poor that merely changing their material circumstances is not the answer to their problems. Perseverance in the midst of trials is!

Should anyone doubt where James is headed with this thinking, he adds, **But the one who is rich should take pride in his low position, because he will pass away like a wild flower** (1:10). In the context of talking about the need for steadfastness and permanence in matters of faith, James vividly illustrates the instability of riches. However perseverance and steadfastness are produced in life, material possessions are not a necessary part of the process.

The rich are to take comfort in the reality that their possession of true religion is not based on anything as temporary as wealth. Indeed, their wealth cannot prevent life from heading toward its inevitable destiny. Like flowers in the fields, the rich are subject to the same processes as the poor: **For the sun rises with scorching heat and withers the plant; its blossom falls and its beauty is destroyed. In the same way, the rich man will fade away even while he goes about his business** (1:11).

Regardless of how singularly beautiful any particular flower in the field may be, that flower is nevertheless subject to the unyielding laws of nature. So it is for the wealthy person. In the course of conducting business and making their fortunes, **the rich** are still human beings. As human creatures, they are subject to forces that pay no attention to things like wealth and worldly standing. So to those on either side of the economic fence who assume that the answer to life's challenges lies in acquisition and material wealth, James is clear: true religion supersedes such ultimately insignificant factors.

This passage recalls the Beatitudes and the general teachings of Jesus about the unimportance of worldly standards and measurements in determining the true value of a person. This passage has much to say to our generation. We have been touched so deeply by the influences of stark materialism. Convincing Christians that their source of well-being, their self-worth (to use contemporary terminology), is ultimately in Christ alone is increasingly difficult.

The understanding that lies at the foundation of true religion is a tough sell, even in the church today. We typically find most of our identity in our professions, our jobs, our income levels. The constant drumbeat of the secular world urges us to evaluate our lives based on where we stand on the socioeconomic ladder. We are bombarded with messages which promise that if we could just make a little bit more, things would be better, life would be easier. In spite of ample evidence to the contrary, Christians are tempted to buy into the lies that emphasize climbing the income ladder above that of humbly celebrating our standing before God.

Given this secular spirit, rather than persevering through tough times, we are more prone to borrow our way through it. Instead of asking God for wisdom to endure, we cast about for self-made solutions. We discover that there is a debate going on within us. Although we think of ourselves as "religious," we're not really sure that we depend on God to meet our needs and lacks in life. So we put our trust in the materialistic culture around us. We too often have been the kind of two-souled persons James condemns. We have envied the wealthy, forgetting the constant biblical reminders as to the fate of such riches.

John Wesley often noted how, in the aftermath of conversion with its reorientation of priorities, a believer's economic condition invariably improved, but with that improvement came the temptation to place one's well-being in economics rather than in real faith. James's question to us is simply this: Why put your trust in something that is destined to **pass away like a wild flower** in a July drought (Jas. 1:10)? Instead, he argues our need to be focused on the bigger picture.

James is not appealing to some fairy-tale kingdom where the poor get the money and the rich get what's coming to them. On the contrary, he reminds them of the essential "leveling" of the kingdom of God as announced by the prophetic voices of Isaiah and John the Baptist. In his work on James's epistle, former Houghton College president Stephen Paine notes that "even apart from the sacred scriptures, philosophers and wise men of all ages have observed that God is a lover of balance; He exalts the lowly and humbles the lofty."[5]

James's strong words to the wealthy here do not signal special contempt for this class of people, as some have tried to argue throughout history. This is simply the realization that those who have abundance are more likely to resist the message of the ultimate insignificance of things like wealth in God's eyes. The rich, therefore, need to be especially sensitive to the transitory nature of life and possessions.

Remember, the typical Jewish idea regarding riches was that it was a sign of God's blessing. That's why Jesus' disciples were so amazed at His words about the difficulty of the wealthy entering the Kingdom. In the Gospel of Mark we find the disciples wondering, "Who then can be saved?" (Mark 10:26). James, squarely in the tradition of Jesus, is here reminding rich and poor alike that "with God, all things are possible."

4. THE BLESSING OF PERSEVERANCE 1:12

James brings his introductory teachings on trials and true religion to a close with a summary statement openly using the language of "blessing" (the word of Jesus in the Beatitudes in Matthew 5, especially verses 10-12).[6] **Blessed is the man who perseveres under trial, because when he has stood the test, he will receive the crown of life that God has promised to those who love him** (Jas. 1:12). To endure is to "pass the test."

Here is an image with a rich biblical history. Abraham **stood the test** when he obeyed God's call to offer Isaac in Genesis 22. God "tested" Israel on several occasions in their journey to Sinai, trying to demonstrate to them the importance of trusting Him with all their hearts. In those passages, Israel put God to the test in ways that were unacceptable. Israel's testing of God was produced by their double-minded faith. The people bore the curse of God's disfavor on those occasions.

But here James speaks of the blessing of passing the test. Note how he portrays the test. He does not say *if* he has stood the test, as if testing is only a possibility. James is not saying that some will not be tested. The opposite is assumed. Everyone will be tested. Testing is part of life itself; no one is exempt. And, like all real tests, this one is scored; it is graded.

The one who perseveres—endures—passes the test. And to pass the test is to be a blessed, happy person. Why? Two reasons: First, because we are accomplishing the end or goal of our faith by standing firm—to be whole, complete persons (see James 1:3-4). Second, the phrase **stood the test** literally refers to one who has become approved, as one worthy to receive something—**the crown of life,** promised by God to those who love Him (Jas. 1:12).

Interesting to note is the fact that the claim of loving God is equated with the willingness to persevere under trial. *Our claims to love God will be put to the test.* And passing the test involves steadfastness. In other words, there is no way to pass the test apart from allowing God to use the trials and challenges of life to shape us into whole, complete persons. From the beginning of the Christian faith, it has been the case—no cross, no crown.

To his beleaguered readers, James must communicate that their present sufferings in the economy of God's grace are producing for them, to use Paul's words to the Corinthians, "an eternal glory that far outweighs them all" (2 Cor. 4:17). Although it is difficult, and other alternatives promise ease and comfort, this is God's method. There is no alternative to perseverance for those who follow the path of true religion. But that hard truth is balanced by the promise of eternal blessing in the form of the crown of life.

This has always been the hope of the weary pilgrim. In the book of Revelation, the promise of Christ is given to a persecuted church: "Do not be afraid of what you are about to suffer. I tell you, the devil will put some of you in prison to test you, and you will suffer persecution for ten days. Be faithful, even to the point of death, and I will give you the crown of life" (Rev. 2:10). Unlike wealth and earthly possessions, the blessings of true religion will never pass away.

ENDNOTES

[1]Blessings and curses refer to the response of God to His people in accordance with their obedience to Him (blessings) or their disobedience (curses). In the Old Testament, God's power was invoked through power-laden words (blessings and curses) often spoken in prayer form. Through these blessings or curses, God's people would call upon Him to provide or care for them by affecting them in a positive way or those around them in a positive or negative way. In Judaism (the belief and cultural system of the Jewish people), some blessings were reserved for the priests, but others were a regular part of the synagogue services. Curses were much less prominent and were forbidden. In the New Testament, the ultimate blessing came from God to mankind in Jesus Christ, and blessings accompanied righteousness. Curses accompanied sin.

[2]Stephen Paine, *Studies in the Book of James* (Old Tappan, New Jersey: Fleming H. Revell Co., 1955), p. 24.

[3]Tom Eisenman, *Temptations Men Face* (Downers Grove, Illinois: InterVarsity Press, 1990), p. 30.

[4]See endnote 1.

[5]Paine, p. 82.

[6]See endnote 1.

3

A DANGEROUS DECEPTION

James 1:13-18

J ames is adamant in his contention that times of trial and testing are critical to accomplishing the purposes of God. For that reason, these times should be embraced and utilized to strengthen one's faith. But James is quick to prevent the readers of his epistle from drawing an unwarranted inference from this truth: **When tempted, no one should say, "God is tempting me"** (Jas. 1:13a). The experience of temptation can conceivably fit the category of a trial or test. And surely the victorious overcoming of such periods in our lives are significant milestones in our struggle for perseverance. But James draws here an unmistakable distinction between testings that result from the difficulties of human life and those that have their source within the heart of the person.

In the midst of trials, we must remember that God ultimately will reward the one who perseveres, but this does not mean that God himself is the source of such trials and testings. While the reward for overcoming temptation comes from God, the temptations themselves do not. The reason for this goes to the nature of God himself: **For God cannot be tempted by evil, nor does he tempt anyone** (1:13b). God is always consistent with His nature. When we consider what His grace has freely provided us, how could we then think that this kind of graciousness would turn on us and tempt us to fall away? God's intention is that we be brought to completion by learning to count on Him in the difficulties of life, not that we suffer incredible temptations aimed at tripping us up.

James brings his readers to a fundamental fact of true religion concerning the source of evil, specifically the temptation to do evil. He begins by ruling out God as the source. In the first place, God himself cannot be tempted by evil. His holiness would make this an impossibility. There is nothing about evil that God would desire or even look upon. Secondly, neither does God employ temptations to evil as one of His tools. That, too, would violate His holiness. While this seems self-evident, James is demonstrating an unusual grasp of human nature.

From the beginning, going all the way back to the Garden of Eden and the book of Genesis, humans have been trying to blame God for the problem of evil: "The man said, 'The woman you put here with me—she gave me some fruit from the tree, and I ate it'" (Gen. 3:12). This is what theologians and philosophers might term a "theodicy," an explanation for evil (it attempts to answer the question of why evil exists if God is all good and all powerful).

One way or another, every person constructs a theodicy—a way of explaining why things are the way they are. For many, God has become the most convenient scapegoat. The subtle implication of this theodicy is that if God is ultimately behind our temptations, then He cannot at the same time hold us accountable and be just. Such untruths lead to the kind of shallow religion and double-minded commitment that James seeks to counteract in his epistle, so he spares no effort to dispel such thinking. As long as people entertain the thought that God places obstacles and traps in their way, they will never properly seek His help in persevering and overcoming such barriers to their discipleship.

But if God isn't the source of these temptations, who or what is? James adds, **But each one is tempted when, by his own evil desire, he is dragged away and enticed** (Jas. 1:14). Note that the testing here has an immoral purpose behind it—it seeks to draw one into sin. That is an important difference between "trials" in general and trials that result from temptation. The problem, according to James, is centered in one's **own evil desire.**

Just as in the original sin of humankind in Eden, evil springs from a source external to God. This source is described as desire. Genesis 3:6 says that "when the woman saw that the fruit of the tree was good for food and pleasing to the eye, and also desirable for gaining wisdom, she took some and ate it. She also gave some to her husband, who was with her, and he ate it." Rather than God being the source of this temptation, the temptation came from an outside source—the serpent—and significantly (this is James's point), the appeal was to desire!

The serpent did not introduce novel ideas into the minds of Adam and Eve. Instead he played upon readily present notions, such as the aesthetic beauty of the tree of the knowledge of good and evil. He exploited the desire of the woman to be wise (to be like God). And most of all, the serpent's success sprang from the failure of the humans to fully believe in the goodness of the Creator. In the critical moment, they doubted whether God could give them what they thought they needed. Adam and Eve were double-minded!

James wants his readers to grasp the concept that when looking for the source of temptation, they need look no further than their own desires. That **desire** (Jas. 1:14)—literally, strong longing combined with the realities of human life and a double-minded heart—is more than enough to produce all the havoc of sin that ravages our world. Why? Because desire is extremely fertile. James continues: **Then, after desire has conceived, it gives birth to sin; and sin, when it is full-grown, gives birth to death** (1:15).

Desire produces "offspring" in that we act on our desires, and consequences result. In the case of temptation, the offspring produced by desire are evil. Desire drags one away and entices. Unchecked, it gives birth to **sin,** and as the Genesis 3 story amply illustrates, sin fully grown always leads **to death** (see additional notes on desire at the end of chapter 10 of the commentary). Double-minded desire will undermine every attempt at authentic religious faith, and then it will try to blame God.

Don't be deceived, my dear brothers. Every good and perfect gift is from above, coming down from the Father of the heavenly lights, who does not change like shifting shadows (Jas. 1:16-17). This is the dangerous deception that James knows will prevent his readers from trusting God fully and returning to the practical righteousness of true religion. To be deceived into thinking that God causes temptation would surely reinforce double-minded commitment, rather than cure it. Such deceptions, as in the Garden of Eden, always result from a faulty view of God.

To view God as the sort of being that turns on His own children represents the epitome of double-mindedness. Failure to know and to appreciate who God is and what He desires for us is typically at the heart of most of humankind's problems. Understanding full well the connection between bad thinking and bad living, James urges his readers not to be deceived by false teaching about God. Whether such teachings were actually being dispensed to James's readers is unclear. James 3 indicates some form of problem with teachers in the churches. We do know that such ideas were surely present in the theological mix that characterized much of the first-century church. This kind of "doctrinal cafeteria" is very much a part of today's world, making James's words particularly relevant.

Instead of viewing God as some kind of celestial police officer—always watching for a way to catch us speeding—we are reminded by

James of the authentic portrait of God that comes to us through the Scriptures. The correct view of God is not that of a being who is stingy and who, therefore, seeks to disqualify as many people as He can from heaven. He is not callously plotting ways to tempt us so that we will fail. That is the dangerous deception that must be avoided.

The correct view of God is that of a Father, an image James has employed already in reference to God's generous giving (see James 1:5). This **Father of the heavenly lights** (1:17b)—a reference to God's creative majesty and sovereign power—is also the One who descends to us and bestows good and perfect gifts. In short, God generously gives us gifts that serve His purposes which are redemptive, not retributive and vengeful in intent.

Notice how James highlights the consistency of God's nature: **[He] does not change like shifting shadows** (1:17c) or like the waves of the sea (see 1:6). In the midst of times of great uncertainty, in situations where we ask if there is anything firm and stable, the answer is yes! God is completely trustworthy. We can give ourselves to Him wholeheartedly, knowing that He is exactly what He reveals himself to be in the Bible. With God, "what we see is what we get." These words describing God hearken back to James's opening statements about reckoning times of trial as occasions for joy. The reason for this lies squarely in one's view of God.

James urges his readers to view their lives through the lens of gratitude, because such an approach to living has proven itself over the years as the secret of abundant life. That victorious attitude for living is centered in one's understanding of God and His nature. To know God, the real God of the Bible, is to know that there are no circumstances of life that can rob us of real joy—that's the blessedness of true religion, the intimate knowledge of the true God.

This emphasis on a correct view of God is why we ought to be extremely wary of those who speak of theology as being useless, saying that we ought to "keep to what's practical." One can't help but think that James would brand such thinking as shortsighted nonsense! Remember that the Epistle of James is without question the epitome of practicality, but James's practical wisdom stems from a classic theological orientation in the truth of God's nature.

Theology cannot be dismissed as useless. Rather, it is all-important. Our theology is ultimately what we believe about God. If our view of God is primarily that He is "judge, jury, and executioner," then our lives will likely be characterized by fear, anxiety, and the constant knowledge of falling short of an unattainable standard. Such views almost necessarily lead one into being a "double-minded man, unstable in all he does" (Jas. 1:8). These views are not likely to move us to asking God confidently for the wisdom we lack. To the contrary, such views of God lead us to the place of making it seem reasonable to blame Him for all that goes wrong with life.

On the other hand, if our view of God is that which James portrays here—**the Father of the heavenly lights** (1:17), majestic and sovereign over creation—then we know that there is no fickle indecisiveness regarding His purposes for us. If God is the One who acts absolutely consistently with what He has revealed of himself in Scripture, and especially with what He has revealed of himself in Jesus Christ, then truly, joy is not dependent upon pleasant circumstances. With this view of God, we can cultivate an orientation of gratitude in life that considers even times of trial joyfully. With James's view of God, we can begin to experience the depth and richness of a life lived in the awareness that we are ever and always in the benevolent gaze of this marvelous Creator.

Knowing this God is what makes it possible to endure the trials of life as occasions of joy. This is the theological foundation of true religion. James's words here recall the words of Jeremiah in the book of Lamentations: "Because of the LORD's great love we are not consumed, for his compassions never fail. They are new every morning; great is your faithfulness" (Lam. 3:22-23). When the prophet Jeremiah wrote those words, he was surrounded by the desolation of a captive and destroyed Jerusalem. Outwardly there was no reason to have such hope. All the circumstances of the prophet's life at that moment would belie such hopefulness. It was in his vision of God that he found reason to sing. James's words combine with the words of the prophet to produce one of the church's most beloved hymns:

> Great is Thy faithfulness, O God my Father; There is no shadow of
>   turning with Thee;
> Thou changest not, Thy compassions they fail not; As Thou hast
>   been Thou forever wilt be.
> Great is Thy faithfulness! Great is Thy faithfulness!
> Morning by morning new mercies I see;
> All I have needed Thy hand hath provided; Great is Thy
>   faithfulness, Lord unto me!
>   (Thomas Chisholm and William M. Runyan 1923)

Building upon this unchanging portrait of God, James reminds his readers of the ultimate reason why God is not the source of their failings: **He chose to give us birth through the word of truth, that we might be a kind of firstfruits of all he created** (Jas. 1:18). What must characterize our understanding of God first and foremost is the truth communicated through James's words: **He chose.** God chose! Those two words are filled with the sublime truth of the gospel. God, the eternal, all-sufficient One (see 1:17), whose Being would not have been in any way diminished by choosing otherwise, nevertheless chose to give us birth into a new kind of life. It is in the fact of God's choice that we ought to place our trust completely in Him.

This new life of faith and its ultimate destiny (see 1:12) is what enables us to persevere in the midst of testings. The means by which this life is brought forth is **the word of truth** (1:18). This simple, yet descriptive designation of God's saving Word is significant, given James's concern with "deception" voiced earlier in verse 13. The God James describes in this paragraph does not deal in deception; rather, His nature is displayed in the truthfulness of His revealed Word.

God is the initiator of new life, and His Word is the means by which this life is made possible. Apart from this Word of truth, the implication is that such life is not possible. The image of **birth through the word** (1:18) is significant because the Judeo-Christian faith finally rests upon the truth of this Word. The vehicle of the Word has always been God's method.

In the beginning, Genesis tells us, there was nothing at all, until God spoke His creating Word. John says that when God revealed himself in the most complete manner, it was as the Word—the Word made flesh (see John 1:14, 18). Jesus Christ was the Word that explained God more completely than anything else could have. This is God's pattern, to use the Word as a vehicle of creation, of revelation, and now, says James, of redemption. Our birth into the kingdom of God is through the Word, the Word of truth.

The purpose of this birth is that we should become **a kind of firstfruits of all He created** (Jas. 1:18). Again, the Genesis story seems to be in the background. Just as all of creation experienced the ravages of sin and death when Adam and Eve sinned, even so, it will be through human beings that God will demonstrate initially and powerfully His redemptive purposes for all of the fallen creation. He will do this by redeeming men and women, making them the firstfruits—the prototypes—of His saving grace.

God's saving choice on our behalf becomes the basis for morality and ethics in human life. James is passionately interested in the practice of religious faith; indeed, from this point onward, that will become the central focus of the epistle. But James's appeal for practicing real faith will be centered in the fundamental assertion that everything we do in the name of religion is a response. We are simply responding to what God has already done when He chose to redeem us.

Our lives are rightly called to account on the basis of God's choice. The essence of true religion is to live in a manner consistent with God's willful choice to save us and fit us for heaven. It is possible to add all sorts of accessories to one's understanding of true religion, but for James, nothing less than this can pass itself off as authentically Christian. There is no such thing as authentic religious faith that fails to live life in the light of God's saving choice.

4

THE NATURE
OF TRUE RELIGION

James 1:19-27

Having argued that our proper faith response is based on who God is and what He has done on our behalf, James now undertakes to bring his readers to a clearer understanding of the true religion to which he calls them. These nine verses constitute one of two critical sections of the entire epistle (the second critical section is James 4:1-10). In these verses, James uses the goal of true religion as a basis for ethical admonitions. He highlights obedience to the Word as the method by which true religion is practiced. And he clearly defines this kind of religion in ways that rule out brash claims of spirituality that cannot be evidenced in real life.

1. THE GOAL OF TRUE RELIGION 1:19-21

My dear brothers, take note of this: Everyone should be quick to listen, slow to speak and slow to become angry, for man's anger does not bring about the righteous life that God desires (Jas. 1:19-20). Again, the use of the endearing term **brothers** indicates a major emphasis on the part of the author. Having argued that a proper understanding of God is the necessary prerequisite for a proper response to God, James now begins to articulate the nature of that response.

Typically, he makes a declarative kind of statement which paves the way for an imperative or command. James's concern has to do with an understanding of what it is that God wants of us. What brings about the kind of **righteous life that God desires?** In other words, what is the kind of life indicated by the idea of "firstfruits" (1:18)? If you and I are to be the first of something that God wants, what does that something look like?

James says that the goal or end of true religion is that its practice produces exactly what God had in mind when He made His redemptive choice in the first place. God desires a **righteous life** (Jas. 1:20). Such a goal demands certain prescriptions in terms of behavior on the part of the "religious." Literally, we are to be **quick to listen, slow to speak and slow to [wrath]** (1:19).

There is some merit in considering these verses, along with much of the rest of the chapter, as something of a preview of topics to come. James certainly will return to these ideas. But, though covered more extensively later, these themes are introduced here as essential to our understanding the nature of true religion.

James's exhortation is comprised of words reminiscent of the Wisdom writings in general and the Proverbs in particular.[1] The conditions in which James wrote would seem to indicate a tension-filled atmosphere where careless words could cause major destruction (see James 3:1-12). In an environment where accusations are being made, battle lines drawn, and shortsighted actions offered as solutions, James counsels coolheaded reflection rather than reaction. To be swift in hearing means to listen actively with a genuine desire to understand.

Here is the kind of practical wisdom for which James is noted. Simply hearing is not sufficient; it must be accompanied by understanding. As mundane as this sounds, it is embarrassing to consider how much of the turmoil in marriages, families, nations, and even churches could be improved by a genuine desire to listen with understanding. As one has wisely noted, the fact that God gave us two ears and only one mouth means that we ought to listen twice as much as we talk!

The inability to make oneself heard or the sense that no one is truly listening lies at the heart of much of the rage and chaos that characterizes our contemporary culture. Countless numbers of people pay professionals exorbitant hourly fees simply to listen sympathetically to them, to understand them. James contends that the church ought to be the kind of place where everyone is truly heard—where they can be truly *understood.* The failure to listen is costing us dearly in our homes, at our jobs and within our churches. The sense that no one is really listening to us has a way of battering our self-worth and feeding the drive—as strong as it already is—to "look out for number one."

Beyond the practical wisdom inherent in such advice, it seems that James is also referring to the idea of the "implanted word" (see 1:18, 21). To fail to listen, when the very means of our spiritual birth is such that listening is necessary, is a recipe for disaster. This theme of truly hearing will be expanded in the discussion on James 1:22-25.

We are to be **slow to speak** (1:19). The human tendency is to be reactive, rather than reflective. James will argue here, and in chapter 3, that words have power. Of all people, Christians, who were brought to spiritual life by a "word," ought to appreciate that truth. We are to weigh our words carefully, knowing that they count.

We are to be **slow to become angry** (1:19). The New International Version has chosen to translate the Greek word for "wrath" here as *anger*. However, *wrath* is a preferable translation because wrath connotes the idea of vengeful retribution, which is what James has in mind.

We know anger is a basic human emotion that, like all emotions, can be morally neutral. Wrath, on the other hand, speaks of a kind of *willful choice* on the part of the person involved. The drive for retribution, even in understandable circumstances, is to be put into low gear, says James. Why? He offers one compelling reason: *The wrath of human beings does not produce the kind of life that God has purposed for us.* Our lives are to be consistent responses to what God has willed, to what God has chosen. Anger, says James, cannot meet that standard; it cannot possibly bring about the kind of life God wills for His children.

If Christians alone would grasp the importance of this verse, it would revolutionize our world. Our anger, our vindictiveness, our retribution will not bring about the Kingdom which we claim to be seeking. Anger, in the sense of wrath, as defined above, is one of the so-called "seven deadly sins." It is a dominant human response that characterizes the beginning of the third millennium.

Our world is filled with this kind of wrath, which is counterproductive in terms of what God desires from us. But such appeals to reason and God's will are barely heard above the angry voices. It is now everyone's "right" to vent his or her anger. Regardless of its validity or cost to the rest of society, venting anger has become an acceptable mode of public therapy. James condemns this for one overriding reason: it doesn't work! It does not produce "firstfruits"; rather it lays waste otherwise fertile ground.

Anger is not among the fruits of the Spirit listed in Galatians 5 for good reason. The anger of men and women never can accomplish the purposes of God. God's desire is to see a righteous life—literally, a life of *rightness*—in relationships with Him and with others. Anger precludes such a life, because in anger, control is surrendered to the point where God and His Word no longer rule us, and we are instead ruled by passion, fear and circumstances.

The Christian community needs to ponder long and well James's words here. The last one-third of the twentieth century witnessed the introduction of so-called "righteous anger" as an acceptable methodology within the evangelical church. Suddenly, people of strong religious backgrounds seem willing to entertain notions that violence and mayhem, and even killing doctors who perform abortions, may be acceptable responses for Christians. Such thinking is on exceedingly thin ice in terms of its faithfulness to historic Christianity, or what James terms "true religion." While we can agree that Jesus expressed His anger in cleansing the Temple, we also must see that His act fell clearly within the context of God's purposes, which Jesus cited (see Matthew 21:12-13; John 2:14-17).

Many of the so-called "culture wars," which characterize the relationships of conservative Christian churches and the non-Christian world, come dangerously close to violating this principle of foregoing anger as a tool for accomplishing the will of God. Scripture is clear that in terms of judgment and condemnation, wrath is something reserved for God and God alone (see Romans 12:19). To an environment charged with tension, James says (to his day and to ours) to be swift to hear, slow to speak and slow to wrath.

Having laid the conceptual groundwork for this kind of response, James follows it with an imperative command: **Therefore, get rid of all moral filth and the evil that is so prevalent and humbly accept the word planted in you, which can save you** (Jas. 1:21). The word **therefore** ties this imperative to what preceded in 1:19-20. The implication is that James is addressing a situation where a lot of careless talk and anger are being evidenced with precious little sympathetic listening. Using exceptionally blunt language, James commands an end to such conditions with a twofold command.

First, the Christians are to **get rid of all moral filth**—literally, "filthiness" or "impurity." The word James uses here in the Greek is found only here in the New Testament. It refers to a kind of "sordid avarice."[2] The latter definition is significant in light of James's emphasis on the problems that can come with wealth (see 2:1-13; 5:1-6). The idea of ridding ourselves of impurity is notable, given James's insistence throughout the letter on purity, authenticity and single-mindedness (versus double-mindedness). Such immoral behavior is not conducive to true religion; therefore it must go.

Second, James includes **the evil that is so prevalent**—literally, superfluous evil. Practical man that he is, James knows that evil is absolutely worthless in producing the goal of true religion—a righteous life. Evil, too, must go.

Specifically what is referred to here by the "prevalent evil" is unknown, although it would be reasonable to associate it with the behavior spoken of in James 1:19-20. This good riddance to, or "putting off," is to be accompanied by a corresponding "acceptance" or "receiving, taking to oneself" **the word planted in you, which can save you** (1:21). (The use of "ridding oneself" here is similar to Paul's writing style—see Colossians 3:9-10; Ephesians 4:22-24.)

James is clearly emphasizing that the Word is instrumental in bringing us to God and keeping us close to God. It is in us because God has put it there; it is implanted. This reveals God's initiative in salvation. But we also have a part in salvation—that is, to accept the Word, as James admonishes his readers. The work of the Word is begun by God and sustained by God, but all who have been given this "imperishable" seed (see 1 Peter 1:23) are responsible both for allowing the seed to grow unhindered and for living in ways that promote its flourishing into full flower. James's advice is emphasized by the truth that this Word implanted is the Word which saves (see James 1:21)—literally, "being able to save your souls." James speaks here of a kind of "synergy"—a working partnership—between God and humans. This partnership will characterize James's understanding of salvation throughout the letter.

2. THE PRACTICE OF TRUE RELIGION 1:22-25

James uses the remaining verses of his opening chapter to explain to his readers how to become faithful practitioners of true religion. The critical element hinges around James's insistence that true religion allows for no divorce between hearing and obeying: **Do not merely listen to the word, and so deceive yourselves. Do what it says** (Jas. 1:22). Earlier, James counseled his readers that they should be "quick to listen" (1:19). There, the immediate context seemed to point to the need to listen to others in ways that would promote peace and harmony. Here he urges that mere listening alone is insufficient when it involves the **word** which is able to "save" (1:21-22).

In terms of this saving word, James insists that hearing must be accompanied by obeying—**Do what it says** (1:22). The author reflects two parallel traditions in his insistence on obedience. First, he appeals to the basic Jewish conception of "hearing." The Hebrew word for "hear" is *shema* and, as such, the "Shema" referred to the well-known words of Deuteronomy 6:4-5: "Hear, O Israel: The LORD our God, the LORD is one. Love the LORD your God with all your heart and with all your soul and with all your strength." Every Jew knew of the Shema. Conscientious Jews repeated these words over and over again as the foundation of their faith. But, what is actually being commanded here when the words "Hear, O Israel" are invoked?

Does the command to hear merely mean that these words are to be listened to and then forgotten? Is this simply about the physical phenomenon of sound waves bouncing off one's eardrums? Of course not. The Jewish sense of the word *shema*—"to hear"—implied that if one did not proceed to act upon the words spoken, it was evidence that the words were never really heard. In short, to hear that one should love God with all of one's heart, soul, and strength meant that one's hearing was evidenced by living according to the words spoken. So there can be no divorcing of hearing from obeying.

The context of this epistle demonstrates that religious practice has become largely a matter of talking about faith and not living it. James appeals to a basic tenet of Jewish religious understanding to make the critical point that the life-giving Word has to be obeyed to remain life-giving. The combination of hearing and doing has always been a fundamental element of the Jewish faith. It is a fundamental element of true religion even yet, says James.

The other line of thinking appealed to here is obviously that of Jesus in the Sermon on the Mount (see Matthew 7:24-27). Jesus' concluding story about the wise and foolish men who build on differing foundations was meant to illustrate the uselessness of merely hearing His words without putting them into practice. In this illustration, Jesus, too, reaffirmed the connection between hearing and doing. We are saved by this implanted Word when we actually practice what it tells us to do.

At different places in the Gospels, Jesus says, "He who has ears to hear, let him hear" (Mark 4:9; Luke 8:8; 14:35).[3] Like the words of Deuteronomy, Jesus' words call attention to the fact that the evidence of truly hearing His words will be seen in what a person does following the hearing. This principle is fundamental to the practice of authentic religion as portrayed in this epistle. It is a principle anchored in Judaism and in the teachings of Christ as well.[4] True religion means true obedience to the Word of truth.

James continues the emphasis upon obedience to the Word by illustrating his point: **Anyone who listens to the word but does not do**

what it says is like a man who looks at his face in a mirror and, after looking at himself, goes away and immediately forgets what he looks like (Jas. 1:23-24). This well-known illustration comparing obedience to the Scriptures with the act of looking **in a mirror** (1:23) has intrigued biblical students across the years. The image underscores that the Scriptures are the means of our coming to see clearly and accurately—they are the Word of truth. This is particularly the case in terms of knowing ourselves. Such illumination can be humbling, discouraging, and even intimidating. There is much in Scripture that we might prefer to ignore or conveniently forget.

To listen to the Word and then fail to practice it, says James, is akin to going to a mirror to learn what one looks like, and then immediately forgetting all details of what has just been seen. The very purpose of looking in the mirror has been displaced. Even after seeing the reflection, the person hasn't a clue what he or she looks like. The mirror has proven to be practically useless.

The critical aspect of the comparison here has to do with why the person forgot what was seen. It wasn't due to a deficiency in the mirror—the reflection was clearly there. The problem was in the carelessness of not committing the reflection to memory. In the same way that one can "hear" without really hearing, here is one who "saw" without truly seeing. That's the danger of not practicing the Word. We must knowingly commit ourselves to observing what we see in God's Word—to doing what we hear. James knows, as do all of us, that this is easier said than done. There is something about the nature of truth that makes fallen human nature tend to ignore it, to forget what it looks like.

We see a group of people in the Gospel of John who illustrate James's point. These were people who prided themselves on their knowledge of Scripture, but Jesus told them that their "knowledge" was extremely deficient, for they did not even recognize their own Messiah! Jesus then made the critical connection between knowing and doing, hearing and obeying: "To the Jews who had believed in Him, Jesus said: 'If you hold to my teaching, you are really my disciples. Then you will know the truth, and the truth will set you free'" (John 8:31-32).

That clause, "the truth will set you free," is one of the most misquoted and abused statements in all of Scripture. People across all spectrums of life and faith employ this phrase as their credo. But the point here is not that truth or mere *knowing* can set one free; Jesus' point was that only if we hold to His teachings—obey or practice them—are we truly His disciples. Then, *and only then,* will we know the liberating truth.

The tendency to divorce hearing from obeying is as old as the Garden of Eden. But true religion is built solidly on this premise: to hear is to obey. James continues his emphasis of this point by illustrating the positive response: **But the man who looks intently into the perfect law that gives freedom, and continues to do this, not forgetting what he has heard, but doing it—he will be blessed in what he does** (Jas. 1:25).

Here is the promise of true religion: Blessing is by way of obedience. To gaze intently into the perfect law is to come to see it for what it truly is: God's liberating will for human life.[5] Here James shifts from the connection between *hearing* and doing to that of *seeing* and doing. To look intently and then act on it . . . **not forgetting what he has heard, but doing it** . . . will bring the blessedness of true religion. This is the essence of what persevering in the faith is about—continuing in obedience to God's Word.

The words chosen here by James hint that Psalm 1 is in the background. "Blessed is the man" who follows closely the ways of God, says the opening verse by the psalmist. Specifically, James's emphasis upon looking intently into the law is the focus of verse 2 of the psalm: "But his delight is in the law of the LORD, and on his law he meditates day and night." The blessings that accrue from such obedience are evidenced in verse 3: "He is like a tree planted by streams of water, which yields its fruit in season and whose leaf does not wither. Whatever he does prospers." The contrasting fate of the wicked, namely those who do not meditate on God's law, shows the curse of disobedience.[6] The way to persevere successfully in the faith is to allow the **law** of God (Jas. 1:25) to capture our lives to the point where our responses are reflections of that law.

James clearly demonstrates a sound Jewish understanding of "law." To the Hebrew, law—or *torah* in Hebrew—was a sublime gift from God to His people.[7] To know what God desired of them and to be able to walk within the confines of His will was the glory of all true Israelites. Rather than seeing law as some confining attempt on the part of God to restrict the self-actualization of humankind, the Jews correctly embraced God's law as a means of living in accordance with the Creator's purposes. This was the way of "wisdom" (see additional notes at the end of this chapter).

This understanding of God's commandments has always characterized the Judeo-Christian faith. Jesus freely confessed that He had come to "fulfill" the law, and He commanded His followers to a level of righteousness that exceeded that of the scribes and Pharisees (see Matthew 5:17-20). The Apostle Paul, the champion of "justification by faith alone," insisted that grace doesn't set one free to go one's own way. On the contrary, real grace binds us ever closer to God and to His will for our lives (see Romans 6). And John said in his first epistle, "This is love for God: to obey his commands. And his commands are not burdensome" (1 John 5:3). John saw no contradiction between a life of obedience and a life of joyful liberty. Neither does James. Although much has been made of supposed discrepancies between the thinking of James and the rest of the New Testament writers, it is clear that James's perception of God's law parallels that of the rest of the New Testament.

This view of God's commands as something that liberates—as something that is in our best interests—is crucial to James's argument that the practice of true religion is the answer to the problems that confront the communities to which he writes. The way of joy is the way of continuing in the faith. The way of continuing in the faith is the way of living in accordance with God's will. God's will is revealed to us in His commandments. True religion is the way of obedience.

In much the same way as James encounters here, our own day is filled with people who insist upon their religious standing by virtue of merely hearing the Word. They claim a redemptive kind of hearing, while its practice is very foreign to them. Beyond that, the popular conception of "law" and "commandments" is too often that they are suffocating to human freedom and are infringements upon self-realization. The temptation for the church in such conditions is to fudge on our commitment to Scripture—to compromise with the unbelieving world in an attempt to prove that we really do believe in "freedom."

Far too often, the confessing church has become an accommodating church, divorcing hearing from obeying in ways that rob the gospel of its transforming power. All such attempts are doomed to failure, for as James puts it so clearly, our freedom is bound to that very law which the critics claim constricts and binds us. The Old Testament Scriptures, Jesus, and James all agree: Our freedom is in obedience to God. Apart from a clear call to obediently practice the word of Scripture, there is no future for true religion.

3. THE TOUCHSTONE OF TRUE RELIGION 1:26-27

A touchstone is a standard or criterion by which something is judged. James contends in his epistle that there is a touchstone by which true religion can be measured. First, he cites an obvious disqualifier for claiming to be truly religious: **If anyone considers**

himself religious and yet does not keep a tight rein on his tongue, he deceives himself and his religion is worthless (Jas. 1:26).

The core argument of James's reasoning—indeed, the whole point of his epistle—is that real religion works! It is practical, it is blessed by God, and it results in harmonious communities. By contrast, there is a kind of **religion** (Jas. 1:26) that is empty, vain and cursed in terms of its value to humankind. It is the kind of religion that destroys communities. For James, this worthless kind of religion is clearly illustrated by those whose undisciplined talk would undermine any religious claim they might make. Careless and harmful speech is a major theme of this epistle, and James will explore it in detail in his third chapter. But here he uses the failure to exercise control over one's tongue as an illustration of false religion.

For James, religious faith is imminently useful. Faith is something that helps us to live in ways that matter. To claim to be **religious** (1:26), and yet be unable to do something as elementary as regulate one's speech, is deception and vanity, not true religion.

True religion, the underlying theme of this entire epistle, is defined by James in 1:27: **Religion that God our Father accepts as pure and faultless is this: to look after orphans and widows in their distress and to keep oneself from being polluted by the world.** This kind of faith qualifies as true **religion,** first of all by the significant fact that God himself accepts such religious endeavor as **pure and faultless.** Something that is pure is entire, whole, undiluted. It is singular in its essence, not fractured nor distracted.

Given James's concern over double-minded people—those who have divided loyalties and distracted motives—this verse is certainly well-chosen by many as the key verse of the epistle. It is a hinge upon which the entire letter swings. Understanding what true religion encompasses is fundamental to grasping James's concern in the remainder of the letter. True religion is literally "clean and undefiled" faith. That kind of faith profession is James's hope for these fractured and troubled Jewish-Christian communities. This kind of religion is two-dimensional. It has both horizontal and vertical aspects to it: it relates in specific ways to both God and our fellow human beings.

Significantly, in light of the opening section of the epistle's next chapter (see James 2), the author places the horizontal dimension of human relationships first. True religion involves the horizontal aspect of caring for people in need. The use here of **orphans and widows in their distress** (1:27) not only refers to a most tangible illustration of people who need care, but also recalls Old Testament teachings.

Exodus 22 contains several admonitions regarding the responsibilities of the Israelites to care for the needy in their midst. Verse 22 specifies, "Do not take advantage of a widow or an orphan." Deuteronomy 14 reminds the Israelites that part of the reason for the tithe is to insure that the fatherless and widows are cared for properly, the result of such obedience being that "the LORD your God may bless you in all the work of your hands" (14:29b). The linkage of compassionate behavior with the covenant-blessing language is extremely significant as it is used here.[8] James may have had these passages of Scripture in mind since he seems to have utilized the formula of blessing, cursing and obedience as found in Deuteronomy (see additional notes at the end of this chapter of the commentary).

Further, Deuteronomy 16 specifies the inclusion of the fatherless and the widows in the celebration of the Feast of Weeks (see 16:11, 14). The needy people in Israel's midst are to be included in the general religious life of the community. Israel's role in the covenant is to be an instrument by which God blesses the rest of humankind, and the neediest subgroups of the community are included in God's design.

In fact, God himself is described in similar compassionate terms in one of the Psalms. There, along with other descriptions of Israel's God, Yahweh is called "a father to the fatherless, a defender of widows" (Ps. 68:5a). In the final analysis, the essence of true religion is to imitate one's God. The God of Israel, the God of Christianity, is a God who cares about the needy in His midst. His worshipers can do no less.

Attempting to pass oneself off as religious while neglecting this kind of social concern was considered the height of folly by the Old Testament writers. Isaiah condemned Israel in the strongest terms when he said, "Woe to those who make unjust laws, to those who issue oppressive decrees, to deprive the poor of their rights and withhold justice from the oppressed of my people, making widows their prey and robbing the fatherless. What will you do on the day of reckoning, when disaster comes from afar? To whom will you run for help? Where will you leave your riches?" (Isa. 10:1-3).

Malachi, who, centuries before James, championed a return by Israel to the practices of true religion, warned those who yearned for Messiah to appear that they may get more than they bargained for: "So I will come near to you for judgment. I will be quick to testify against sorcerers, adulterers and perjurers, against those who defraud laborers of their wages [see James 5:4], who oppress the widows and the fatherless, and deprive aliens of justice, but do not fear me,' says the LORD Almighty" (Mal. 3:5). It is apparent that these foundational Old Testament teachings are in the mind of James when he so defines true religion. Religion with no heart for other people is not real religion at all.

Moreover, James surely must remember the teachings of the Lord, his half brother, on such topics. Jesus made a point in Mark's gospel of criticizing the scribes and Pharisees—people who claimed the highest kind of religious ideals, and yet were apt to "devour widow's houses and for a show make lengthy prayers. Such men will be punished most severely" (Mark 12:40). Given James's open identification with the poor, together with the likely opposition wealthy Jewish classes had to the Christian efforts toward justice (see introduction), it is probable that these teachings of Jesus are clearly in mind here as well.

Finally, the incident in Acts 6 concerning the distribution of food for the widows in Jerusalem—an event James likely witnessed and perhaps helped resolve—may be in his mind here. This tangible expression of compassion on the part of the early church, along with the numerous references to caring for the widows, in the rest of the New Testament (see 1 Timothy 5) demonstrate that caring for the needy was long considered a fundamental practice of the Christian faith. Religious claims can sound hollow apart from such evidence of practical concern for the needy.

Employing the same touchstone to our contemporary religious claims, we must ask ourselves, "Who are the needy among us?" and then investigate our willingness to care for them. Certainly Wesley's legacy with the poor and needy of his own day models the commitment to true religion that James admonishes here. In his well-documented love and concern for the poor, Wesley properly modeled the way for all who share the heritage of his name and his example.

Ultimately, our fidelity to the historic Christian faith is evidenced not by our religious claims but by our religious acts. James will pursue that theme vigorously in his next chapter, but he uses it here to invalidate the religious claims of those who "talk the talk" without "walking the walk." As one British missionary put it so bluntly, "Your theology, plain or simple, is what you do when the talking stops and the action starts." All religious claims must be evidenced by our response to the neediest in our midst. If they "do not know us," then it is likely, says James, that Jesus doesn't "know us" either.

In addition to the call to compassionate love for others, there is a vertical dimension to true religion. This dimension more particularly reflects one's relationship to God himself, and this is summarized in the call to keep oneself from being polluted by the world. The theme of separation from the world will arise later in more detail in this epistle (see James 4), but here James employs it to underscore the reality of one's religious claims.

True religion involves purity in the guise of separation. Being truly religious is being different from the world. And James's wording—**to keep oneself from being polluted** (Jas. 1:27b)—indicates that it is a matter of one's choices or will. This reaffirms James's emphasis on the "desires" that lead us closer to or away from God (see comments on 1:14-15; 4:1-5; and see additional notes on desire at the end of chapter 10 of the commentary). Our relationship to God is evidenced by our orientation to Him, and likewise it is undermined by our willingness to be oriented to a world that has rejected God (see 4:4).

While the horizontal dimension of true religion—caring for the widows and the orphans—necessarily involves engagement in the world, the vertical dimension insures distance from the world. Jesus himself prayed that His followers might be in the world but not of the world (see John 17:15-16). That kind of dual relationship seems to be the illustration for what James is trying to portray here as the touchstone or standard by which true religion is measured.

James calls his readers to this kind of authentic religion: to be actively engaged in the world around us, and yet to be sufficiently separated from the world so that its ways and destiny do not affect us as believers. The beauty of this description is in its balance.

Unfortunately, the history of Christianity largely reveals a lack of balance. Typically, one element of authentic religion takes preeminence and smothers the other. The result has been all sorts of distorted pictures of religious faith. There have been, and still are, religious practitioners who have neglected any real involvement in the lives of people around them, and who have instead holed up in spiritual ghettos to practice a faith that appears totally irrelevant to the rest of the world.

On the other hand, there have been those whose eagerness to engage the world around them is so overwhelming that often there is no discernible difference between the lives and values of those claiming religious faith and those to whom they minister. Each is a tragic distortion of balanced spirituality, which is the kind of vital religious faith God has always desired for His people. Jesus modeled this as the kind of wholeness of the Incarnation, and it is the kind of faith that has made a genuine difference in the world through the centuries.[9] It is the faith that James champions in his epistle, and it is this kind of faith—true religion—that all those who claim to follow Jesus are called to imitate.

The task of keeping our faith profession in proper balance so that it truly does meet the criterion of true religion is the daunting task of discipleship. Every age will have differing challenges that tempt believers to err to one side or the other of the extremes of religion. But every age must resist the twin temptations of imagined relevance at the cost of purity and imagined purity at the cost of relevance.

ADDITIONAL NOTES ON JAMES AND THE OLD TESTAMENT

Before James was a Christian in the New Testament sense, he was a Jew in the Old Testament sense. In fact, James was a Jew all of his life. To forget that fact when reading his epistle is to omit a critical resource in understanding what James is trying to say to us. The Jewish-Christian churches to whom James wrote were also profoundly influenced by their Jewish roots in the Old Testament Scriptures. Therefore, it is little surprise that James leans heavily upon the Old Testament for his understanding. This is doubly true when we remember that at the time of writing, there was no New Testament! While the Old Testament influence is pervasive throughout the epistle, there are two specific aspects of the Old Testament that help us grasp the meaning of this epistle: law and wisdom.

To the Jew, the Law—or Torah—was a supreme gift from God. To know the Law was to know what God expected of His creatures. To walk in the ways of the Law was to know the way of life, peace, and harmony with God. To disobey the Law was to break covenant with God and walk alone in the world.[10]

Given James's tendency toward practicality, there are two specific aspects of the Law that influence his writing more obviously than the rest. First, James's letter generally reflects the theology of the book of Deuteronomy. This final book of the Law—its name literally means "second law"—is essentially Moses' last will and testament to Israel. This book records Moses' retelling of the Law to Israel and his urge to them to remember and practice it after they took possession of the Promised Land. Moses' final admonition to Israel in chapter 30 reveals the overall emphasis of the book.

> Now what I am commanding you today is not too difficult for you or beyond your reach. It is not up in heaven, so that you have to ask, "Who will ascend into heaven to get it and proclaim it to us so

we may obey it?" Nor is it beyond the sea, so that you have to ask, "Who will cross the sea to get it and proclaim it to us so we may obey it?" No, the word is very near you; it is in your mouth and in your heart so you may obey it. See, I set before you today life and prosperity, death and destruction. For I command you today to love the LORD your God, to walk in his ways, and to keep his commands, decrees and laws; then you will live and increase, and the LORD your God will bless you in the land you are entering to possess. But if your heart turns away and you are not obedient, and if you are drawn away to bow down to other gods and worship them, I declare to you this day that you will certainly be destroyed. You will not live long in the land you are crossing the Jordan to enter and possess. This day I call heaven and earth as witnesses against you that I have set before you life and death, blessings and curses.[11] Now choose life, so that you and your children may live and that you may love the LORD your God, listen to his voice, and hold fast to him. For the LORD is your life, and he will give you many years in the land he swore to give to your fathers, Abraham, Isaac and Jacob (Deut. 30:11-20).

The theological importance of Deuteronomy is demonstrated again and again through the remainder of the Old Testament. Whenever the people of Israel "remembered" the Law and practiced it in their lives, they were blessed as a people. However, the Old Testament is filled with examples of when Israel "forgot" the Law, paid it only lip service, and experienced the resulting curse of disobedience promised in Deuteronomy. James, a man faithful to his Jewish heritage, had heard these Mosaic texts again and again. He knew that "playing" at religion was a most dangerous course to choose. The absolute necessity of obeying God's commands was deeply ingrained in him; it worked itself out in his insistence upon his readers' being doers of the Word. We can appreciate James's emphasis in this epistle upon the double-minded approach to religion that would try to have it both ways—friendship with God and friendship with the unbelieving world (see James 4:4-5).

The other aspect of the Law that shows itself clearly in this epistle is the so-called "holiness code" of Leviticus 19.[12] The book of Leviticus was critical to the religious life of the Israelites because they found themselves linked in covenant to a holy God, which meant that they must find proper ways of relating to Him. The thrust of Leviticus was to teach the Israelite people how they too could be holy and live in fellowship with their God.

Thus the book taught the people the sacrificial system, the rules for ritual cleansing, and laws regarding diet and such.

The nineteenth chapter of Leviticus introduces an element into the call to holiness which proves to be very near and dear to the heart of James in his epistle. Concerned with the relationship between holiness and one's personal conduct, specifically as it relates to the way we treat one another, Leviticus 19 is sometimes referred to as the "law of love." The area of special importance to James is the section of verses 12 through 18. Comparing the words of these verses to specific verses in James, we find the following allusions to the "law of love" in James's writing.

Leviticus 19:15—Do not pervert justice; do not show partiality to the poor or favoritism to the great, but judge your neighbor fairly.	**James 2:1**—My brothers, as believers in our glorious Lord Jesus Christ, don't show favoritism. **James 2:9**—But if you show favoritism, you sin and are convicted by the law as lawbreakers.
Leviticus 19:18b—. . . love your neighbor as yourself. I am the Lord.	**James 2:8**—If you really keep the royal law found in Scripture, "Love your neighbor as yourself," you are doing right.
Leviticus 19:16—Do not go about spreading slander among your people. Do not do anything that endangers your neighbor's life. I am the Lord.	**James 4:11**—Brothers, do not slander one another. Anyone who speaks against his brother or judges him speaks against the law and judges it. When you judge the law, you are not keeping it, but sitting in judgment on it.
Leviticus 19:13—Do not defraud your neighbor or rob him. Do not hold back the wages of a hired man overnight.	**James 5:4**—Look! The wages you failed to pay the workmen who mowed your fields are crying out against you. The cries of the harvesters have reached the ears of the Lord Almighty.
Leviticus 19:18a—Do not seek revenge or bear a grudge against one of your people.	**James 5:9**—Don't grumble against each other, brothers, or you will be judged. The Judge is standing at the door!

Leviticus 19:12—Do not swear falsely by my name and so profane the name of your God. I am the LORD.	**James 5:12**—Above all, my brothers, do not swear—not by heaven or by earth or by anything else. Let your "Yes" be yes, and your "No," no, or you will be condemned.
Leviticus 19:17—Do not hate your brother in your heart. Rebuke your neighbor frankly so you will not share in his guilt.	**James 5:20**—Remember this: Whoever turns a sinner from the error of his way will save him from death and cover over a multitude of sins.[13]

James's emphasis on practical religion—being a doer, rather than merely a hearer of the Word—is powerfully underscored by the allusions to Leviticus 19. That chapter of the Old Testament Law reminded every member of Israel that holiness is not merely saying the right things or dressing the right way or even performing the right religious acts. Holiness also involves a distinctive approach to life, specifically as it relates to the way we treat others around us. That's the language James speaks in his letter, and it is the ancient language of the Torah.

The other major Old Testament influence on James is "wisdom." The so-called Wisdom books of the Old Testament represent a distinct philosophy of life that began to appear in Israel soon after the appearance of the Law.[14] Whereas the Greeks thought of wisdom as the search for the "real" or the "street smarts" that enable a person to be successful in life, Hebrew wisdom was different. The primary meaning behind the Hebrew word for "wisdom" *(hokmah)* is that of moral discernment. To be wise in the Hebrew sense was much more than gaining worldly success. To be truly wise meant doing what was right according to God's law and God's way. Wisdom or knowledge, therefore, was the obedient application of God's law to every part of one's life. As the book of Proverbs says, "the fear of the LORD is the beginning of knowledge" (Prov. 1:7).

The Hebrews were advised to get wisdom, and with wisdom to get understanding. In other words, it was never enough simply to *know* something; you also had to have the ability, the understanding and the will to put that knowledge to practical use! Walter Kaiser has written, "Wisdom is the cure for one of the greatest diseases of religion—a lack of reality, or unreality. Wisdom shows us how life is to be lived. It demonstrates how to be real, identifiable and meaningful."[15] These words which describe the Wisdom writings of the Old Testament also describe the Epistle of James.

In his introduction to James, Eugene Peterson uses similar language: "Wisdom is not primarily knowing the truth, although it certainly includes that; it is skill in living. For, what good is a truth if we don't know how to live it? What good is an intention if we can't sustain it?" (The Message). This is what makes James fit so nicely as the New Testament expression of "wisdom." It's not James's Proverb-like writing that places him in the tradition of Jewish Wisdom Literature; rather it is his adoption of the philosophy of life that says the law of God applies to every aspect of our being and is meant to be lived out, not simply talked!

Specifically, James's use of wisdom is seen in his emphasis on prayer and in relying on wisdom in times of testing (see 1:5). He sees wisdom as a gift from above that brings with it the kind of virtues necessary to sustain authentic Christian community. Some commentators have argued for a close identification of James's wisdom with the person of the Holy Spirit because Jewish thinking had long associated the gift of wisdom with the coming new age inaugurated by Jesus (see comments on 1:5; 3:17-18).[16] Regardless of the validity of this view, James's relationship to the Wisdom tradition of Israel is an indispensable tool in understanding the practical nature of his teachings.

ENDNOTES

[1]The Wisdom Literature includes the books of Job, Proverbs, Ecclesiastes, and Song of Songs (Song of Solomon). Also known as the Books of Poetry. These writings are collections of statements of wisdom, often dealing with the great issues of life, such as the problem of suffering, practical ethics and morality, and the meaning of life and love.

[2]Walter Bauer, *A Greek-English Lexicon of the New Testament and Other Early Christian Literature,* 2nd ed., translated by William F. Arndt and F. Wilbur Gingrich (Chicago: University of Chicago Press, 1979), p. 738.

[3]The Gospels include the New Testament books of Matthew, Mark, Luke, and John.

[4]Judaism is the belief and cultural system of the Jewish people, referring to the Jews' way of life as those in a covenant relationship with God, rather than just to their religious doctrine. Judaism in Jesus' day differed according to different sects, and there are still various branches of Judaism today, but the underlying theme among them has been a belief in one God and a recognition of the Law of God. Law here refers to the Pentateuch (the first five books of the Old Testament: Genesis, Exodus, Leviticus, Numbers, and Deuteronomy).

[5]Law refers to either the Levitical Code (all God's rules and regulations), the Ten Commandments, or the Pentateuch (the first five books of the Old Testament: Genesis, Exodus, Leviticus, Numbers, and Deuteronomy). Often capitalized when it means the Pentateuch or the Ten Commandments.

[6]Blessings and curses refer to the response of God to His people in accordance with their obedience to Him (blessings) or their disobedience (curses). In the Old Testament, God's power was invoked through power-laden words (blessings and curses) often spoken in prayer form. Through these blessings or curses, God's people would call upon Him to provide or care for them by affecting them in a positive way or those around them in a positive or negative way. In Judaism (see endnote 4), some blessings were reserved for the priests, but others were a regular part of the synagogue services. Curses were much less prominent and were forbidden. In the New Testament, the ultimate blessing came from God to mankind in Jesus Christ, and blessings accompanied righteousness. Curses accompanied sin.

[7]Torah is another name for the Pentateuch (the first five books of the Old Testament: Genesis, Exodus, Leviticus, Numbers, and Deuteronomy). The Hebrew word which *Torah* comes from is translated *law* and refers to divine instruction and guidance. The Torah (or Law) was the instructions and directions given to Israel by God. God had a covenant relationship with His chosen people, in which their fulfillment of a promise to live in obedience to His instructions was rewarded.

[8]See endnote 6.

[9]The Incarnation was God's coming to us in the person of Jesus.

[10]See endnote 7.

[11]See endnote 6.

[12]Much of this material is taken from Luke T. Johnson, "The Use of Leviticus 19 in the Letter of James," *Journal of Biblical Literature,* vols. 101–3 (1982), pp. 391–401.

[13]Johnson, p. 399.

[14]See endnote 1.

[15]Walter Kaiser, *The Old Testament in Contemporary Preaching* (Grand Rapids, Michigan: Baker Books, 1973), p. 119.

[16]Peter Davids, *James,* New International Bible Commentary (Peabody, Massachusetts: Hendrickson Publishers, Inc., 1983), p. 19.

Part Two

BARRIERS TO TRUE RELIGION

James 2:1-26

James's purpose in writing this epistle is to call his readers back to the practice of true religion. We can assume that he had reasons to feel it necessary to issue such a call. Beginning in his second chapter, the author attempts to address specific issues that have caused him concern over the authenticity of the faith and the unity of the Christian community.

Specifically, he addresses two separate, yet related, problems which serve as effective barriers to the practice of true religion. First, there is the problem of *favoritism*—showing partiality within the church. Second, James addresses the problem of *meaningless faith*—faith without the accompanying deeds to demonstrate its authenticity. Both issues are seen by James as behaviors barricading his people from the course of true religion. These are practices resulting in curse rather than the blessing that is promised to those whose religion is "pure and faultless."

5

THE BARRIER
OF FAVORITISM

James 2:1-13

ames begins this passage with a personal appeal: **My brothers, as believers in our glorious Lord Jesus Christ . . .** (Jas. 2:1a). The appeal to **brothers** announces another major emphasis on the part of the author, springing directly from James's conviction of what it means to be **believers in our glorious Lord Jesus Christ.** He has been calling for consistency in the response of his readers to what God has done (1:18-21). Here, he calls attention to their status as believers in Christ in order to address a specific problem.

This verse contains one of the only two direct references to Jesus in the epistle (see comments on 1:1). The use of the adjective **glorious** (2:1a) is the best way to bring out the significant meaning in the Greek, which links the person of Christ inseparably to the quality of glory. Again, James's doctrinal understanding of Jesus Christ is shown as primarily concerned with the exalted Lord who will return someday as Judge. This reference to his readers' belief in this kind of Christ underscores the reason for James's upcoming appeal to them.

James's concern is summed up with the blunt rendition, **don't show favoritism** (2:1b). The Greek word for **favoritism** here is rarely found in the New Testament, but has a rich Old Testament history behind it that demonstrates the gravity of such behavior (see additional notes on favoritism at the end of this chapter). The word refers to the practice of "respecting persons" or, literally, "receiving their faces." To respect persons is to do something which James considers wholly inconsistent with the status of being a believer in the exalted Christ. He goes on to demonstrate what he means by respect of persons and therein gives us insight into the kinds of problems that plagued these relatively young Jewish-Christian communities.

Suppose a man comes into your meeting wearing a gold ring and fine clothes, and a poor man in shabby clothes also comes in (Jas. 2:2). The word translated **meeting** in the New International Version is the word for "synagogue." The use of this word strongly indicates that this epistle was actually addressed to Jewish Christians who continued the use of the synagogue when the majority had embraced Christianity. This was a well-known practice for Jewish believers.

The contrast that James sets here is obvious. He locates the basis for distinguishing between the two people at the level of their outward appearance—but the appearance alone is enough to prompt differing responses. **If you show special attention to the man wearing fine clothes and say, "Here's a good seat for you," but say to the poor man, "You stand there" or "Sit on the floor by my feet," have you not discriminated among yourselves and become judges with evil thoughts?** (2:3-4).

James's concern about this issue is vividly illustrated. Based on appearance, the "well-dressed" man is honored while **the poor man** is humiliated. The genius of this illustration is, unfortunately, that it is so believable. It's exactly the way people typically respond to the rich and the poor among them. The wealthy are used to being (and even expect to be) shown to the seat of honor, while the poor are likewise resigned to being treated as something of a bother. But (and this is James's basic point) while that kind of response may be all too typical in our world, inside the faith community—among those who profess belief in the glorious Lord Jesus Christ—such behavior is scandalous.

The problem with such respect of persons is twofold. First, it involves discrimination **among yourselves**—"making class-distinctions in your minds" (Jas. 2:4, J. B. Phillips). Such actions involve the deliberate segregation of God's people into classes based on something that, as James argued earlier, is temporary at best (see 1:9-11). Second, these actions indicate the far more serious problem of people taking upon themselves the office of judge even though their thoughts are evil and prejudiced. Such a description is exactly the opposite of what makes for a competent judge. The one indispensable quality a judge must possess is complete impartiality. When distinctions are made on external factors like how one dresses or one's wealth, impartiality has disappeared and the cruelest sort of favoritism has been substituted.

Given James's emphasis on true religion in 1:27, this illustration may serve as an immediate indicator pointing to those who have, in fact, been "polluted" by the world. Such behavior is not in keeping with belief in

Christ and thus does not qualify as true religion. It does, however, indicate the presence of worldly influences—pollution—of the sort that would definitely disqualify someone's claim to being "religious."

This issue barricading the believers of James's day from the practice of true religion is also epidemic in our contemporary society. Our world is torn asunder by the sting of prejudice and class warfare. We have perfected the art of discriminating—of drawing lines between people based on factors every bit as superficial as in James's illustration.

People demonstrate their biases in a number of ways. They close themselves off from meaningful contact with those perceived to be different from them. They perpetuate a system which subtly continues to encourage separatism between classes and races and which serves to strengthen the obstacles to mutual understanding and fellowship. Such behaviors and attitudes betray the influence of the unbelieving world, for they represent the level of thinking which characterizes those who are in the world—"in the flesh," Paul would say. The "flesh" judges other people by socially approved external standards such as race, wealth, or economic class.

Such attitudes, misguided and destructive as they are, can be expected in the unbelieving world, but when they characterize the community of faith, something extremely sinister has taken place. Little wonder that this apostle who oversees the Jewish-Christian communities is so alarmed. Both the passion of his words and the amount of space devoted to the topic point out how fully James recognizes the danger of such attitudes in the church.

As a Jew, James thoroughly understood the motivations and attitudes of exclusion. Perhaps nothing was as much of a stumbling block to Jews coming to Christ as was the knowledge that to do so was to embrace the Gentiles as well. And yet, despite such overwhelming psychological and sociological barriers, this is precisely the point where the early church made its decisive break with Judaism.[1] One of the few other uses of James's word for **favoritism** (Jas. 2:1) is Peter's spiritual enlightenment at the house of Cornelius in the book of Acts where, having witnessed God's acceptance of the Gentiles, he exclaimed, "I now realize how true it is that God does not show favoritism" (Acts 10:34).

The story of the Jerusalem council (see Acts 15) was a watershed event in the life of the early church. There the leaders of the church determined that God's agenda for the whole world—for all peoples—would also be the agenda of His church. That council, led by James himself, decreed that nothing should be done that would hinder the work of God among the Gentile peoples. So James knew well the power of prejudice and the danger it presented to the health of the faith community.

This demonstrates again the significance of a correct view of God. Understanding that God himself does not show favoritism leads to the kind of transforming vision that characterized Peter and James and the leaders of the early church. Failing to incorporate the implications of God's universal love of human beings, regardless of external differences, is to fall too easily into the influence of a world bent on prejudice and favoritism.

Beyond this, the context of the epistle indicates a growing rift between the haves and have-nots. The disparity between people's economic status appears to be an increasingly sore point within the communities to whom James writes. If such issues cannot be reconciled within the community of believers, the future of Christianity is bleak. When people begin to choose sides, the faith can quickly fall into disrepute, and even more stirring incidents between classes are likely to follow.

It is little wonder, then, that James is determined to deal decisively with the problem of favoritism within the body. Acknowledging Jesus as Lord means grasping His love of all—rich and poor—and submitting to His authority over all peoples equally. Serving the God who cares for the "orphans and widows" means cherishing all persons equally, regardless of temporary earthly distinctions.

What is at stake here is nothing less than the integrity of the church of Jesus Christ. James and the apostles decreed the foundational truth of the good news in Acts 15: that God does not play favorites; that Christ's death is effective for all persons, no matter who they are or what their worldly status may be. While the simple act of showing deference to a rich person may not seem like the worst of sins, James correctly sees its destructive possibilities, especially in the tinderbox atmosphere of potential class warfare.

How relevant James's words are to our day, when "money talks." How carefully we ought to heed his warnings as we watch people—even within the church—drawing lines based on race and economic status. What an indictment against the gospel and against our claims of belief in the glorious Lord Jesus Christ. Think of the damage that has been done to the vitality and credibility of the church by submitting to the cultural standards that value and prefer people on the basis of things like income and social class. Believers have too easily ignored the fundamental equality of all people in terms of our status before God. Typically, this is because of the misguided notion our world has about the "worth" of certain people.

What makes such actions all the more shameful is the sad truth that sometimes favoritism has been shown to some (let's be honest) because of the potential of their *income* for the church. When this happens, the whole question of values has been divorced from the context of New Testament Christianity and particularly from the teachings of Jesus. The irony here is that Christ not only would condemn our favoritism, but also would condemn our mistreatment of the wealthy!

When viewed through the lens of material worth, people are reduced to objects, or a means to an end: the financial health of the church. In similar fashion, the poor are also typically judged as objects. They are considered not valuable because of their lack of resources, and thus lack significance for the health of the church. Both classes have been devalued as persons.

While James's concern here is portrayed against the backdrop of economic discrimination, his words give us pause, in light of the racial strife that tears at our society and which, all too often, pervades our churches. No amount of rationalization can justify the discriminating judgments that have been leveled at whole races of people. No amount of sociological babble can justify the mournful reality that the 11:00 A.M. Sunday worship service is the most segregated hour in America. James and John Wesley alike would wear sackcloth at such strange behavior on the part of the Christian community.

Unfortunately, such "discriminating" thinking has shown itself time and again when church planting experiments are deliberately located within the most financially secure neighborhoods and as far from the ghettos as possible. Defending these actions on the grounds of "long-range thinking" and "good stewardship" does little to convince us that James would find such thinking compelling in any way. Sadly, discrimination on the basis of race, wealth and social standing is a besetting sin in American church life. Socioeconomic prejudice runs as deep as racial prejudice. By overlooking the needs of the poor to serve the rich, we effectively give the seat of preference to the wealthy and show the poor to the corner of inattention, willing (perhaps) to let them have the crumbs from the table.

The problem of showing partiality in the church profoundly demonstrates James's concern over the growing rift between the rich and poor. It is a problem we see throughout the epistle. James now turns in 2:5 to this underlying problem: **Listen, my dear brothers: Has not God**

**chosen those who are poor in the eyes of the world to be rich in faith
and to inherit the kingdom he promised those who love him?**

The construction of the admonition, **Listen, my dear brothers** (Jas.
2:5), is such that if expressed in our day it might sound like this: "Now
get this straight. I don't want to have to say it twice!" Including the term
brothers heightens our sense of James's concern.

His undisguised outrage at this kind of behavior in the church is fired
by two realities. Here he deals with the first: Showing partiality toward
the rich goes against the way God works in His world. James is pointing
out the irony of the church's choosing the rich while God chooses the
poor (2:5). The author falls squarely into the prophetic tradition of the
Old Testament which sees the poor as especially cherished in the eyes of
God. Jesus himself reiterated this truth on different occasions, notably
in the Gospel of Luke, when He proclaimed, "Blessed are you who are
poor, for yours is the kingdom of God" (Luke 6:20). The fact that James
phrases the question as he does suggests that he believes there is no
question but that God has chosen the poor—it is beyond dispute.

The idea of God's choosing the poor has to be balanced with the truth
of God's impartiality. How can James first appeal to God's historic refusal
to play favorites, and then turn right around and suggest that God favors
the poor? The answer lies in James's task of combating the false teachings
that equate material blessing with spiritual attainment.

Already the author has debunked such ideas (see James 1:9-11).
Here he comes from the opposite side of the issue to suggest that there
is a possible link between richness in faith and one's social standing.
Jesus suggested, much to the amazement of the disciples, that it was
easier for a camel to go through the eye of a needle than for a rich man
to enter the Kingdom (see Matthew 19:24). The point Jesus was
making was that riches easily become a barrier to the sense of
dependence upon God, and dependence upon God is absolutely
necessary to enter the Kingdom.

In a parallel statement to Luke 6:20, Jesus used the phrase "poor in
spirit" (Matt. 5:3) to speak of those who enter the Kingdom. Much has
been written about how those two verses differ, but many would conclude
that there is much agreement between the two statements. It's not that
God shows partiality in turning His back on the wealthy, but that He
directs himself to those whose hearts are most open to Him. *The
Kingdom is given by God to those who recognize the poverty of their
status before Him.* The Kingdom is given to those who love Him. Wealth
and social standing have nothing whatsoever to do with it.

For the one who has failed to understand the transitory nature of wealth (see James 1:9-11), committing one's entire life in dependency upon God may prove to be most difficult. On the other hand, the poor would naturally hold far fewer illusions about their ability to sustain life on their own merits and resources. For this reason, the poor have historically responded much more openly to the gospel than the wealthy. Faith becomes the bulwark of life in the world for those in poverty. They are the ones who most generally demonstrate the realities of the Kingdom in their attitudes and behaviors. This is what James means when he says that God has chosen those who are poor. The nature of the Kingdom is such that ideas of self-sufficiency and independence represent an insurmountable barrier to entering.

In light of God's "choice" of the poor, then, how can the church ever feel good about the choices it makes where the poor are discriminated against? In such instances, the church ceases to be the body of Christ acting out the designs and will of the Head. Instead, it demonstrates that it has become "polluted" by the world, imitating earthly values in regard to playing favorites. James rightly sees this as a most destructive and unacceptable state of affairs.

But you have insulted the poor (Jas. 2:6a). Rather than imitate God's choice of the poor by investing them with dignity and value, James contends that the behavior of the Christian community has resulted in grievous insult. The word **insulted** literally means "to treat shamefully." The original Greek word used is the same word Paul used in Romans 1:24 in speaking of God's giving people over to the sinful desires of their hearts to the extent that they degrade their bodies with one another. That usage is significant because James considers favoritism a behavior that "degrades" the body of Christ. Class distinctions—showing partiality— are to the health of the body of Christ what unbridled sexual lust is to the health of the human body—ultimately destructive.

James's words are sobering and frightening in light of our present culture's tendency to make social, racial and class distinctions ever more significant in the way we relate to one another. Surely this is a case where we must be hearers and doers of the Word, lest true religion be swallowed up by societal evil.

James's concern over this issue also has to do with his inability to understand the reasoning behind showing favoritism. He sees a puzzling incongruity between the church's desire to show partiality to the rich and the fact that the rich typically show contempt for the church: **Is it not the rich who are exploiting you? Are they not the ones who are dragging**

you into court? Are they not the ones who are slandering the noble name of him to whom you belong? (Jas. 2:6b-7).

Here is James's practicality showing through once again. Playing favorites might be understandable if it represented a mutually beneficial relationship. But he points out that the relationship that generally exists between the rich and the Christian community is anything but mutually beneficial. The rich don't treat the church any better for the favoritism they are shown. James levels a three-pronged charge against the rich. By doing this, he expects to undermine any naive assumptions that simply treating the rich preferentially will benefit the Christian community.

First, James reminds his readers that as a class, it is **the rich who are exploiting** (oppressing) them (Jas. 2:6b). While he is clearly speaking in generalities (not all rich people are exploiters), James means to emphasize the lessons of history in regard to material power. Failure to accept the transitory nature of possessions (see 1:9-11) results in a skewed vision of life where wealth equals power. With this power comes the liberty to use other people as the means to keep one's wealth or to acquire more. The Old Testament prophets preached often and eloquently about how God views such treatment of people by those with wealth. James is shocked that Jewish-Christians, steeped in the Old Testament Scriptures, would be duped into bowing before their oppressors.

Second, James reminds his readers that it is the rich **who are dragging you into court** (2:6b). Evidently, the wealthy were exercising their economic power over the courts and employing it to their advantage against the Christian community. Ironically, such states of affairs ought to have taught believers how important it is to keep partiality out of the church. The courts were supposed to be the place where one could obtain justice regardless of social or economic standing. Unfortunately, history is filled with examples of the way influence has been purchased—literally and figuratively—to tilt the scales of justice. Knowing this to be case, and knowing how frustrated they must be by such conditions, James cannot believe that Christians ever would attempt to reproduce such biases within the church. Why would they resort to treating the poor the way the rich were treating them?

Third, James returns to the opening line of thought he expressed in this chapter, by appealing to his readers' status as **believers in our glorious Lord Jesus Christ** (2:1). That description was intended to encompass the whole of their lives. Calling Jesus **Lord** was admitting His sovereign control over every aspect of their being. In light of that, how could they show favor to people **who are slandering the noble name of him to whom [they] belong** (2:7)? The willingness to live with such contradictions is part of the double-minded approach to religion that James attacks throughout his letter. Valuing those who blaspheme the source and essence of one's Christian identity demonstrates the "pollution" of the world and its values, rather than the pure and faultless religion that God accepts. Desiring the intoxicating approval of the wealthy to the point of discriminating against the poor undermines any valid claim to being associated with Jesus.

In keeping with his overall emphasis on hearing and doing the word, James casts his concern about the issue of favoritism into conditional form: **If you really keep the royal law found in Scripture, "Love your neighbor as yourself," you are doing right** (Jas. 2:8). This reference to Leviticus 19:18 serves as a summary of God's commands regarding the treatment of neighbors by Israel. Jesus himself reiterated the significance of this command on different occasions in the Gospels (see Mark 12:31, 33; Luke 10:27).[2]

The importance of these words was clearly understood by all who grew up within Judaism. The description of this law as royal demonstrates the way Jesus' teachings regarding the "greatest of the commandments" were followed in the early church. To love your neighbor as yourself represented the height of the law; it was the supreme law.[3] To those who count themselves as **believers in our glorious Lord Jesus Christ** (Jas. 2:1), disregarding the royal law—the "kingly" word of Jesus—would be unthinkable.

James presses home the utter inconsistency of claiming to adhere to these words while practicing favoritism: **But if you show favoritism, you sin and are convicted by the law as lawbreakers** (2:9). This recalls the specific admonition of Leviticus 19:15: "Do not pervert justice; do not show partiality to the poor or favoritism to the great, but judge your neighbor fairly." The call to neighborly love is not issued in a vacuum. Loving one's neighbor calls for certain attitudes and practices. The keeping of this royal **law** of neighborly love is praiseworthy and is evidence of doing right, while practicing **favoritism** completely undermines such claims (Jas. 2:9).

James adds the indictment that this royal law which validates our claims also judges us. According to this law, practicing favoritism is lawbreaking. The author's appeal to lawbreaking here is informative. While showing favoritism may be culturally acceptable and even beneficial at times, it invalidates our religious claims based on the ancient standard of God's law for His people. We can have the approval of those around us, or we can have the approval of God's will as expressed in His commandments. But let us be clear: no amount of cultural affirmation can overcome the charge of breaking the royal law.

The tendency in cases such as these is to view the issue solely in light of pragmatic concerns. So the thinking goes, "Paying special attention to the rich can sometimes 'pay off' for the church. Whereas if we don't treat them special, we know we won't get their loyalty. Therefore, in the interest of strengthening the church, let's show the wealthy a little special favor now and then. It couldn't hurt, and it might help. After all, we want to build the church." But James insists that the issue must be placed within the larger context of the command to neighborly love. Building the church is important, but not at any cost and especially not at the cost of disobeying the royal law. James replaces cultural and pragmatic concerns with the primary call to obeying what God says (see James 1:22).

Ultimately what turns a group of people into a church is their commitment to be molded by total obedience to this royal law. To claim to believe in Jesus and then practically ignore His teachings is hypocrisy of the highest degree. The reason is obvious to James: **For whoever keeps the whole law and yet stumbles at just one point is guilty of breaking all of it. For he who said, "Do not commit adultery," also said, "Do not murder." If you do not commit adultery but do commit murder, you have become a lawbreaker** (2:10-11).

Here is another powerful example of James's commitment to attack halfhearted religious practice. There cannot be selective obedience. All of the law expresses God's intentions. One cannot obey most of the law and then disobey one command without becoming a **lawbreaker.** There is no such thing as disobedience followed by the claim of keeping the commands of God. The **law** as a whole is an expression of God's will for His people. God never intended that His commands become a kind of moral cafeteria where people pick and choose what appeals to them. James insists that obedience is not a matter of finding things one agrees with, or those rules which one finds easiest to keep, and ignoring the difficult issues.

James's choice of terms here is meant to properly identify this for people steeped in the Jewish tradition of keeping the law. But his words also speak powerfully to our own day where selective obedience is a particularly crippling sin within the Christian community. We have become suspiciously selective in our obedience to God's Word. We have found that most of our society will allow us the privilege of picking out a few commands, obeying them, and then claiming to be "religious folk." James tells us that while such selective obedience passes for religion in the world, it does not find acceptability with God (see 1:22-27).

This section is intended to instruct the community on how to solve the troubling issue of favoritism. Favoritism is best handled by recalling clearly the eternal perspective—including judgment—which ought to characterize all true believers: **Speak and act as those who are going to be judged by the law that gives freedom, because judgment without mercy will be shown to anyone who has not been merciful. Mercy triumphs over judgment!** (Jas. 2:12-13). Note here the linkage of speaking and acting. Again, James insists on consistency between one's words and deeds. Both words and acts are to take place in the context of those who will themselves face judgment.

To people who seem overly interested in usurping the position of judges, James gives a reminder of the standard by which they themselves are to be measured. Implicit in this warning against **judgment** are the words of Jesus that those who show **mercy** are in turn shown mercy themselves (see Matthew 5:7), and that to those who withhold mercy, judgment will be severe (see Matthew 18:32-35). The law of love which extends mercy to all "lawbreakers" is not available to those who violate that same law of love by showing preference for people on the basis of wealth.

James's use of mercy stands in stark contrast to the idea of favoritism. Mercy is what all of us have received from God. It is not deserved or merited in any way. Mercy is not extended on the basis of any earthly standing or possession; it is given as an expression of God's care and love for us.

To people who were being pressured into responding to others on the basis of their wealth and standing, James offers the only standard which those who claim the name of Christ can use when responding to others: **mercy** (Jas. 2:13). We are to respond to other people in the way that God through Christ has responded to us. No other standard is acceptable for those who claim to follow the way of Jesus. Regardless of the possible benefits of judging and showing favoritism, regardless of the pressure to adopt the standards of worldly achievement within the church, the bottom line is the command to show mercy rather than judgment. **Mercy triumphs over judgment** (2:13b).

ADDITIONAL NOTES ON FAVORITISM

My brothers, as believers in our glorious Lord Jesus Christ, don't show favoritism (Jas. 2:1). James's use of the Greek word translated here as **favoritism** (*prosopolampsia*) serves as still another example of the Old Testament roots of this epistle. The word itself is extremely rare, found in only four other places in the New Testament (see Acts 10:34; Romans 2:11; Ephesians 6:9; Colossians 3:25). What makes the use of this word even more intriguing is that it is not found at all in ancient Greek literature outside of the Bible. Its existence is best explained by considering it to be a Hebraism (somewhat akin to a Hebrew "slang" word) that gained popular usage in Hellenistic Judaism (Greek-encultured Judaism; see glossary for *Judaism*).

The word itself *(prosopolampsia)* is formed from the two Greek words *lambanein prospon,* meaning "to receive or accept face." While the word evidently found its way into the New Testament through its being used in everyday speech, the origins of the concept are found in the Old Testament. *Lambanein prospon* (and, therefore, James's word **favoritism** [Jas. 2:1]) was a shortened form of *lambanein prosopon,* which would have appeared in the Septuagint.[4]

The idea behind the term is that God is an unbiased judge who shows no regard for persons. The book of Deuteronomy says, "For the LORD your God is God of gods and Lord of lords, the great God, mighty and awesome, who shows no partiality and accepts no bribes" (Deut. 10:17). This is communicated in the Old Testament with a Hebrew word that literally refers to "lifting up" either the face or the head of someone.

For example, in Genesis 40, Joseph prophesied to Pharaoh's cupbearer, "Within three days Pharaoh will lift up your head and restore you to your position, and you will put Pharaoh's cup in his hand, just as you used to do when you were his cupbearer" (Gen. 40:13). The prophecy was fulfilled: "Now the third day was Pharaoh's birthday, and he gave a feast for all his officials. He lifted up the heads of the chief cupbearer and the chief baker [in the case of the baker, 'lifting up the head' was to be literal!] in the presence of his officials" (Gen. 40:20). To "lift up" the head or face of someone is to show them particular favor. The psalmist demonstrated this when he wrote, "But you are a shield around me, O LORD; you bestow glory on me and lift up my head" (Ps. 3:3).

The significance of this for James is that the Hebrew word behind his Greek word for **favoritism** (Jas. 2:1) is typically translated *partiality* and most often refers to the practice of human judges. Deuteronomy particularly stresses the need for impartiality in human judges: "Do not show partiality in judging; hear both small and great alike. Do not be afraid of any man, for judgment belongs to God. Bring me any case too hard for you, and I will hear it" (Deut. 1:17). Also, "Do not pervert justice or show partiality. Do not accept a bribe, for a bribe blinds the eyes of the wise and twists the words of the righteous" (Deut. 16:19). The author of the Chronicles—heavily influenced by the theology of Deuteronomy—said, "Now let the fear of the LORD be upon you. Judge carefully, for with the LORD our God there is no injustice or partiality or bribery" (2 Chron. 19:7). Israel was continually warned against the practice of showing partiality (lifting up the faces of people) because it perverted justice and, most importantly, because it betrayed God's own example.

James's adoption of this Hebraism which literally means to "lift up or receive the face" of someone in an act of partiality flows out of the Old Testament concern that people within the community be confident that they would be treated by human judges as God himself would treat them. The New Testament emphasizes God's refusal to show partiality in terms far beyond what any Old Testament Jew could have envisioned. The acceptance of Gentiles into the covenant demonstrates that God's love for humankind knows no barriers—He will not play favorites.[5] Therefore, James sees it as extremely troubling that God's people—**believers in our glorious Lord Jesus Christ** (Jas. 2:1), who himself never showed partiality—would engage in the practice of favoritism.

Beyond that, James makes it clear that judgment is something ultimately reserved for God alone. As people who will be judged by the royal law of neighborly love, James's readers must refrain from taking on themselves the privilege of judging who is acceptable and who is not.[6] Rather, they are to take their cues from God and from the Lord Jesus (who refused to show partiality) and demonstrate their love for all, rich and poor alike (see Luke 20:21).

ENDNOTES

[1]Judaism is the belief and cultural system of the Jewish people, referring to the Jews' way of life as those in a covenant relationship with God, rather than just to their religious doctrine. Judaism in Jesus' day differed according to different sects, and there are still various branches of Judaism today, but the underlying theme among them has been a belief in one God and a recognition of the Law of God. Law here refers to the Pentateuch (the first five books of the Old Testament: Genesis, Exodus, Leviticus, Numbers, and Deuteronomy).

[2]The Gospels include the New Testament books of Matthew, Mark, Luke, and John.

[3]Law refers to either the Levitical Code (all God's rules and regulations), the Ten Commandments, or the Pentateuch (the first five books of the Old

Testament: Genesis, Exodus, Leviticus, Numbers, and Deuteronomy). Often capitalized when it means the Pentateuch or the Ten Commandments.

[4]The Septuagint is the Greek version of the Old Testament, translated from the original Hebrew scrolls. It is often indicated by the Roman numerals LXX in accordance with the legend that it was translated by seventy scribes.

[5]A covenant is a solemn promise made binding by a pledge or vow, which may be either a verbal formula or a symbolic action. A covenant often referred to a legal obligation in ancient times. In Old Testament terms, the word was often used in describing the relationship between God and His chosen people, in which their sacrifices of blood afforded them His atonement for sin, and in which their fulfillment of a promise to live in obedience to God was rewarded by His blessings. In New Testament terms, this relationship (the new covenant) was now made possible on a personal basis through Jesus Christ and His sacrifice of His own blood.

[6]See endnote 3.

6

THE BARRIER
OF EASY FAITH

James 2:14-26

Another barrier to true religion is the curse of easy faith.[1] James's insistence on "walking the talk" as opposed to merely "talking the talk"—making empty claims of religious belief—comes through loud and clear in this section. No other passage in the epistle has undergone greater scrutiny. Indeed, few passages in the entire New Testament have been debated more so than James's words here about faith and deeds. At least some of the initial hesitancy to include the Epistle of James in the New Testament is owed to the perceived conflict between James's teaching here and the Pauline doctrine of "justification by faith alone" (see additional notes on James and the New Testament at the end of this chapter). But, given the background of Jewish Christianity combined with the early date of these teachings and the situation James is addressing, disagreement with Paul's teaching is more perception than reality (see below).

As in the opening section of James 2 (see verses 1-13), the author makes an initial statement here defining the issue and then offers concrete examples of what he means. But there is a major difference between these two passages: 2:1-13 refers to favoritism of the rich which was actually taking place, whereas here in 2:14-26 James speaks of *hypothetical* situations to illustrate the problem. He then appeals to biblical examples to demonstrate his proposed solution to the problem.

What good is it, my brothers, if a man claims to have faith but has no deeds? Can such faith save him? (Jas. 2:14). The word for **good** is actually *profit*. What profit is there in claims of belief that do not result in actions? Obviously, the essential question of the entire passage centers around the meaning of **faith.**

There are two very different ways in which faith can be defined. In the context of this passage, James assumes that some of his readers understand faith to mean simple intellectual assent. This is what might be termed *cognitive* faith—it is limited to one's intellect, or merely agreeing in one's mind that something is true. But James will argue for another definition of faith: belief that evidences itself in the way people behave and live. By contrasting these two kinds of faith, James links this passage with the overall emphasis of the epistle: the call to true religion (see James 1:27).

The substance or content behind the claim to faith is what is at issue here. What does it mean to say that I have faith or that I believe? In other words, what is the nature of authentic faith? Is faith that leads to salvation (sometimes called "saving faith") nothing more than the intellectual affirmation of certain ideas or doctrines? Is faith only a matter of believing certain things? Or does it entail something more? These are the kinds of questions James has in mind as he writes.

The hypothetical situation that follows illustrates the center of his concern: **Suppose a brother or sister is without clothes and daily food. If one of you says to him, "Go, I wish you well; keep warm and well fed," but does nothing about his physical needs, what good** [profit] **is it?** (2:15-16). The heart of this example centers around the clear assessment of a need which is then "addressed" in a useless—or at least impractical—fashion.

A situation of real human need that is addressed solely by good wishes and warm sentiment is certifiably inadequate. The real need is effectively ignored. Despite the words and sentiments, it doesn't work, precisely because nothing is done about the situation. The situation that provokes the need is unchanged. Undoubtedly, the expression of care and well-wishes could be sincere and well intended—indeed the needy persons themselves might be momentarily cheered by them—but ultimately nothing of significance happens to alter the need. Words alone cannot solve the problem. Something more than talk is required to meet the need of our hypothetical **brother or sister.**

The fact that James includes the word **sister** in the illustration may reflect back upon 1:27 where he defined "pure religion" in terms of looking after widows. At any rate, this is the only time in the epistle where James uses the specific term referring to female members of the congregations.

Having presented his argument by using hypothetical situations, James then drives home his conclusion: **In the same way, faith by itself, if it is not accompanied by action, is dead** (2:17). The use of the phrase

in the same way demonstrates the comparison between the unmet needs of the hungry person(s) and the empty claims of faith. James's argument is that just as mere words (expressions of sentimental concern), no matter how sincere, cannot meet the need of the naked and hungry, faith that is unaccompanied by tangible evidence of its reality will ultimately prove inadequate as well. In fact, that kind of deedless faith **is dead.** The irony is that James has contended from the beginning (see James 1:18) that God desires to impart "life" to us through His Word, but the divorce of belief from doing—religion from ethics, faith from deeds—has become a barrier to God's intention.

It is clear at this juncture that James has an understanding of faith that would be heartily affirmed by John Wesley and all those who fall into the tradition that bears his name. Wesley's grasp of faith and its vital power for making a real difference in human life differentiated him from many others in his own day and time. His resolute belief in good works being the "fruit of faith" led him into many areas of human endeavor that raised the eyebrows of his contemporaries, religious and nonreligious alike (see introduction). He seemed to appreciate James's concern here that authentic faith must necessarily—by its nature—bring forth fruit.

In his *Explanatory Notes on the New Testament,* Wesley contends that James "refutes not the doctrine of St. Paul, but the error of those who abused it."[2] To claim to be filled with the Spirit of God, and yet never *do* anything as a result of such infilling, was inconceivable to Wesley. So, although many figures in history—notably Martin Luther—have struggled with James at this point, John Wesley has been a model of the kind of faith that James encourages his readers to seek.

James further strengthens his argument by making four specific appeals: two to reason, two to Scripture.

The first appeal to reason supposes a dialogue between a person claiming faith and one who performs deeds: **But someone will say, "You have faith; I have deeds." Show me your faith without deeds, and I will show you my faith by what I do** (2:18). James constructs here the equivalent of a first-century "man from Missouri." The challenge is, "Show me! Enough talk—show me!"

How can faith all by itself possibly be validated? Should not what a person truly believes necessarily express itself in the circumstances of everyday life? The original Greek word translated **show** has the idea of "prove." The argument is that whereas claims of faith alone cannot validate themselves, our actions have a way of demonstrating what we truly believe.

This speaks clearly to the dangers of what might be termed "creedal Christianity"—mere intellectual assent to certain ideas and doctrines, apart from any real, discernible affect on one's life. The history of Christianity is filled with occasions where this kind of approach to the faith has been utilized. It is always a danger among people who stress certain beliefs as the identifying mark of a real believer. Surely beliefs matter. What we believe is an intricate part of Christianity, but when belief gets separated from practical living, all sorts of problems can arise.

Interestingly, Jesus himself recognized this danger when He emphasized that the ultimate test of faith was not subscribing to certain beliefs, but following Him (see Matthew 16:24). He also linked real life to belief when he said in John's gospel, "By this all men will know that you are my disciples, if you love one another" (John 13:35). So, while belief clearly matters, *our lives* are the clearest evidence of what we truly believe.

James's second appeal to reason follows immediately from the preceding point: **You believe that there is one God. Good! Even the demons believe that—and shudder** (Jas. 2:19). Here is a graphic demonstration of the ultimate inadequacy of belief divorced from accompanying deeds. The nature of authentic faith, as opposed to mere belief, is to *motivate*—to influence behavior, choices and attitudes. Real faith in Christ is meant to be a transforming kind of experience. That's why Jesus compared it to being born all over again (see John 3:3).

James argues that apart from such a transformation, mere belief puts one into a similar category as that of **demons** (Jas. 2:19), who are faithfully orthodox in terms of what they believe to be true. In fact, their intellectual commitment to their belief in God is so strong that it causes them to **shudder** (no doubt because of the implications God's existence holds for them). They genuinely **believe** in God. But the irrefutable fact is that despite the depth of their belief, they remain demonic in their orientation and practice. In other words, their belief makes no essential difference in their lives and behavior.

James means to question those who claim that faith can be authentic when it does nothing to change the basic orientation and habits of their lives. Such "faith" becomes a barrier to authentic Christian faith. This is what James might term "easy faith." It's easy to hold, easy to claim, but it doesn't mean much of anything in terms of life.

One of the great dangers of modern Christianity is precisely that of "easy faith." The polls of Gallup and others consistently show the great chasm between what people claim to believe and how such "beliefs" actually affect their lives and choices. The spiritual commitment of the evangelical community of recent years has often been characterized as being "a mile wide and an inch deep." This is James's concern for the Jewish-Christian communities of his day as well.

In light of the huge number of people in North America who *claim* to be "born again"—approaching as much as one-fourth of the population—one must wonder at how little effect they seem to have on the culture around them. As one person has quipped, "A quarter-pound of salt ought to have some effect on a pound of meat." When the effect of such "salt" is as negligible as it seems to be in our culture, then James's words here become uncomfortably relevant.

Jesus spoke clearly about the connection between faith and fruit. In fact, this appears to be another case where James reminds his readers of the Lord's teachings. Jesus addressed the phenomena of faith and works when He said in Matthew's gospel, "By their fruit you will recognize them. Do people pick grapes from thorn bushes, or figs from thistles? Likewise every good tree bears good fruit, but a bad tree bears bad fruit. A good tree cannot bear bad fruit, and a bad tree cannot bear good fruit. Every tree that does not bear good fruit is cut down and thrown into the fire. Thus, by their fruit you will recognize them. Not everyone who says to me, 'Lord, Lord,' will enter the kingdom of heaven, but only he who does the will of my Father who is in heaven" (Matt. 7:16-21). James's concern about the worthlessness or profitlessness of empty faith seems to have in mind Christ's words here.

Many of the controversies swirling about the evangelical Christian community are owing to the lack of clarity on what conversion actually means. In the rush to claim huge success in our evangelistic endeavors, we may end up, in effect, counting "demons"! That is, people who may have assented intellectually to Christian doctrines (made decisions) without ever actually appropriating authentic, saving faith. That blunt judgment is warranted by the truth James presents here: that real faith is manifested by true repentance, a change of mind and heart, and the easily documented evidence of a new way of life.

The sad state of affairs brought about by "easy faith" is particularly ironic in its effect on the Wesleyan tradition. Wesley preached with an unyielding sense of commitment the utter necessity of the "fruits of faith." If we claim huge numbers of conversions without a corresponding increase in the fruits of righteousness, we have succumbed to the kind of virtual religion that James rightly condemns here and elsewhere in his letter.

Having appealed to the reason of his readers, James sets forth two further arguments based in Old Testament Scripture: **You foolish man,**

do you want evidence that faith without deeds is useless? (Jas. 2:20). The passion with which James considers this theme is borne out with his exclamation, **You foolish man**—literally, "you empty man." James is not being mean-spirited; he is simply reflecting the importance he attaches to his readers' proper understanding of the issue.

The idea is that only a fool—a vain, empty person, one who willingly ignores the evidence—could fail to be convinced of the futility of professions of faith that make no difference in one's life. The word used here for **useless** literally refers to "barrenness." Faith without accompanying deeds is barren. This is a concept that not only underscores the necessity of "fruitfulness" in regard to faith, but it attaches nicely to the Old Testament in general and in particular to the example of Abraham, to which James refers immediately.

To be "barren," in terms of being without children, was considered a serious threat to the claim that one was in a marriage covenant. The evidence or fruit of a real marriage was considered to be the children produced by the union. The inability to produce children was considered as a legitimate reason for divorce. That's what made Abraham's election by God as the "father of nations" so ludicrous in the eyes of a faithless world. How could he who had no "fruit"—no children—be the father of many? That God chose Abraham and then blessed him with "fruit" demonstrates the necessity of something beyond mere belief. At some point, Abraham and Sarah had to have a child, or else the promise would be empty.

This also sets the stage for James's employment of Abraham as the example of real faith: **Was not our ancestor Abraham considered righteous for what he did when he offered his son Isaac on the altar?** (2:21). The example of **Abraham** as James cites it here actually combines two different occasions mentioned in the text of Genesis. The attempted offering of **Isaac,** recorded in Genesis 22, perfectly serves James's case because God's purpose behind this incident was to determine the reality and quality of Abraham's faith.

Abraham was being tested by God (see comments on James 1:12). The result of Abraham's obedience to God is seen where God said, "Now I know that you fear God, because you have not withheld from me your son, your only son" (Gen. 22:12c). Abraham's actions revealed what he truly believed. The author of the book of Hebrews interpreted this event in similar fashion: "By faith Abraham, when God tested him, offered Isaac as a sacrifice. He who had received the promises was about to sacrifice his one and only son, even though God had said to him, 'It is through Isaac that your offspring will be reckoned.' Abraham reasoned that God could raise the dead, and figuratively speaking, he did receive Isaac back from death" (Heb. 11:17-19).

James selects this incident from Abraham's life because it represents the absolute depths of Abraham's faith. Abraham was not prepared to rest on mere intellectual assent. His faith was vital and affected every aspect of his being, including that which represented the heart and soul of God's covenant with him—Isaac.[3] **You see that his faith and his actions were working together, and his faith was made complete by what he did** (Jas. 2:22). The Greek word translated here as **working together** is the same term that gives us our English word *synergy*. It basically means "to work in partnership." To labor synergistically is to work together, producing through a partnership something that could never have been produced separately. This is James's point.

Faith as mere belief would not have been sufficient for God to reach the conclusion He reached about Abraham. Only as Abraham *acted on what He believed* did God conclude that Abraham really did trust in Him. The result was that Abraham's **faith was made complete.** In other words, Abraham's faith reached the point that God desires all of us to reach by persevering through times of testing (see 1:2-4). Through utilizing the test as an opportunity to demonstrate what he truly believed, Abraham's faith was made complete or "perfected."

And the scripture was fulfilled that says, "Abraham believed God, and it was credited to him as righteousness," and he was called God's friend (2:23). The scripture James refers to here is actually Genesis 15:6, taking place prior to the Genesis 22 narrative about the offering of Isaac. But the context of Genesis 15 shows how it fits nicely here for James's purposes. The context is that of God's making the initial promise of an heir for Abraham who would be other than that of Abraham's servant. Abraham accepted God's promise in Genesis 15 and is called righteous.

Here, James suggests that the Genesis 22 story represents the fulfillment—the filling full—of Abraham's initial faith response. For James, Abraham's "credited" **righteousness** (Jas. 2:23) is most vividly illustrated not in the simple act of receiving the promise of God in Genesis 15, but in acting upon that promise in Genesis 22. This is where the Hebrews 11 treatment of Abraham becomes important. Abraham's faith was so strong that he obeyed, knowing that God was able to raise Isaac from the dead.

Righteousness—literally, rightness in terms of our relationship with God and humankind—is God's stated purpose for us in faith (see James 1:20). Abraham achieved that God-desired purpose by putting his faith to work. He is known as **God's friend** (2:23; see Isaiah 41:8). In other words, as the friend of God—one desired by God—Abraham is an appropriate example of the pure religion that God accepts and which James champions in his epistle (see James 1:27).

Had James stopped here, or perhaps simply gone ahead to his second example from Scripture, he may have avoided much of the controversy that surrounds this passage. But to leave no doubt as to his point, he includes these words: **You see that a person is justified by what he does and not by faith alone** (2:24). Here are words that Martin Luther and others saw as incompatible with the New Testament teaching of justification by faith alone. That James uses the words here so clearly makes it hard to imagine that it is mere coincidence. For whatever reason, James seems willing to open the door to criticism in order to drive home his point. How can this statement be reconciled with that of Paul?

First, we must always remember the Jewish background of James. As was emphasized earlier in the epistle (see 1:22-25), the Jewish concept of belief was inseparable from action. To hear and not act upon what was said was the same as not hearing at all. To believe and not act accordingly was equal to not believing at all. Again, Jesus' story of the wise and foolish builder from Matthew 7 could be in the mind of James here (see James 1:22). How can we possibly claim to believe the gospel and yet allow it to make no difference in the way we conduct our lives? To a good Jew like James, such a claim was preposterous.

In Jesus' story of the builders, the issue at stake was not works that in turn merit the status of faith. The point of the story was that what one does with Jesus' words, "hearing and putting them into practice," is the sign of authentic faith. It is like building one's house on the kind of foundation that can stand the inevitable storms of life (see James 1:2-4). James is addressing people who have divorced the profession of religious faith from the daily realities of human life. They evidently desire to substitute some cheap believism for the rigors of vital faith.

Paul's vehement argument against "works"—in Galatians, for example—addressed people who were attempting to replace grace with works, specifically, the works of the Jewish law.[4] They wanted to replace the good news of God's gracious provision in Christ with the dead works of legalistic Judaism.[5] The "legalists" in Galatians claimed that faith alone cannot save a person—they must continue to keep the old Jewish law. When we remember what James is arguing against here versus what Paul was combating, the supposed problem between them disappears.

Paul was as insistent as James in calling his readers to practical holy living, saying to the Ephesians, "I urge you to live a life worthy of the calling you have received" (Eph. 4:1b). Paul exhorted the Roman church, on the basis of God's provisions, to "offer" their bodies as "living sacrifices" to the Lord (Rom. 12:1). He also urged them to "put aside the deeds of darkness and put on the armor of light" (Rom. 13:12b). To the Colossian church he wrote, "So then, just as you received Christ Jesus as Lord, continue to live in him" (Col. 2:6). And, in his writings to Timothy, Paul constantly urged this young apprentice in the faith to follow closely the ways of godliness in contrast to the ways of others who have lived profane and evil lives (see 1 Timothy 1:18-20; 6:11-14; 2 Timothy 2:14-19).

In short, the teachings of the Apostle Paul (the preacher of justification by faith alone) are in unity with those of James on the necessity of allowing faith to do its desired work in us: transforming our lives. There is no essential disagreement between James and Paul when we remember the special circumstances in which they presented their cases. Thus James can so strongly claim that a person is truly **justified** (Jas. 2:24) by the kind of faith that is allowed to accomplish its transforming mission in one's life—not by mere intellectual assent to doctrines and forms. As one person has put it, "We are justified by faith alone. But the faith that justifies is never alone."

James's final scriptural witness is a most unlikely candidate for inclusion, especially when compared to the revered Abraham: **In the same way, was not even Rahab the prostitute considered righteous for what she did when she gave lodging to the spies and sent them off in a different direction?** (2:25). Perhaps James's choice of **Rahab** (see parallel use in Hebrews 11:31) is explained by the fact that, unlike Abraham, she had made no hint of faith profession prior to the act cited as illustrating her faith. She is simply presented as one who, when confronted with a choice between believing in the God of Israel or in the walls of Jericho, cast her lot with God and as a result saved her household.

The fact that she is cited here as an example of real faith refers to the appropriateness of her actions following her belief. When confronted with this choice, she believed, and we know that she believed precisely because of **what she did** (Jas. 2:25). She acted in a way that corresponded to what she believed. Again, faith and deeds worked together. No one ever heard a word of testimony from Rahab. Instead, what we have is the incident in Joshua 2, and the claims of both James and the anonymous author of Hebrews agreeing that Rahab's deeds were "saving deeds"—her faith saved her, and that faith was inseparable from her actions.

James brings this topic to a close, aptly summarizing all he has argued by introducing one last, helpful analogy: **As the body without the spirit is dead, so faith without deeds is dead** (Jas. 2:26). A **body without the spirit** is still a body, but it has no life in it. It has no usefulness, no value. It is a corpse. It may resemble the person it once was in certain ways, though not for long! It may enable us to remember what someone looked like, but beyond that, a corpse serves no real purpose. It is a poor imitation of real life.

The faith that has nothing to show for itself other than words or claims—no deeds to underscore its living vitality—is like that spiritless body. It **is dead!** At best, it is a poor imitation of the real thing. To people who are long on talk and short on backing it up with their lives, James suggests in the strongest possible terms a return to true religion, lest the inevitable decay of dead faith render them useless and empty before God and the world.

It is interesting to note that James's analogy appears to reverse the application that Paul and others might have made. For it is easy to see how one might argue that "faith" is the spirit which gives life to the body, which quickens or makes it come alive (see Ephesians 2:1-6). But James's point is the critical truth that there is no such thing as fruitless faith. What the spirit (the soul) is to the body, so deeds are to faith professions.

ADDITIONAL NOTES ON JAMES AND THE NEW TESTAMENT

James's connection to the rest of the New Testament is a two-sided coin. On one hand, his writing falls among the class of letters designated as General Epistles, which means that less is known about the recipients and circumstances of these letters than is the case with other New Testament writings.[6] Further, the notable lack of doctrinal material in the epistle has often relegated it to the "second tier" of New Testament books. That is one side of the coin. The other side of the coin shows James to have a relationship to the New Testament that few, if any, of the other books can exhibit. The specific characteristic that sets this epistle apart from the rest of the New Testament has to do with the author's relationship to and dependence upon the teachings of Jesus.

Throughout the entirety of his epistle, James mentions Jesus by name only twice (see 1:1; 2:1). He never claims to quote his half brother, who is Lord of the church to whom he writes. He never even uses the phrase "the Lord said." It seems curious that the Lord's own brother would not take advantage of such a close relationship to refer more directly to Him.

One New Testament scholar suggests that the reason for this glaring omission on the part of James is that much of James's words actually are sayings of Jesus not recorded.[7]

Remember that at the time James wrote, there was no New Testament in print. The teachings of Jesus were preserved primarily in oral form. That is, people spoke from memory the words and sayings of Jesus. In our modern Western culture, we find it difficult to think of an "oral tradition" as having much validity or accuracy. But there are many evidences of oral traditions in the cultures of Africa, Asia, and elsewhere. Missionaries, anthropologists, and others have been amazed to see young children recite generations of family history with pinpoint accuracy. In short, oral tradition can be extremely accurate.

Knowing what we do of the culture of Jesus' day, it is safe to assume that much of His teachings had been committed to memory. For the readers of James, the Old Testament and the oral teachings of Jesus comprised the Scriptures. In the same way that James leans upon the Old Testament, assuming that his readers know the source he is quoting, it is plausible to suppose that James quotes the teachings of Jesus as well, knowing that his readers will know their source.

What an exciting possibility this is! While we cannot prove this in any scientific manner, it does seem reasonable to think that when we are reading the book of James, we could be actually reading some of the words of Jesus Christ. If James's words openly reflect the words of the Lord himself, something his original readers would know, it is little wonder James can speak so confidently.

Beyond this reasonable possibility, it is indisputable that James leans heavily upon Jesus' teachings. This is particularly true in the case of Matthew's gospel, specifically the Sermon on the Mount (see Matthew 5–7). The following chart demonstrates some possible correlations between the writings of James and the teachings of Jesus in Matthew.

Matthew 5:12—Rejoice and be glad, because great is your reward in heaven, for in the same way they persecuted the prophets who were before you.	**James 1:2**—Consider it pure joy, my brothers, whenever you face trials of many kinds.
Matthew 5:48—Be perfect, therefore, as your heavenly Father is perfect.	**James 1:4**—Perseverance must finish its work so that you may be mature and complete, not lacking anything.

continued

105

Matthew 7:7—Ask and it will be given to you; seek and you will find; knock and the door will be opened to you.	**James 1:5**—If any of you lacks wisdom, he should ask God, who gives generously to all without finding fault, and it will be given to him.
Matthew 24:13—But he who stands firm to the end will be saved.	**James 1:12**—Blessed is the man who perseveres under trial, because when he has stood the test, he will receive the crown of life that God has promised to those who love him.
Matthew 5:22—But I tell you that anyone who is angry with his brother will be subject to judgment. Again, anyone who says to his brother, "Raca," is answerable to the Sanhedrin. But anyone who says, "You fool!" will be in danger of the fire of hell.	**James 1:20**—For man's anger does not bring about the righteous life that God desires.
Matthew 5:3—Blessed are the poor in spirit, for theirs is the kingdom of heaven.	**James 2:5**—Listen, my dear brothers: Has not God chosen those who are poor in the eyes of the world to be rich in faith and to inherit the kingdom he promised those who love him?
Matthew 19:23-24—Then Jesus said to his disciples, "I tell you the truth, it is hard for a rich man to enter the kingdom of heaven. Again I tell you, it is easier for a camel to go through the eye of a needle than for a rich man to enter the kingdom of God."	**James 2:6-7**—But you have insulted the poor. Is it not the rich who are exploiting you? Are they not the ones who are dragging you into court? Are they not the ones who are slandering the noble name of him to whom you belong?
Matthew 5:7—Blessed are the merciful, for they will be shown mercy. **Matthew 6:14-15**—For if you forgive men when they sin against you, your heavenly Father will also forgive you. But if you do not forgive men their sins, your Father will not forgive your sins. **Matthew 7:1**—Do not judge, or you too will be judged.	**James 2:13**—Because judgment without mercy will be shown to anyone who has not been merciful. Mercy triumphs over judgment!

Matthew 7:21-23—Not everyone who says to me, "Lord, Lord," will enter the kingdom of heaven, but only he who does the will of my Father who is in heaven. Many will say to me on that day, "Lord, Lord, did we not prophesy in your name, and in your name drive out demons and perform many miracles?" Then I will tell them plainly, "I never knew you. Away from me, you evildoers!"	**James 2:14-16**—What good is it, my brothers, if a man claims to have faith but has no deeds? Can such faith save him? Suppose a brother or sister is without clothes and daily food. If one of you says to him, "Go, I wish you well; keep warm and well fed," but does nothing about his physical needs, what good is it?
Matthew 25:35—For I was hungry and you gave me something to eat, I was thirsty and you gave me something to drink, I was a stranger and you invited me in.	**James 2:16**—If one of you says to him, "Go, I wish you well; keep warm and well fed," but does nothing about his physical needs, what good is it?
Matthew 5:3—Blessed are the poor in spirit, for theirs is the kingdom of heaven.	**James 3:13**—Who is wise and understanding among you? Let him show it by his good life, by deeds done in the humility that comes from wisdom. **By contrast:** **James 4:6**—But he gives us more grace. That is why Scripture says: "God opposes the proud but gives grace to the humble." **James 4:16**—As it is, you boast and brag. All such boasting is evil.
Matthew 5:5—Blessed are the meek, for they will inherit the earth. **Matthew 5:9**—Blessed are the peacemakers, for they will be called sons of God.	**James 3:17-18**—But the wisdom that comes from heaven is first of all pure; then peace-loving, considerate, submissive, full of mercy and good fruit, impartial and sincere. Peacemakers who sow in peace raise a harvest of righteousness.
Matthew 6:24—No one can serve two masters. Either he will hate the one and love the other, or he will be devoted to the one and despise the other. You cannot serve both God and Money.	**James 4:4**—You adulterous people, don't you know that friendship with the world is hatred toward God? Anyone who chooses to be a friend of the world becomes an enemy of God.

continued

Matthew 7:1-2—Do not judge, or you too will be judged. For in the same way you judge others, you will be judged, and with the measure you use, it will be measured to you.	**James 4:11**—Brothers, do not slander one another. Anyone who speaks against his brother or judges him speaks against the law and judges it. When you judge the law, you are not keeping it, but sitting in judgment on it.
Matthew 6:19—Do not store up for yourselves treasures on earth, where moth and rust destroy, and where thieves break in and steal.	**James 5:2-3**—Your wealth has rotted, and moths have eaten your clothes. Your gold and silver are corroded. Their corrosion will testify against you and eat your flesh like fire. You have hoarded wealth in the last days.
Matthew 5:33-37—Again, you have heard that it was said to the people long ago, "Do not break your oath, but keep the oaths you have made to the Lord." But I tell you, Do not swear at all: either by heaven, for it is God's throne; or by the earth, for it is his footstool; or by Jerusalem, for it is the city of the Great King. And do not swear by your head, for you cannot make even one hair white or black. Simply let your "Yes" be "Yes," and your "No," "No"; anything beyond this comes from the evil one.	**James 5:12**—Above all, my brothers, do not swear—not by heaven or by earth or by anything else. Let your "Yes" be yes, and your "No," no, or you will be condemned.
Matthew 24:33—Even so, when you see all these things, you know that it is near, right at the door.	**James 5:9**—Don't grumble against each other, brothers, or you will be judged. The Judge is standing at the door!
Matthew 5:12—Rejoice and be glad, because great is your reward in heaven, for in the same way they persecuted the prophets who were before you.	**James 5:10**—Brothers, as an example of patience in the face of suffering, take the prophets who spoke in the name of the Lord.[8]

Many New Testament scholars differ in their interpretations of exactly what these findings mean. But the basic truth we want to take from this comparison is that "James has a point of view . . . similar to that which marks the teachings of Jesus during His lifetime. Much of James reads like the gospel of Jesus rather than the gospel about Jesus."[9] When reading the Epistle of James, we should read it knowing that this short letter stays very, very close to the person and ministry of Jesus of Nazareth.

Some biblical scholars have raised questions about James's authorship of this epistle because of what they view as an apparent contradiction with the theology of Paul by James in 2:14-26. Specifically, these people have claimed that Paul's teachings on justification by faith alone in Romans 3 and 4 are undermined by James's teaching that **faith without deeds is dead** (Jas. 2:26b). Martin Luther is infamous for his disregard of this epistle. He too considered it out of agreement with Paul's teaching on justification by faith alone. Since it didn't meet Luther's requirement of presenting Christ as the other epistles did, he gave it a secondary position and labeled it a "right strawy epistle."[10]

Some critics have charged that since James uses Abraham to illustrate his contention that we are *justified by what we do* and not merely by faith, then this epistle couldn't possibly have been written by anyone who knew—and agreed with—what Paul taught: that we are *justified by faith* and not by works. And since James the Just served as the voice of reason in the Jerusalem conference of Acts 15, he certainly understood what Paul was teaching on this subject and thus never would have written such contradictory words.

Careful analysis of the texts in question show that the "contradictions" are only surface level at best. James and Paul are not on opposing sides of an argument, but they use language very differently and for different emphases. Whenever we forget that James's epistle is the most Jewish book of the New Testament, we are likely to encounter difficulties like this. James uses the words in their older Jewish sense, while Paul's tendency was to adopt his own meaning for words (the word *flesh* being a vivid example).[11]

When James speaks of faith, he wants his readers to see it as the complete opposite of hypocrisy and double-minded religion. That is why he says that *apart from accompanying deeds,* there is no faith. The "faith" James condemns is mere intellectual belief, without any demonstration of its effectiveness in one's life. James always views real faith as resulting in obedience to God's commands. According to Paul, "faith" summarizes the nature of our response to God's gracious offer of salvation as opposed to any lingering Jewish ideas about the merit of works. James isn't speaking of meriting or earning salvation by what we do. His interest is that we actually live out our salvation! That's why he emphasizes Jesus' teachings about hearing and doing the Word. When we understand what kind of faith James is attacking, then we see that there is no real argument with Paul at all.

Overall, the relationship of the Epistle of James with the rest of the New Testament is one of harmony and support. The more one studies this short epistle, the more he or she will be convinced that James, while clearly speaking from the vantage point of Jewish Christianity, is in the mainstream of New Testament thinking.

ENDNOTES

[1]Blessings and curses refer to the response of God to His people in accordance with their obedience to Him (blessings) or their disobedience (curses). In the Old Testament, God's power was invoked through power-laden words (blessings and curses) often spoken in prayer form. Through these blessings or curses, God's people would call upon Him to provide or care for them by affecting them in a positive way or those around them in a positive or negative way. In Judaism (see endnote 5), some blessings were reserved for the priests, but others were a regular part of the synagogue services. Curses were much less prominent and were forbidden. In the New Testament, the ultimate blessing came from God to mankind in Jesus Christ, and blessings accompanied righteousness. Curses accompanied sin.

[2]John Wesley, *Explanatory Notes on the New Testament,* vol. II (Peabody, Massachusetts: Hendrickson Publishers, Inc., 1986), p. 54.

[3]A covenant is a solemn promise made binding by a pledge or vow, which may be either a verbal formula or a symbolic action. A covenant often referred to a legal obligation in ancient times. In Old Testament terms, the word was often used in describing the relationship between God and His chosen people, in which their sacrifices of blood afforded them His atonement for sin, and in which their fulfillment of a promise to live in obedience to God was rewarded by His blessings. In New Testament terms, this relationship (the new covenant) was now made possible on a personal basis through Jesus Christ and His sacrifice of His own blood.

[4]Law refers to either the Levitical Code (all God's rules and regulations), the Ten Commandments, or the Pentateuch (the first five books of the Old Testament: Genesis, Exodus, Leviticus, Numbers, and Deuteronomy). Often capitalized when it means the Pentateuch or the Ten Commandments.

[5]Judaism is the belief and cultural system of the Jewish people, referring to the Jews' way of life as those in a covenant relationship with God, rather than just to their religious doctrine. Judaism in Jesus' day differed according to different sects, and there are still various branches of Judaism today, but the

underlying theme among them has been a belief in one God and a recognition of the Law of God. Law here refers to the Pentateuch (the first five books of the Old Testament: Genesis, Exodus, Leviticus, Numbers, and Deuteronomy).

[6]The General Epistles are the books of James; 1 and 2 Peter; 1, 2, and 3 John; and Jude. They are called General Epistles because they are books or letters written to broad groups of people, rather than being addressed to specific individuals or churches the way that, say, Paul's letters to the Corinthians were.

[7]Peter Davids, *James,* New International Bible Commentary (Peabody, Massachusetts: Hendrickson Publishers, Inc., 1983), p. 22.

[8]Ralph Martin, *James,* Word Biblical Commentary (Waco, Texas: Word Books, Publisher, 1988), p. lxxvi.

[9]R. R. Williamson, cited in James B. Adamson, *The Epistle of James* (Grand Rapids, Michigan: Wm. B. Eerdmans Publishing Co., 1976), p. 22.

[10]Everett F. Harrison, *Introduction to the New Testament* (Grand Rapids, Michigan: Wm. B. Eerdmans Publishing Co., 1971), p. 383.

[11]Davids, p. 5. Paul's use of the Greek word for "flesh," *sarx,* goes far beyond the Old Testament and common Jewish understanding of the term. See also Gerhard Kittel and Gerhard Friedrich, eds., *Theological Dictionary of the New Testament,* vol. VII (Grand Rapids, Michigan: Wm. B. Eerdmans Publishing Co., 1968), pp. 125–38.

Part Three

TEACHERS
AND
TRUE RELIGION

James 3:1-18

The role of teacher has always been critical within the Christian community. Those who teach—who give leadership and direction to the people of God—have consistently held an important place in the Scriptures. The stories of the Old Testament prophets and kings essentially tell the whole story of the nation called Israel. The significant place held by those offices in the Old Testament is largely shifted in the New Testament to those who were teachers.

The importance of the teaching office revolves around the kind of effect teachers have on those around them. Teachers, then and now, have the potential to deeply influence the lives and thinking of people. Jesus was viewed initially by the people of Israel as a teacher. He was called "Rabbi" (meaning "Teacher") by His followers. Teachers were held in great esteem by the culture in general and particularly by their students. James's epistle emphasizes the importance of the teaching office by leaning heavily on the teachings of Jesus. Having observed the teaching ministry of his exalted half brother, Jesus, James knows full well the significance attached to teaching others about God and His ways.

The importance of teachers was doubly true in the life of the early church. In a day when written documents were extremely rare and largely inaccessible to the masses, when oral tradition (communication through the spoken word) was the major means of transmitting ideas, it fell to teachers to accurately transmit the substance of the Christian religion. Given this critical role filled by teachers, it is not difficult to understand how teachers could bring great problems into the church, as well as great benefits. Indeed, the problem with teachers who led others astray was, and continues to be to this day, a perpetual thorn in the flesh (see 2 Corinthians 12:7) to the Christian community.

The early church was filled with examples of problems with the teaching office. Paul had to deal with the misleading and outright false ideas of teachers in many of his epistles, particularly in the letters to the Galatians and Colossians. He counseled Timothy and Titus regarding the presence of people who have no use for sound doctrine, but insist upon pursuing senseless arguments about "myths" and "genealogies" (1 Tim. 1:3-4; Titus 3:9). The Second Epistle of Peter is largely aimed at combating false teaching that threatens the faith of the Christian community, especially regarding the second coming of Christ. John, in his first epistle, hinted at the presence of false teachers (he called them "antichrists" [1 John 2:18]) who have influenced the flock under his care. So the significance of the teaching office and the problems that could result from false or inadequate teaching was an ongoing issue for the early church.

In his third chapter, James focuses his concern on the teaching office. This epistle is generally aimed at the community as a whole. But a strong case can be made for approaching this third chapter as being aimed primarily at the teachers in the community.

While specific details are lacking, the context of the epistle suggests the presence of inadequate and even false teaching that is causing much of the difficulty in the communities. Both of the issues James addresses in this third chapter—the problem of the tongue and the attainment of true wisdom—are especially appropriate for those who teach. Therefore, even though the teachings of this chapter have general applications to all of James's readers, it seems that he has particularly singled out teachers—those entrusted with instructing the believing community. James is determined that these people grasp the heightened expectations and responsibilities that go with the teaching vocation.

THE TONGUE
AND
TRUE RELIGION

James 3:1-12

Not many of you should presume to be teachers, my brothers, because you know that we who teach will be judged more strictly (Jas. 3:1). As usual, the term **brothers** signals a major emphasis. Here, James begins with a rather surprising piece of advice: that not many should pursue the teaching vocation. This is surprising because of the importance attached to the teaching office; it was surely viewed as a most noble vocation. The reason offered for such counsel is that **teachers,** including James himself (note the use of **we**), are subject to stricter judgment. This does not imply some divine double standard in terms of judging particular vocations differently from others, but simply emphasizes the critical nature of the teaching profession. Being entrusted with leading people into the truth means accepting the sobering responsibility of eternal decisions.

The essence of the teaching task is to influence others with the content of what one teaches. Teachers mean to influence their students toward their own understanding of truth. The content of the Christian faith is literally an eternal matter of life and death. Therefore, such weighty matters carry with them heavy consequences for those who seek to influence others in eternal ways.

Jesus himself noted the heavy judgment involved in leading "little ones" astray (see Matthew 18:6-7). Paul counseled Timothy not to lay hands on others too quickly, thrusting unworthy people into the teaching vocation (see 1 Timothy 5:22). The Scriptures always portray the office of the teacher with the kind of seriousness that James indicates here. In light of the great harm that can befall those who are taught wrongly or even inadequately, anyone entering the teaching vocation in the Christian community ought to reflect soberly on James's words.

The office of teacher as James portrays it can be thought to encompass any of the varied positions where instruction in Christian truth is given to the church. While shortages of Christians in these offices is a perennial problem, the cost of neglecting James's warning here is much too high to disregard.

As we consider the health and vitality of the contemporary church, how can we escape the conclusion that many of our problems can be attributed to the absence of sound teaching? But then we must further acknowledge that "quality control" in teaching, especially in the teaching of children, is something sorely lacking in many churches. How can we entrust the minds of our people, especially our little ones, to anyone who has not been sobered by the awesome responsibility of James's words?

The danger that exists for the contemporary church is that we have become so "program" oriented (focusing on providing certain programs or ministries) that we have in effect looked the other way concerning some instructors who cannot rightly claim the teaching office. James's words here ought to give us great pause as we think about the consequences that can follow in the wake of inadequate teaching.

We all stumble in many ways. If anyone is never at fault in what he says, he is a perfect man, able to keep his whole body in check (Jas. 3:2). It's not that teachers are expected to be **perfect,** as James is quick to admit. We (note again James's inclusion of himself) all trip up or **stumble**—literally, "commit many sins." The standard for teachers is not one of absolute perfection, for such perfection does not exist in any human form outside of the earthly Jesus. A good teacher is one who understands his or her imperfections—who knows how to say, "I don't know," or "I was wrong," or even "I'm sorry." Such self-understanding is an important virtue in teaching.

At the same time, the second part of the verse emphasizes the point of James's concern with the teaching vocation. It also reveals why accepting the position of teacher ought to be approached with great sobriety. On one hand, nobody's perfect in the role of teacher. To not "trip up" in what one says indicates perfection (completion) for anyone who teaches. In fact, James equates control over one's speech with control over one's **whole body.** The sense is that this is an ideal standard which is virtually unattainable, at least by human power.

On the other hand, James's introductory remarks about the "stricter judgment" facing teachers makes the pursuit of such an ideal—even if unattainable in an absolutely perfect sense—the proper concern of anyone who teaches. Self-control is the prominent issue here. James speaks of controlling one's speech as having the effect of keeping the **whole body in check**—literally, "bridled" (Jas. 3:2). James used this same Greek word in 1:26 (NASB) to point out that failing to "bridle" one's tongue nullifies a person's claim of being religious! Thus, even though absolute perfection in speech is not the standard demanded of teachers, James insists that failure to exercise due control over one's speech disqualifies one as a teacher and as a practitioner of true religion.

The idea of bridling one's whole body leads naturally into another one of the analogies for which James is famous: **When we put bits into the mouths of horses to make them obey us, we can turn the whole animal** (3:3). The Greek word for **bits** is another form of the word for "bridle." Bridling one's tongue has the same effect, in terms of controlling one's whole body, that bridling a horse does in controlling the whole horse.

In each case, there is no comparison between the size of the object used to control the body or animal as the case may be. Bits are much smaller than horses, and tongues are much smaller than entire bodies. In fact, the precise point of the comparison is this: The power of the bit over the horse is way out of proportion to its size in comparison with the horse. James says we should find it amazing that such a powerful animal is so influenced and controlled by such a small piece of hardware. In the same way, the discipline of controlling the tongue, as small as it is in comparison with the rest of the body, yields results far in excess of its physical size. Controlling the tongue is in effect controlling the whole person.

The comparison continues with another example: **Or take ships as an example. Although they are so large and are driven by strong winds, they are steered by a very small rudder wherever the pilot wants to go** (3:4). Again, the same principles come through. **Ships** can be of indeterminate sizes, but they share three characteristics. First, each ship has a **rudder**—some mechanism for steering. Second, the size of a ship is always much greater in proportion to the size of its rudder. Third, regardless of the size of the ship and the size of the rudder, all ships are guided by those small instruments. Small ships, large ships, and still larger ships are steered via the rudders in accordance with the wishes of their pilots. The reference here to ships being **steered by a very small rudder wherever the pilot wants to go** (literally, "directed by the very small helm where the impulse of the one steering resolves") reaffirms James's intent to hold the one who possesses—steers—the tongue as ultimately responsible for its actions.

What James wants his readers to grasp is the significance that words coming from this little member—the tongue—have over the rest of the body and life itself. In particular, he wants those who teach to appreciate the importance of their words over the rest of their lives and the lives of their students. Many people, large or small in physical stature, have been done in by their inability to properly "steer" their lives by controlling their tongues. During the Second World War, the government—attempting to preserve national secrets—appealed to people to keep quiet by reminding them that "Loose lips sink ships!" James would make the same point to all who teach.

Likewise, the tongue is a small part of the body, but it makes great boasts. Consider what a great forest is set on fire by a small spark. The tongue also is a fire, a world of evil among the parts of the body. It corrupts the whole person, sets the whole course of his life on fire, and is itself set on fire by hell (Jas. 3:5-6). Despite its smallness in comparison to the rest of the body, **the tongue** can make **great boasts.** Claiming to be "religious," when one cannot bridle the tongue, comes immediately to mind as one great boast—literally, "wild claim."

Continuing the emphasis on the physical insignificance of the tongue in comparison to the consequences it can effect, James compares its impact to the damage done by a **great forest . . . set on fire** by a single spark. Annually, we are reminded by thousands of burned acres just how destructive one small spark can be when not controlled. The fiery nature of inappropriate statements is such that small, seemingly insignificant words have the capability of destroying almost anything. Human history is filled with examples of individual lives, families and even nations effectively destroyed by intemperate, carelessly spoken words.

If anyone in the world needs to understand the power of words, it is those who teach, and in particular those who teach within the Christian community. The context of James's epistle demonstrates that loose and careless talk makes difficult situations even worse. The possibility that this kind of talk may have its source among those who teach is particularly troubling to James. Teachers should know better. Of all people, teachers should appreciate the power of words.

James's designation of the tongue as **a fire, a world of evil among the parts of the body,** vividly demonstrates his own appreciation for the power of this small member. Fire can be either a tool of constructive good or an instrument of indiscriminate destruction, depending on one thing—its control. When fire is harnessed, it produces the power to generate incredible benefit to others and provides refuge from the chill of cold. When fire is out of control, it becomes one of the most destructive forces known to humankind. Anyone who has observed the aftermath of a forest fire or has stepped through the smoldering ruins of a burned home understands well the point James makes.

How is it that James can possibly compare the destructive capability of fire with the words that roll off the human tongue? It is that the tongue has a tendency or disposition toward evil in humans. It has the power to corrupt the entire body in the same way that small rudders have of determining the direction of whole ships.

The Greek word for "corrupt" here (Jas. 3:6) is the same root word used in James's definition of true religion in 1:27, where he insisted that keeping oneself "unspotted" (KJV) or uncorrupted from the world is essential to the kind of religion of which God approves. Lack of control over the tongue is so serious precisely because of its capacity for starting fires that destroy others, as well as "corrupting" the person to whom the tongue belongs. It becomes increasingly subject itself to the influences of evil—**and is itself set on fire by hell** (3:6).

Whether this refers to the tendency for careless and harmful words to double back and destroy those who uttered them or is a reference to the ultimate destiny of the one who fails to exercise control, James means to leave no doubt as to the destructive potential of the tongue. Actually, any or all of the above understandings could be supported by the text. Surely the words we utter have a way of coming back on us. Loose lips do sink ships! Sometimes those ships are our own. Further, the less we discipline our speech, the more our speech becomes influenced by the power of evil. Having those whose tongues are charged with teaching the truth become the instruments of evil is a frighteningly real possibility.

All kinds of animals, birds, reptiles and creatures of the sea are being tamed and have been tamed by man, but no man can tame the tongue. It is a restless evil, full of deadly poison (3:7-8). Continuing his appeals to the world of nature, James suggests that human ingenuity has been sufficient to **tame** (subdue) any number and variety of creatures. But in spite of such ingenuity, no human has been able to subdue **the tongue.**

The Greek word for **tame** is used only here in James 3 and once in the Gospel of Mark, where, in describing the demon-possessed man, Mark says, "For he had often been chained hand and foot, but he tore the chains apart and broke the irons on his feet. No one was strong enough to *subdue* him" (Mark 5:4, my emphasis). In the same way that chains and irons and all the efforts of humans were insufficient in taming the demon-possessed man, James says that no human can tame or subdue the tongue.

This explains James's contention that perfect control of the tongue is beyond human capacity (see James 3:2). To erase any remaining doubt about that, he adds, **It is a restless evil, full of deadly poison** (3:8). Portraying the human tongue as being **full of deadly poison** graphically illustrates the power of words—something James wants his readers to grasp. With tensions rising between the rich and poor, and depth of commitment by many questionable at best, James knows how easily even the smallest spark could start a destructive fire storm in the church.

The origins of most human conflicts lie in the realm of the verbal—spoken words. Someone's words inflame, offend or are misconstrued, and the fire rages. Beyond that, human words can wound and "kill" in ways that make the analogy to deadly poison most apt. Parents, spouses, friends and, yes, church members forget the potential poisoning effects of words and cause suffering in numerous ways as a result. James's warning about the power of the tongue is ignored at great peril.

The issue of the tongue bridges this epistle's connection to the Jewish Wisdom tradition.[1] The book of Proverbs contains many wisdom sayings directed at the phenomena of human speech. In particular, Proverbs stresses the importance of exercising proper control over one's words: "When words are many, sin is not absent, but he who holds his tongue is wise" (10:19); "The words of the wicked lie in wait for blood, but the speech of the upright rescues them" (12:6); "Reckless words pierce like a sword, but the tongue of the wise brings healing" (12:18); "A gentle answer turns away wrath, but a harsh word stirs up anger" (15:1); "A man of knowledge uses words with restraint, and a man of understanding is even-tempered" (17:27); "A word aptly spoken is like apples of gold in settings of silver" (25:11).

The Jewish Wisdom tradition considers that words have what philosophers call "being." Words take on being—reality or existence—when spoken, and cannot be revoked. Characterizing words as having "being" makes God's creative Word and His redemptive Word powerfully significant for all humankind. While people may speak of "mere words," Christians clearly know that when words come from the mouth of God, there is nothing "mere" about them. They are real! The power of words to affect the real lives of real people is why James is insistent that words be respected and the tongue be controlled.

Words have always played significant roles in the human experience. Indeed, we see in Genesis that false words instigated the fall of humanity— "has God said?" (Gen. 3:1 NASB). The punishment of God upon those at Babel who sought to make a great name for themselves (make **great boasts** [Jas. 3:5]) was to confuse their speech (Gen. 11:7-8). God knew that nothing would divide and scatter people like words out of control!

As believers, we are part of a church redeemed by the Word of God made flesh. Jesus is the explanatory Word *of* God *about* God. Pentecost reminds us of God's intention to make His speech clear and redemptive to all who would hear.[2] Of all people, Christians are without excuse when it comes to knowing about the power of the tongue, and yet this continues to be a major source of difficulty within the contemporary Christian community. The Bible is clear regarding the necessity of coming to grips with the power of words. James urges his readers to correctly understand the power of their own speech.

Perhaps the key to understanding these verses lies in noting that the Greek word James uses in 3:8 for **restless** often refers to persons who are unsettled or vacillating. In fact, this is the word James employed in 1:8 to describe the "double-minded man" who is "unstable in all he does." Double-minded persons are those who are unsettled and vacillating. They are restless.

The connection between failing to control the tongue and the double-mindedness that dooms the faithless person to instability is critical to understanding James's concern over this issue. The relationship between a faith profession and one's speech was clearly made in 1:26, and now we understand why failing to control the tongue is so damning. It reveals the heart of a person as unstable or two-souled. Our words have a way of revealing our hearts.

This double-minded character that expresses itself in one's speech is what James proceeds to illustrate: **With the tongue we praise our Lord and Father, and with it we curse men, who have been made in God's likeness. Out of the same mouth come praise and cursing. My brothers, this should not be** (3:9-10). When religion is surface only, or when the soul is divided in its loyalties, odd, incongruous situations occur. For example, James says that one can employ the tongue to **praise our Lord** (literally "bless"—likely a reference to Jesus; see comments on 1:1) **and Father,** but then turn around and curse those **made in God's likeness.** Both blessings and curses come from the same source.[3]

The use of **brothers** here only strengthens James's plea that such unseemly and contradictory acts have no place in the practice of true religion. James evaluates such acts literally as "not fitting"—they don't match up with one's profession (see 1:26). This kind of incompatibility between one's professed love for God and treatment of one's brother is targeted by John's first epistle: "If anyone says, 'I love God,' yet hates his brother, he is a liar. For anyone who does not love his brother, whom he has seen, cannot love God, whom he has not seen" (1 John 4:20).

James's concern closely parallels John's. A person who can bless the Father and then turn around and curse those whom the Father loves shows a fundamental inconsistency. It doesn't fit! Given James's overall concern with the blessing that comes from authentic faith, and the curse that comes in the form of all kinds of trouble from superficial and halfhearted religion, his words here are carefully chosen. That such contradictory speech originates from the same mouth illustrates the essence of the double-minded person and stands in stark contrast to the God in whom there is no such inconsistency (see James 1:17).

To show just how unseemly this state of affairs really is, James continues the illustrations by posing a question: **Can both fresh water and salt water flow from the same spring?** (3:11). Again, the emphasis of Jesus' teaching about the fruit of one's life being an accurate gauge of what truly resides within is apparently in James's mind here. **Fresh water** springs would be highly prized by the water-starved residents of the Middle East in that day. Discovering a spring was like uncovering all the rich possibilities of life. Entire villages and cites grew up around springs whose sweet waters provided the necessary resources for human life. Imagine the disappointment, despair, and even disgust of discovering that the life-giving **spring** was also producing worthless **salt water.** Can such opposites coexist? The answer is clear: They can't!

The utter impossibility of such double-minded productivity leads James to add to the illustration: **My brothers, can a fig tree bear olives, or a grapevine bear figs? Neither can a salt spring produce fresh water** (3:12). It's simple—like begets like; same produces same. One doesn't plant **fig** seeds, expecting to harvest **olives.** No one expects to pick **figs** from **a grapevine.** In the same way, **a salt spring** will never **produce fresh water.** The double-minded nature of human speech is a contradiction to the profession of authentic faith every bit as much as the presence of salt water and fresh water from the same spring is a contradiction of nature. Blessing and cursing from the same lips is a contradiction of spirit.

These concerns certainly apply to all within the Christian community, but they hold true especially for those who teach and instruct others. In his second chapter, James argued that mere words, apart from accompanying deeds, were dead. Now in chapter 3 he demonstrates that uncontrolled words are deadly. The practice of true religion cannot be successful apart from significant control over the power of the tongue.

How can such a troublesome member be controlled? James poses that exact question in varying ways in verses 2 and 8 of this chapter. Having argued first the absolute necessity of controlling the tongue, James then despairs that human effort is not sufficient to accomplish such a task. It could be that he has intentionally set the stage for what is to come by focusing on the need for something beyond human ability to accomplish the important task of becoming wise in our words.

The problem of the double-minded person, unstable in all he says and does, is not a problem that can be solved by mere human efforts. In bringing the issue of one's basic character to the fore, James has prepared his readers for the second emphasis pertaining especially to teachers: the issue of wisdom.

Endnotes

[1]The Wisdom Literature includes the books of Job, Proverbs, Ecclesiastes, and Song of Songs (Song of Solomon). Also known as the Books of Poetry. These writings are collections of statements of wisdom, often dealing with the great issues of life, such as the problem of suffering, practical ethics and morality, and the meaning of life and love.

[2]In the New Testament, Pentecost primarily referred to the event when the Holy Spirit was given to the church; this occurred on the Day of Pentecost. The Greek term which *Pentecost* comes from means "fiftieth" or "the fiftieth day," and is literally the fiftieth day after the end of the Passover. It is also known as the Jewish Feast of Weeks. This day is part of the Jewish observances, and was the beginning of the offering of first fruits.

[3]Blessings and curses refer to the response of God to His people in accordance with their obedience to Him (blessings) or their disobedience (curses). In the Old Testament, God's power was invoked through power-laden words (blessings and curses) often spoken in prayer form. Through these blessings or curses, God's people would call upon Him to provide or care for them by affecting them in a positive way or those around them in a positive or negative way. In Judaism (the belief and cultural system of the Jewish people), some blessings were reserved for the priests, but others were a regular part of the synagogue services. Curses were much less prominent and were forbidden. In the New Testament, the ultimate blessing came from God to mankind in Jesus Christ, and blessings accompanied righteousness. Curses accompanied sin.

8

TRUE WISDOM
AND
TRUE RELIGION

James 3:13-18

The double-minded nature of the tongue clearly points to the need for divine help in taming what no human has been able to tame. The question of where one turns for help in times of need has been answered previously (see James 1:5). Here, James returns to the resources of this God who "gives generously to all without finding fault" (1:5) by turning to the issue which guided his discussion of the tongue—wisdom. The commerce of all teachers is wisdom, and the vehicle or means by which they conduct their profession is speech. The joining of these two issues is not coincidental.

Who is wise and understanding among you? (Jas. 3:13a). Being **wise and understanding** is fundamental to those who hold the teaching office. Of all people, teachers are supposed to lead lives of wisdom. James emphasizes the necessity for the twin virtues of wisdom and understanding by posing this question.

Surely all who claim the title "teacher" would feel compelled to assert their possession of these two qualities. But James will contend throughout this paragraph that there are different kinds of wisdom. The wisdom James speaks of here refers to knowledge that is "divine in nature and origin."[1] The wisdom that enables one to guard his or her speech and, therefore, direct his or her life in positive ways is something beyond human intellectual accumulation. Its origins are divine.

The addition of **understanding** insures James's emphasis upon the practical advantage of true wisdom, namely that one understands how to

125

put it into practice. Having argued as he has in the first two chapters, James would be the last person to advocate the mere possession of knowledge as an end in itself. In fact, James wouldn't consider that "wisdom" at all. If it doesn't work itself out in real life, it isn't true wisdom, and it has nothing to do with true religion. Stephen Paine defined wisdom as "the ability to deal successfully with the factors of life."[2] This fits well with the overall emphasis of the so-called Wisdom tradition that views wisdom as a way of life rather than the accumulation of knowledge for knowledge's sake.[3]

The fact that James raises this as a question seems to suggest that he is trying to engage people who have declared themselves to be wise and understanding. He wants them to measure themselves and their professions against the true standard. The presence of undisciplined teachers in James's day whose careless talk was inflaming the community would certainly justify James's questioning of their claims. Identifying the authentic becomes much more critical in the presence of a counterfeit. James seeks to expose the counterfeit by revealing the genuine article.

He does this in his typical fashion; he marries the claims of wisdom and understanding to deeds. The "man from Missouri" is alive and well. James's credo is "Show me!" The challenge is given to those who claim wisdom and understanding: **Let him show it by his good life, by deeds done in the humility that comes from wisdom** (Jas. 3:13b).

In the final analysis, **wisdom** isn't something one talks about; it is something one lives. Being wise is living in a certain way. The real test of wisdom is the test of life. Real wisdom can be measured, but it has nothing to do with IQ tests. It has everything to do with a person's attitude and approach to life. Real wisdom is always connected to life in significant ways.

In Luke's version of the Sermon on the Mount (see Luke 6), Jesus cited the necessary connection between real **wisdom** and **deeds** (Jas. 3:13) in dealing with the criticisms of the religious leaders. A variety of scenes follow in Luke 7 that demonstrate this connection between His wisdom and His deeds. Even John the Baptist was compelled to believe that Jesus was truly the expected Messiah on the basis of how His deeds demonstrated His wisdom. Jesus fulfilled John's expectations of the Messiah by *living* wisdom, not just talking it. When the Pharisees criticized Christ for "eating with sinners," Jesus roundly condemned their failure to connect His words and His deeds, as we read in Luke's gospel: "To what, then, can I compare the people of this generation? What are they like? They are like children sitting in the marketplace and calling out to each other: 'We played the flute for you, and you did not dance; we sang a dirge, and you did not cry. 'For John the Baptist came neither eating bread nor drinking wine, and you say, 'He has a demon.' The Son of Man came eating and drinking, and you say, 'Here is a glutton and a drunkard, a friend of tax collectors and "sinners."' But wisdom is proved right by all her children" (Luke 7:31-35). Jesus contended that the truth of His words was finally demonstrated by their consistency with His deeds.

James fully intends to make this type of connection between real wisdom and real life as well. Wisdom is always vindicated by its deeds. This fits particularly well with James's prior assertion that lofty claims backed by no deeds have little or nothing to do with real religion (see James 1:22–2:13).

The evidence of true wisdom, and thus true religion, is that of a **good life** (3:13)—literally, "the good conduct of his works done in meekness of wisdom." The New International Version's rendition—**by deeds done in the humility that comes from wisdom** (3:13)—fits well because the original Greek actually speaks here of a wisdom resulting in "a wise meekness." Wise meekness? While many in James's day and our own would consider that an oxymoron (a self-contradictory phrase), that is precisely what characterizes the deeds of the truly wise. Anyone who has rubbed shoulders with truly great, truly wise people has doubtless been struck by the **humility** attached to their actions. The truly wise have never found it necessary to broadcast or advertise their possession of **wisdom**—true wisdom pervades their lives.

With the likelihood of teachers jousting for position, each claiming to be the "wisest of the wise," James indicates that such claims deny the presence of the kind of wisdom that characterizes the truly great teachers. As mentioned, the Greek term translated **humility** in 3:13 actually means "meekness." It is Jesus' word in Matthew 5:5, where He said, "Blessed are the meek, for they will inherit the earth." Given the sorry record of power-hungry leaders in our world, the meek may well be the only people wise enough to be entrusted with such responsibility!

The combination of humility and wisdom has been a decidedly Christian contribution to the world's thinking. The Greeks viewed humility as a weakness and, thus, did not connect it in any fashion to wisdom. But from the outset, Jesus presented himself as the humble Son of Man. The prophecy of Zechariah, employed by Matthew's gospel concerning Jesus' triumphal entry, was dressed in meekness: "Say to the Daughter of Zion, 'See, your king comes to you, gentle [humble] and riding on a donkey, on a colt, the foal of a donkey'" (Matt. 21:5). Jesus' teachings and deeds were "clothed" with the humility Paul admonished for all who would be like Christ (see Colossians 3:12).

In James 1, the author counseled humility: "Therefore, get rid of all moral filth and the evil that is so prevalent and humbly accept the word planted in you, which can save you" (verse 21). Connecting humility with wisdom sends a clear message to those whose claims to be wise are undermined by the arrogance of pretense and pride. Again, "faith without deeds is dead!"

To make sure he is understood, James paints a contrasting picture as well: **But if you harbor bitter envy and selfish ambition in your hearts, do not boast about it or deny the truth** (3:14). It's not enough to know what real wisdom is; James wants his readers to know what it is *not,* as well. Ironically, James puts his finger on the besetting sin among those who so often claim to be wise.

Envy and **ambition** are the two deadly sins of those who fancy themselves teachers. This is not simply envy—jealousy—but **bitter envy.** The Greek word for **bitter** is used to describe water that is not potable (not drinkable).[4] Here the word refers to the hearts of the self-proclaimed "wise." But it is not merely the *presence* of bitter jealousy which disqualifies the claims of the wise; it is the *reason it is there* in the first place. It is there because these self-proclaimed wise accommodate it. The word **harbor** is the New International Version's way of showing the ready welcome afforded to envy and selfish ambition by the self-proclaimed wise person. These qualities flourish because they are accommodated so readily in one's life.

Jealousy in our lives is a choice, and apart from our choosing it, it cannot survive. Jealousy, especially "bitter jealousy," must be nurtured and attended to in order to thrive. It cannot survive if ignored. Where there is false wisdom, jealousy is welcomed; it is "harbored."

Further, in stark contrast to deeds done in humility, there is the outcome of **selfish ambition.** The phrase here can be rendered literally, "you have rivalry in your hearts." Whereas the wisdom James commends is the wisdom which reveals itself through deeds of humble service, false wisdom seeks the promotion of self as a true reflection of the heart's contents.

Sadly, much of James's words find suitable parallels in our world today. The places of "wisdom" in our culture—university campuses, research facilities, the halls of government—are characterized more often than not by envy. And it is precisely the kind of **bitter envy** that results in the worst kind of interpersonal conflict and a pettiness that denies the very spirit of wisdom. There is **selfish ambition** at work among the supposed wise persons of our age, the results of which remind one of kindergarten fights over cheap toys. To harbor—make welcome—such attitudes is the opposite of what the teaching vocation is about. Little wonder that James labels such claims as a denial of (literally, "lying against") **the truth.** The truth that is effectively denied in this case is the claim to wisdom itself.

Although it is never attractive in any scenario, in teachers claiming to be Christians, the presence of these attitudes and habits of heart truly does represent a total denial of the truth, because of the nature of this brand of wisdom: **Such "wisdom" does not come down from heaven but is earthly, unspiritual, of the devil** (Jas. 3:15). James makes this blunt assessment of the kind of wisdom described in verse 14 because the Christian world view holds that real wisdom ultimately is not an achievement of human ingenuity, but is a gift—a gift from above. The wisdom James lauds comes down from heaven (see 1:17). But the kind of **"wisdom"** (3:15) that produces the fires of bitter jealousy and ambitious strife cannot originate from the courts of heaven.

This divisive kind of wisdom betrays its place of origin all too readily to the discerning person: **Such "wisdom" . . . is earthly, unspiritual, of the devil.** The threefold indictment against false wisdom reveals that such "knowledge" is limited by its origins: it is earthbound; it is unspiritual; it is doomed by its associations (it is **of the devil**). The charge of being **earthly**—literally, "of the earth"—means that the ample resources of the God of heaven are not included in this wisdom. It is humanistic to the core and cannot overcome the obstacles such limitations impose upon it.

Because it originates in the earth, it is severely limited in what it can do. Remember that earlier James said earthly, or human, wisdom can tame all manner of animals, but it cannot tame the tongue (see 3:8). These inherent limitations of human wisdom are one more reason why we need to ask God for what He alone can supply (see 1:5). However exalted the wisdom of humans may be, we must never forget that it is extremely limited in solving the fundamental problems of life. As Paul put it to the Corinthians—people who fancied themselves wise—"the world through its wisdom did not know [God]" (1 Cor. 1:21). Any wisdom which cannot introduce a person to the ultimate truth of the universe is incompetent.

That such wisdom is termed **unspiritual** (Jas. 3:15)—literally, "natural"—adds emphasis to the understanding of it as earthbound and deficient. What sets real wisdom apart from the human brand is its essential *spirituality*. It is not bound to the realm of physical understanding, but includes the all-important realm of spirit. As such, it is not explainable in mere human terms, but requires a heavenly explanation. The wisdom described here by James is sorely lacking in that quality, being all too easily explained as "natural" in its scope.

But by far, the most damaging indictment James levels is that this particular kind of wisdom is **of the devil** (3:15). The Greek word used here literally means "demon-like," which makes for an absolute contrast as the wisdom that comes down from heaven is compared to the wisdom that has its origins in the habitations of demons. This is a most damaging charge because the Devil, as the father of lies, is incapable of speaking the truth, which is the raw material of wisdom. The clear implication is this: Why bother with something incapable of ever producing the desired result? Given the analogy James drew in chapter 2 comparing deedless faith to the demons who believe but never change, it seems likely that the wisdom originating from such places also has the characteristic of not bearing proper fruit.

The reason it can't produce the right kind of fruit is obvious: **For where you have envy and selfish ambition, there you find disorder and every evil practice** (3:16). James's confidence in asserting the demonic origins of such wisdom is warranted by the consequences that result from the presence of this wisdom. The seeds of bitter envy and selfish ambition always produce a predictable harvest.

Where such seed is sown, the harvest is **disorder and every evil practice.** The Greek word used for **disorder** is from the same root word James used in 3:8 to describe the tongue as a "restless evil," which in turn is related to the word used in 1:8 to describe the instability of the "double-minded" person. That such "fruit" is counter to true wisdom and originates from the Devil rather than God is demonstrated by the Apostle Paul's use of the same word: "For God is not a God of disorder but of peace" (1 Cor. 14:33a). Disorder is the Adversary's mode of operation. The word is also used to describe the conditions of a riot (see 2 Corinthians 6:5) and a revolution (see Luke 21:9). In short, this kind of wisdom disqualifies itself on the basis of the havoc it wreaks.

In addition to disorder, James contends that this kind of earthly, devilish wisdom produces **every evil practice** (Jas. 3:16). Remembering James's insistence that our professions and claims must be borne out by the practices of our lives, this is a final, telling blow against the claims of those who want to be considered wise but whose lives deny such claims. The conclusive evidence against this sort of wisdom is its fruit. Just as faith without works is dead, any wisdom that results in disorder and every evil practice is deficient and suspect. And, we should note, it springs from claims (boasts) that are made with the tongue!

Behind these verses of chapter 3 (and, for that matter, the entire chapter with its overall emphasis upon the significance of teachers), James appears to track closely the teachings of Jesus in the Gospel of Matthew: "Watch out for false prophets [teachers]. They come to you in sheep's clothing, but inwardly they are ferocious wolves. By their fruit you will recognize them. Do people pick grapes from thornbushes, or figs from thistles? Likewise every good tree bears good fruit, but a bad tree bears bad fruit. A good tree cannot bear bad fruit, and a bad tree cannot bear good fruit. Every tree that does not bear good fruit is cut down and thrown into the fire. Thus, by their fruit you will recognize them" (Matt. 7:15-20).

The words and phrasing of James and the words of Jesus in Matthew are too close to be coincidental. Here is a vivid illustration of how James leans heavily on the teachings of the brother who has become his Lord. While the Epistle of James may lack references to the person of Jesus, there is no lack of appeal to the teachings of Jesus.

But the wisdom that comes from heaven is first of all pure; then peace-loving, considerate, submissive, full of mercy and good fruit, impartial and sincere (Jas. 3:17). In severe contrast to the earthbound, unspiritual, and devilish wisdom of the false teachers, James presents here the nature of the true **wisdom** that characterizes true religion. Its place of origin is the polar opposite to false wisdom. Rather than being earthly and demon-like, true wisdom is the product of heaven.

The kind of wisdom that can claim heaven as its place of origin is distinctive in several ways. It **is first of all pure.** The Greek word for **pure** shares the root of the word *holy.* The central characteristic of true wisdom is holiness. How could it be otherwise, coming from heaven? To be holy is to be clean, single-hearted, and unpolluted by foreign matter (1:27). It is being wholly devoted to the aims of its place of origin. The bottom line evidence of true wisdom is that of becoming more and more like the One who walked this earth and demonstrated the holy life of wisdom in our midst—Jesus Christ. Any claim to wisdom that does not connect to Christlikeness is false—it is "impure."

The question now becomes, how "wise" can anyone be who has not accepted Christ as Lord or, as James might put it, given himself completely, as opposed to halfheartedly? The emphasis of James's entire epistle is on the blessedness of wholehearted, true religion. The foundation of wisdom is the fear or reverence of the Lord. It always has been, and always will be.

Our world shuns commitments, yet fancies itself wise. The message of the gospel is that genuine wisdom is committing ourselves "lock, stock, and barrel" to the wisdom of God which has come **from heaven** (Jas. 3:17) in the person of His Son, Jesus Christ.

2)

Real wisdom is also **peace-loving**—literally, "peaceable." In Proverbs 3, where wisdom is spoken of as a person, we read, "Her [Wisdom's] ways are pleasant ways, and all her paths are peace" (verse 17). The way of wisdom is the way of peace. The Wisdom tradition which influenced James's thinking is evident here in the connecting of wisdom to the practice of peacemaking.[5] The contrast of true wisdom with the false wisdom of James 3:16 is demonstrated in Proverbs: "There is deceit in the hearts of those who plot evil, but joy for those who promote peace" (Prov. 12:20); "A heart at peace gives life to the body, but envy rots the bones" (Prov. 14:30). There is no comparison between the fruit of wisdom characterized by peace-loving and the fruit borne by envy, deceit, and evil plots.

The way of peace has always been the way of wisdom, from Old Testament times to now. James's Jewish readers ought to know that. Moreover, the words of Christ from the Sermon on the Mount are likely also in view here: "Blessed are the peacemakers, for they will be called sons of God" (Matt. 5:9). What could be considered greater evidence of possessing true wisdom than having a life that qualifies us to be one of God's children? God's wisdom with His world is the way of peace. Jesus' statement in His Sermon reminds us that "like Father, like son(s)" is the way of true wisdom.

In our increasingly violent world, are we committed enough to the peaceable Kingdom to be judged wise in the eyes of God? Is the peace-loving character of our lives sufficient to prove to others that we are members of God's own family? Do we really possess the kind of wisdom that will not seek violence, knowing that our anger cannot please God (see James 1:20)?

3)

The **wisdom that comes from heaven** is also **considerate** (3:17). The Greek word here speaks of a gentle, yielding spirit. Paul commended Titus to look for this quality in those who should serve as leaders (Titus 3:2). It is the quality Peter urged husbands to show their wives in 1 Peter 3:7. In both of these instances, "power," in its various forms, is at the center. In leaders and, sadly, too often in husbands, authoritarian notions of power overshadow any sense of consideration of others. But in both cases, as James says here, being gentle or considerate is the evidence of true wisdom.

Consideration is a quality that seems oddly out of touch with a "me first" world. No one who wants to make it to the "top" is counseled to be considerate of others. Politicians, celebrity athletes, and all manner of people in the public eye routinely look for opportunities to "step" on those who would get in their way. But the possessor of true wisdom shuns such calculated moves, demonstrating instead an "uncommon civility."

Yes, old-fashioned as it seems, a truly wise person is simply a nice person. That being nice is considered strange is a commentary on our world. Yet it is one more bit of evidence as to how different the ways of God are from those of the unbelieving culture around us. How oddly countercultural the gospel becomes when, instead of "looking out for number one," the way of gentle consideration is proclaimed as the fruit of authentic wisdom. Sometimes truth really is stranger than fiction.

Real wisdom is **submissive** (Jas. 3:17). Interestingly, this is the quality Peter said that wives should demonstrate to their husbands, right before he told husbands to be considerate of their wives. Wisdom is not limited to gender! Neither is submissiveness. Peter also counseled submissiveness from the younger men toward the older as the way of wisdom (see 1 Peter 5:5).

Like many of the qualities we've looked at so far, *submission* is also not typically associated with wisdom in the world of today. Being submissive is viewed as being weak, spineless—extremely unwise. Thus, intentionally cultivating this quality in our lives takes the kind of commitment to real faith that is far beyond the abilities of the double-minded person who cannot make up his or her mind.

For the true believer, however, commitment to the wisdom of submissiveness needs only one model—Jesus. Jesus Christ is the One who submitted himself to death on a cross. Was that wise? The mocking, unbelieving world, and the Jewish religious leaders among them, did not think so. What did God think of such "unearthly wisdom"? Paul revealed in his letter to the Philippians exactly how God responded: "Therefore God exalted him to the highest place and gave him the name that is above every name, that at the name of Jesus every knee should bow, in heaven and on earth and under the earth, and every tongue confess that Jesus Christ is Lord, to the glory of God the Father" (Phil. 2:9-11).

Such exaltation as the result of submissiveness indicates that worldly wisdom, which brands submission as foolishness, is way out of step with reality. That's precisely what James believes. Remember that the essence of the Wisdom tradition is to see wisdom as a way of life that marches in step with reality. Being submissive in our actions and attitudes places us in the company of the wisest of the wise.

Real wisdom is also **full of mercy and good fruit** (Jas. 3:17). James reminds communities of believers, who more than likely have felt the sting of injustice and unfairness, of God's fundamental commitment to mercy. The prophet Micah elevated mercy as indispensable to real wisdom when he said, "He has showed you, O man, what is good. And what does the Lord require of you? To act justly and to love mercy and to walk humbly with your God" (Mic. 6:8). The fruit that is produced by mercy characterizes real wisdom.

Mercy (Jas. 3:17) is a frighteningly rare commodity in our world today, even among professing Christians. When believers join in the madness of vengeance and violence, even against those who have done terrible things, they effectively undermine their profession of the wisdom of heaven. Those who practice true religion need no better reason to show mercy than the staggering truth that they also have been shown mercy.

Jesus' words regarding the wicked, unmerciful servant in Matthew ought to sober all who are tempted to imitate the unmerciful world around them: "'Shouldn't you have had mercy on your fellow servant just as I had on you?' In anger his master turned him over to the jailers to be tortured, until he should pay back all he owed. 'This is how my heavenly Father will treat each of you unless you forgive your brother from your heart'" (Matt. 18:33-35). As James put it earlier, "mercy triumphs over judgment" (Jas. 2:13).

Real wisdom is **impartial and sincere** (3:17). The Greek word for **impartial** here has the idea of something that is "unshakable." It is closely related to the word James used in 1:6 to express the need to ask God for wisdom without "doubting" or "wavering." Again this links the presence of real wisdom to the depths of our commitment to God in faith. Real wisdom is steady, solid, secure. In fact, real wisdom has the kind of perseverance to stand firm in times when others waver. Again, James relates the need for wisdom (see 1:5) with the need to persevere in times of testing (see 1:2-4).

The incompatibility of double-minded, wavering commitment and true religion is strengthened by the addition of "sincerity" as a characteristic of wisdom. The Greek word for **sincere** (3:17) has the idea of something that is "without hypocrisy, and free from insincerity."[6] Insincerity is the hallmark of the double-minded. In their wavering and their attempts at self-protection, they are not the kind of people you would want to lean upon. They are not wise. Insincerity has no place among the truly wise.

James ends his description of real wisdom by summarizing the consequences where this kind of wisdom is present: **Peacemakers who sow in peace raise a harvest of righteousness** (Jas. 3:18). The ongoing interest of James in "fruit" as evidence of the real thing prompts this summary judgment. Throughout the epistle he is concerned about the possibility of conflict breaking out in the Jewish-Christian communities. This background concern is all the more evidenced when we note that of all the qualities of real wisdom listed, James chooses the subject of peacemaking to bring this subject to its conclusion.

Remember that earlier James stated that the anger of man cannot produce the righteousness God desires (see 1:20). Here that conviction is restated, though in a different way. What God desires for our lives— righteousness—comes as a result of the peaceable character of real wisdom. The "law" of the Spirit is absolutely sound: What we sow, we shall also reap. If we sow discord and hatred, we will reap the fruit of such folly. But if we sow the seed of the peaceable Kingdom, we shall see the harvest of true wisdom—the righteous life that God desires.

It is impossible to read James's description of wisdom in 3:17 without thinking of Paul's list of the "fruit of the Spirit" in Galatians: "But the fruit of the Spirit is love, joy, peace, patience, kindness, goodness, faithfulness, gentleness and self-control" (Gal. 5:23-24). This similarity and the emphasis on the wisdom that comes down from heaven has led some to suppose that in James, wisdom is a reference to the Holy Spirit (see comments on James 1:5). Again, this seems to be reading more from the text than is warranted, but even if James's wisdom is not the Spirit himself, the Galatians 5 passage certainly demonstrates that apart from the presence of this Spirit, such fruit—such wisdom—is an impossible human achievement.

Beyond this, we must remember James's move, in his treatment of the tongue, to push his readers to seek help beyond themselves. Such help is surely available in the presence of this heavenly wisdom described in James 3:17. The solution to the problem of teachers out of control is imparting to them the heaven-sent wisdom that produces the fruit of **righteousness** (3:18). Such wisdom can be imparted only through the dynamic presence of the living Lord, specifically through the infilling of His Spirit. So while we may need to stop short of equating wisdom with the Holy Spirit in this epistle, there can be no argument that where true wisdom resides, there the Spirit of Christ resides as well.

James's concern for the teaching leadership of the church is well founded. What ought to concern any and all who love the church is the general failure to hold teachers and leaders accountable to the standards of James 3. The contemporary church is filled with people claiming to be leaders and teachers, but whose lives clearly deny any hint of the wisdom James describes in these verses. Our day is the day of "style over substance." As long as someone "looks" the part, we are more than willing to assume they possess enough wisdom to teach and lead.

Unfortunately, our religious landscapes are littered with the debris of empty claims, empty lives, empty religion. These aspiring teachers claim authority without ever manifesting the fruit of genuine heavenly wisdom, and we have either applauded their exercises of insincerity or stood by and kept our tongues when we should have spoken out. Little wonder, then, that the modern church seems powerless to make peace even within its own ranks—to say nothing of the world around it. We have reaped what we have sown, and, sadly, the fruit is not righteousness. James is right. Not many of us should be teachers.

ENDNOTES

[1]Walter Bauer, *A Greek-English Lexicon of the New Testament and Other Early Christian Literature,* 2nd ed., translated by William F. Arndt and F. Wilbur Gingrich (Chicago: University of Chicago Press, 1979), p. 760.

[2]Stephen Paine, *Studies in the Book of James* (Old Tappan, New Jersey: Fleming H. Revell Co., 1955), p. 120.

[3]The Wisdom Literature includes the books of Job, Proverbs, Ecclesiastes, and Song of Songs (Song of Solomon). Also known as the Books of Poetry. These writings are collections of statements of wisdom, often dealing with the great issues of life, such as the problem of suffering, practical ethics and morality, and the meaning of life and love.

[4]Bauer, p. 657.

[5]See endnote 3.

[6]Bauer, p. 76.

Part Four

THE GREATEST BARRIER TO TRUE RELIGION

James 4:1-10

Having taken aim at the problems surrounding those who aspire to teach (see James 3), the author of the epistle shifts his focus in chapter 4 to consider additional barriers to true religion. But before addressing these problems, he gives full attention to the issue that plagues the lives of his people. It is a fundamental issue which prevents the blessing of true religion from being realized. He has been carefully building his case in anticipation of his words to follow. Up to this point, James's focus has been primarily on symptoms—favoritism, empty faith professions, uncontrolled speech, and invalid claims of wisdom. Now James will look at the underlying cause of these symptoms and will, more importantly, suggest the solution to the problem.

The first ten verses of chapter 4 become the climactic point of the entire epistle. Specifically, verses 6 through 10 represent the height of James's exhortations to his readers. In a letter filled with imperative commands, these are the supreme imperatives, for here James bares the soul of his purpose in writing. This passage thus serves as the climax for those who see a unifying purpose in the epistle, which is what I have argued throughout. Here, the apostle will press his case to the heart of the matter, which, as we shall see, is just that—a matter of the heart.

9

THE PROBLEM OF DOUBLE-MINDED DESIRES

James 4:1-5

hat causes fights and quarrels among you? (Jas. 4:1a). The wording of this verse in the New International Version—**What causes fights**—is unfortunate. The Old English of the King James Version, however, is well chosen: "From whence come wars and fightings?" And so, the question here is better rendered, "Where do these **fights and quarrels among you** come from?" The question posed by this opening line provides a clear turn in the subject matter. We move from the fruit of true wisdom to the source of divisions among people.

James is more interested in the *source* of these conflicts than merely in what causes them. Locating a problem's source implies that it then can be dealt with effectively. The problems cited here are literally "wars" and "fights." James may be using especially graphic terms to illustrate the logical end of the class warfare that seems on the verge of erupting. On the other hand, these terms may simply be descriptive of the state of the problems. In either case, the application of such words to the Christian community is a scandal and an embarrassment to the church. The presence of such open conflicts makes the question of their source all the more urgent.

Don't they come from your desires that battle within you? (4:1b). Having posed the question, James now answers it himself, and his answer is not in the least ambiguous: "Don't they have their source—don't they originate—from the **desires that battle within you?**" The problems of wars and fights may be external, but the origin of such problems is strictly internal. The pressures of the unbelieving world may produce problems for Christians on the outside, but the real problems are produced on the inside.

Desires here (Jas. 4:1) are literally "pleasures." This is the word Jesus used in the Gospel of Luke to speak of the conditions that choke the seed and prevent it from bearing fruit: "The seed that fell among thorns stands for those who hear, but as they go on their way they are choked by life's worries, riches and *pleasures,* and they do not mature" (Luke 8:14, my emphasis). Likewise, Paul reminded Titus, "At one time we too were foolish, disobedient, deceived and enslaved by all kinds of passions and pleasures. We lived in malice and envy, being hated and hating one another" (Titus 3:3). Note here the similar results or fruit that come from the presence of such "pleasures"—namely malice, envy, and hatred.

These desires are not simply present within James's readers, but are doing **battle** (Jas. 4:1)—literally "soldiering," making war. The militant, aggressive character of this word in the Greek comes through when it is used by Paul in 2 Corinthians: "For though we live in the world, we do not wage war as the world does" (2 Cor. 10:3). Peter also showed the aggressive bent of this term when he wrote, "Dear friends, I urge you, as aliens and strangers in the world, to abstain from sinful desires, which war against your soul" (1 Pet. 2:11).

James has identified the source of the wars that exist externally among the believers by putting his finger directly on the war that exists internally within the believers: *The wars without are caused by the war within!* James contends that the source of the problems he has been addressing thus far have their origins in the desires that are at war with one another in the individual members' hearts. The community itself is being threatened by the outward effects of an inward civil war. Here, James has crossed the point of no return, declaring in the clearest fashion the essential incompatibility of true religion and divided spiritual affections.

He proceeds to illustrate his point: **You want something but don't get it** (Jas. 4:2a). The external problems of things like favoritism and loose talk spring from the wanton desires of people who are finding their desires difficult, if not impossible, to satisfy. The Greek word for "desire" means to "set the heart" upon something. It can reflect good or evil desires. For example, Paul told Timothy that "if anyone sets his heart on being an overseer, he desires a noble task" (1 Tim. 3:1). But this is also the word Jesus used in Matthew's gospel to condemn adultery in the heart: "But I tell you that anyone who looks at a woman lustfully has already committed adultery with her in his heart" (Matt. 5:28). The Epistle to the

Galatians also shows the powerfully negative side of such desire: "For the sinful nature desires what is contrary to the Spirit, and the Spirit what is contrary to the sinful nature. They are in conflict with each other, so that you do not do what you want" (Gal. 5:17). Note that the result of this desire is conflict and confusion about what is truly desired! Paul's words here are strangely akin to those of James.

The problem of desire hearkens back to James 1 where the author warned his readers that the temptations for evil do not originate with God but from within themselves. These desires or longings have a way of exercising control over the lives of people in problematic ways. Specifically, these desires seem to be continually thwarted: **You want something but don't get it** (Jas. 4:2a). There is some fundamental breakdown between the point of desire and its fulfillment. Understanding the nature of desire and its implications is crucial to grasping James's overall argument regarding true religion and the way to attain it (see additional notes on desire at the end of chapter 10 of the commentary).

Briefly, this longing—this desire—has its roots in the human will. The impulses to know God and to follow His ways are subject to being diverted by any number of other lesser desires or impulses. Attempting to substitute anything for the God-given longing for fellowship with Him is doomed to confusion and conflict. But that is exactly the course chosen by humankind in the decision to sin against God. And the aftermath of that terrible choice has demonstrated the lengths to which misplaced human desire takes us.

This is graphically illustrated by James: **You kill and covet, but you cannot have what you want. You quarrel and fight. You do not have, because you do not ask God** (4:2b). Desire that is misplaced easily turns to covetousness. Covetousness is essentially the sin of never being satisfied—always wanting more. The reference to killing likely refers to the lengths to which such unbridled desires can lead. James already has indicated that fights and wars are in evidence, figuratively and beyond. Human desire gone amiss is capable of producing the most terrible kinds of consequences. Even the briefest survey of human history shows the violence and destruction that unfulfilled desires can bring. Little wonder James is so concerned.

Most ironically, even given the total expression of such wanton lust, desire remains frustrated. Killing and coveting, quarreling and fighting cannot satisfy the desires that war within. The proper focus for meeting such desires is God alone, but God has never been consulted! Those who have these desires have not bothered to ask God to meet this deepest need of life. As James already has indicated, it is God who must be asked to provide what is lacking (see comments on 1:5).

But how can such a charge be leveled at "religious people"? Remember, James is not talking to those who spend their Sunday mornings on the golf courses. He's talking to the church! He's talking to people who pray, and pray regularly. As if James anticipates their protests, he quickly adds, **When you ask, you do not receive, because you ask with wrong motives, that you may spend what you get on your pleasures** (4:3). On such occasions where God is consulted, the nature of the requests disqualifies them as anything that God could grant. James has previously described what kind of God it is to whom these people pray (see 1:17-18). The requests of these persons are rejected because they **ask with wrong motives** (4:3)—literally, "ask ill." They ask for the express purpose of getting something more to expend on their **pleasures** (see 4:1). But the reality of God's nature means that requests must conform to His nature in order to be granted.

To those James is talking about, God is little more than a heavenly errand boy who is summoned when something is needed to keep the party going. This view of God is the opposite of what James portrayed in chapter 1 (see verses 17-18). There we see God as one who gives good gifts in accordance with His desire to provide for the genuine needs of His children. Here we see that God is being used as a mere convenience, the possession of which affords more ways to try to satisfy our pleasures.

What a frightening picture of degraded religion James paints here. Rather than the peaceable fruit of wisdom from above, this kind of "faith" bears the kind of fruit that rightly deserves its designation as "earthly, unspiritual, of the devil" (3:15). A quick look around the contemporary church tells us that we ought to take James's words to heart. People are being killed—both literally and figuratively—in the pursuit of desire dressed as religion.

The inability to satisfy the misplaced longings of humankind has turned our cities into gutters of unthinkable filth and moral depravity. Hucksters posing as preachers hawk a brand of religious faith where God is offered as the answer to all our wants and fantasies. It grows ever more difficult to distinguish the believers from nonbelievers as lifestyles in the church increasingly mirror the culture around us. Christians have replaced the standard of "Behold how they love one another," with the more likely words, "Behold how they sue one another!" Fighting and quarrels between Christians commonly end up before the civil courts, publicly paraded by a cynical media.

The misplaced longings that theologians tell us can be satisfied only in God remain frustrated as we go about our endless search for satisfaction at the level of the flesh. Indeed, we *have* not because we *ask* not, and when we do ask, we "ask amiss" (Jas. 4:3 KJV). Our desire for God is halfhearted and double-minded. Our pursuit of true religion is mirrored in the words of a poem by Wilbur Rees:

> I would like to buy three dollars worth of God, please,
> Not enough to explode my soul or disturb my sleep
> But just enough to equal a cup of warm milk or a snooze in the sunshine.
> I don't want enough of him to make me love a black man or pick beets with a migrant.
> I want ecstasy, not transformation;
> I want the warmth of the womb, not a new birth.
> I want a pound of the Eternal in a paper sack.
> I would like to buy three dollars worth of God, please.

In our consumeristic world, where everyone is looking for a bargain— a real "steal"—some have the misguided notion that God is selling himself cheap. The idea that possessing God can be accomplished like possessing any number of other trinkets of the "good life" is exacting a terrible toll inside and outside of the church. The problem of this kind of religion is where James now turns his attention.

You adulterous people, don't you know that friendship with the world is hatred toward God? (4:4a). These words clearly show the passion that James feels as he observes the halfhearted, shallow practice passing itself off as authentic Christianity. The indictment of adultery must bring a chill to James's spine. As a Jewish Christian, he is well aware of the prophetic history of adultery.

Israel was often portrayed by the prophets as the spouse of God. Israel's unfaithfulness was often described in terms of infidelity and adultery. For example, Jeremiah wrote, "During the reign of King Josiah, the LORD said to me, 'Have you seen what faithless Israel has done? She has gone up on every high hill and under every spreading tree and has committed adultery there'" (Jer. 3:6). Or read Ezekiel's words: "Then in the nations where they have been carried captive, those who escape will remember me—how I have been grieved by their adulterous hearts, which have turned away from me, and by their eyes, which have lusted after their idols. They will loathe themselves for the evil they have done and for all their detestable practices" (Ezek. 6:9; see also chapter 16).

Note how the prophets stress that the sins of Israel—where the people turn away from God—are a problem of the "heart." Nowhere does this analogy come through more clearly than in the powerful story of the prophet Hosea. Without doubt, Hosea had the strangest of assignments from God: "When the LORD began to speak through Hosea, the LORD said to him, 'Go, take to yourself an adulterous wife and children of unfaithfulness, because the land is guilty of the vilest adultery in departing from the LORD'" (Hos. 1:2).

James's use of the indictment of adultery shows how seriously he takes the problems plaguing his readers' lives, and also shows how he characterizes the nature of these problems. It is a matter of spiritual infidelity—adultery.

He is sobered as well by the knowledge of how God has dealt historically with His people when they have broken faith with Him and run after other "lovers." The words of Jeremiah, Ezekiel, and Hosea, among others, regarding the judgment that was to befall Israel must be in the back of James's mind as he levels this frightening charge. The reason for such harsh judgment is demonstrated by what the charge of adultery implies.

James says that the misplaced desires of the people demonstrate their preference for the world's friendship over that of God. The result of such **friendship** is **hatred** (Jas. 4:4)—enmity—toward God. Enmity is hostility. This is how Paul, in his letter to the Romans, described the fundamental incompatibility of the sinful mind and God: "The sinful mind is hostile to God. It does not submit to God's law, nor can it do so" (Rom. 8:7). And James insists that such a relationship is not by default; it is a choice consciously made: **Anyone who chooses to be a friend of the world becomes an enemy of God** (Jas. 4:4b). The sentence can be literally rendered, "Whoever therefore resolves to be a friend of the world is constituted an enemy of God."

The intentionality of the human heart and will is the root of these conditions of hostility. That one becomes an enemy of God is not God's choice, any more than was His walking away from His bride, Israel, in the centuries before Christ. This infidelity is all one-sided. And the consequences are devastating in terms of our relationship to the God who alone can supply what is needed in times of testing (see 1:5).

Keeping oneself unpolluted from the world is to have true religion (see 1:27). Here James contends that true religion has been sold out by sinful desire. The consequence is hostility. Little wonder that the heart of humankind, created to be in fellowship with its Creator, now restlessly seeks to satisfy its gnawing sense of desire.

Or do you think Scripture says without reason that the spirit he caused to live in us envies intensely? (Jas. 4:5). Lest anyone think that James is overstating the consequences of friendship with the world, he makes an allusion to the Old Testament which has been the subject of a variety of interpretations. The New International Version renders a very different meaning than that of the Revised Standard Version, which states, "Or do you suppose it is in vain that the scripture says, 'He yearns jealously over the spirit which he has made to dwell in us?'" In this translation, it is God who is made jealous, by inference, because of "our" flirtations with the world. Given the Old Testament references surrounding Israel and her adulterous infidelity, there is some warrant to this reading. It fits into the context of the prior verses.

The New International Version, on the other hand, clearly portrays the spirit in us as envying intensely. The thought here seems to point to the insatiable desires of the spirit which God has placed within human beings. This rendering seems to indicate some relationship to Genesis 6:5, where in the days preceding the flood, God assessed the scope of humankind's fall into sin: "The LORD saw how great man's wickedness on the earth had become, and that every inclination [desire] of the thoughts of his heart was only evil all the time" (see additional notes on desire at the end of chapter 10 of the commentary). This verse shows how the inclination or desire of the human heart can become so depraved that hostility with God is not only warranted, but issues forth in God's judgment, in this case through the flood.

While the Revised Standard Version's rendering makes some sense in terms of God's being jealous for Israel's affections, the New International Version fits better overall with the context of James's thinking here. He is focused on the problem of the divided heart. The heart that wanders halfheartedly is a heart that inevitably will try to satisfy its longings in counterfeit ways. And that kind of heart is a heart capable of the most unthinkable kinds of evil—evil which brings one into open hostility with God. The picture James presents here is not pretty.

James directs communities reeling under the weight of testings and trials, plagued with class divisions and a growing war of words, to look inward and examine their hearts. Their affections are divided. They are playing the classic game of religiously trying to "have their cake and eat it too." They want God and the world together. They are using their faith as a means of satisfying their pleasures.

God is not about to be partner to such an arrangement. These people must understand that they are on a most dangerous road to judgment. The fate of adulterous Israel would be well-known among these Jewish Christians. James has spoken bluntly because they are in grave danger. Playing at religion is even more costly than ignoring religion wholesale. Trying to keep company with God and the world that rejects Him has all the makings of disaster. This is virtual religion, a faint shadow of the authentic faith that James has commended to his beloved people.

In terms of the spiritual significance of James's epistle, this is the climactic point of the letter. Here, James has put his finger directly on the problem that underlies all the other issues that both precede and follow this passage. The two-souled, double-minded approach to religion is the most dangerous road of all. In the book of Revelation, Jesus' words to the church at Laodicea tell us how such "faith" is considered in His eyes: "I know your deeds, that you are neither cold nor hot. I wish you were either one or the other! So, because you are lukewarm—neither hot nor cold—I am about to spit you out of my mouth" (Rev. 3:15-16). The combination of Israel's adulterous fate and the haunting words of Jesus compels James to speak the terrible truth in love.

It is at this climactic point in the epistle where we discover the frightening relevance of James's words in terms of the modern church. There has never been a time in history when more people make professions of faith without that faith making a difference in their lives. "Virtual Christianity" is a sad fact of life. And the source of the problem has not changed one iota from the days when James originally wrote these words. The divided human heart—trying to have it both ways—continues to deliver the chaos of unsatisfied desire.

Church Father Augustine is famous for confessing to God that "our hearts are restless until they rest in Thee." Unfortunately, much of the religious history of humankind is the sad story of humans trying desperately to find rest anywhere *except* in God. We have attempted to have God, but only on our own terms, with the world thrown in.

The truth of the gospel is that God will not accept such terms. He stands in judgment of such wishy-washy religion. The sad state of affairs that seems to reflect the even sadder state of authenticity within much of the North American church is a direct result of our two-souled approach to religion. We have reaped what we have sown. We have chosen friendship with the world—cozy relations with its values and pleasures—and we have discovered the absence of God. Little wonder, then, that in the most churchgoing society in the history of humankind, things seem to be falling apart. Virtual spirituality, earthly wisdom and double-minded religion simply don't work.

James has painted a very dark picture of the human situation. He has touched upon themes of a person's basic spiritual orientation. He has built his case for laying the blame for the unrest, dissensions and dissatisfactions of the community at the point of one's affections. The heart of the matter, in James's view, is a matter of the heart.

James has followed carefully in the tradition of the Old Testament prophets who were the first to hint that God's ultimate solution to Israel's waywardness (double-mindedness) would be to perform a kind of spiritual heart transplant. Consider the words of Jeremiah and Ezekiel in light of James's concern about the divided hearts of his readers:

> I will give them a heart to know me, that I am the LORD. They will be my people, and I will be their God, for they will return to me with all their heart (Jer. 24:7).

> I will give them singleness of heart and action, so that they will always fear me for their own good and the good of their children after them (Jer. 32:39).

> I will give them an undivided heart and put a new spirit in them; I will remove from them their heart of stone and give them a heart of flesh (Ezek. 11:19).

> I will give you a new heart and put a new spirit in you; I will remove from you your heart of stone and give you a heart of flesh. And I will put my Spirit in you and move you to follow my decrees and be careful to keep my laws (Ezek. 36:26-27).

The prophets of Israel saw through all the symptoms that plagued God's people and diagnosed the real problem as a matter of the heart. The people's affections for God were divided. James stands in that same prophetic tradition here as he moves past the various issues that threaten the health and harmony of the churches to the issue that threatens the community's very life with God.

This treatment of the human heart and its tendency to wander and divide its affections is also found clearly in the teachings of Jesus. Jesus constantly taught that the real problem of humankind originated in the heart. To the legalistic Pharisees, who preferred to concentrate on external matters of the law, Jesus flatly stated in Mark's gospel, "For from within, out of men's hearts, come evil thoughts, sexual immorality, theft, murder, adultery, greed, malice, deceit, lewdness, envy, slander, arrogance and folly. All these evils come from inside and make a man 'unclean'" (Mark 7:21-23). The parallel between these evils that come from the heart and James's list of problems with "earthly, unspiritual" wisdom (see James 3:14-16) is much more than coincidental; it reflects the widespread consensus of the New Testament writers that unclean, double-minded hearts are capable of all manner of evil.

Jesus' teachings are also reflected in James's argument that friendship with the world constitutes enmity with God. James's words recall those of Jesus in the Gospel of Matthew: "No one can serve two masters. Either he will hate the one and love the other, or he will be devoted to the one and despise the other. You cannot serve both God and Money" (Matt. 6:24). The impossibility of living with two masters is another way of saying that one cannot divide the affections of the heart without suffering consequences.

Jesus consistently portrayed discipleship as a matter of clearly choosing Him above all others. Nowhere is that more evident than in Luke's gospel, where Jesus said, "If anyone comes to me and does not hate his father and mother, his wife and children, his brothers and sisters—yes, even his own life—he cannot be my disciple" (Luke 14:26). If one's own family cannot come between his or her commitment to Christ, then it goes without saying that open friendship with the world clearly indicates that one has chosen false over true religion.

So James's portrayal of the human heart reflects both the Old Testament teachings as well as those of Jesus himself. And when honesty prevails, we must admit that James has correctly read the tendencies of our hearts. The pull of double-minded faith is strong. The "natural" tendency is to try to have it both ways. James's uncovering of the heart is so precise that it can create despair of ever escaping such adulterous spiritual motives. How can such a pervasive and damaging problem be overcome? It is to the answer of this all-important question that James now turns.

10

THE SOLUTION TO DOUBLE-MINDED DESIRES

James 4:6-10

But he gives us more grace. That is why Scripture says: "God opposes the proud but gives grace to the humble" (Jas. 4:6). The divided, double-minded heart of humankind wreaks havoc on one's spiritual quest and all of his or her relationships. James has amply demonstrated that fact in his letter to this point.

Now in response to such a destructive problem, he offers one solution—**grace.** As widespread and destructive as the problem is, grace is sufficient. As Paul put it so succinctly in his letter to the Romans, "But where sin increased, grace increased all the more" (Rom. 5:20b). The good news of the gospel is that God has committed himself to solving the problem that divides the human heart and creates enmity between himself and His creation. He does not intend for the solution to be halted halfway or to fall short in the lives of extremely difficult cases. Grace is more than adequate. James says this is the God who gives **more grace.**

Remember that James already has assured his readers of God's willingness to provide for their needs (see James 1:5) and that God is perfectly consistent with His redemptive purposes in all that He does for us (see 1:17-18). That understanding of God is what makes James so confident. James sees grace as the unmerited favor of God which no human can earn, but which is freely given as the outcome of God's nature and of His choice of us in redemption. James's words here in his fourth chapter underscore his intention that none of his readers—weighed down by the brokenness of their divided hearts—should despair or even question whether there is a way out of their distress. Grace is adequate! It always has been and always will be.

The only question that is raised is whether or not this abundant grace is receivable. Amazing as it seems, some may not take advantage of God's gracious provision. And they will disqualify themselves on the basis of their own pride. That's what prompts James's quote from Proverbs 3:34: "He mocks proud mockers but gives grace to the humble." Literally, this verse tells us that "God resists arrogant men."

Human pride is the one insurmountable barrier to grace. Over and again in the Gospels, Jesus lamented the inability of the scribes and Pharisees to get past their pride so that they might receive God's grace like the poor and openly sinful had done.[1] God's provision of grace is sufficient to solve the problems that plague these Jewish-Christian believers, but stubborn pride and spiritual pretense will prove to be an effective barrier to God's redeeming purposes.

Throughout Judeo-Christian history, pride has occupied a place at or near the top of every attempt to catalog the insidious sins of humankind. The Devil himself is said to have fallen from heaven as a result of this sin. Pride will undoubtedly do more to populate the darkness of hell than any other human failing. It is one of the so-called "seven deadly sins," although many Christians have considered it *the* sin, putting it in a category by itself. This innate human desire to "stand tall" works to our harm and even, perhaps, to our eternal damnation if we refuse to bow to the Almighty God who offers us His amazing grace.

Pride and its counterpart—humility—are the primary determining factors of our spiritual selves and eternal destinies. C. S. Lewis was surely right when he said that "in the end there are only two kinds of people: those who say to God, 'thy will be done,' and those to whom God says, 'thy will be done.'" In a sense, the troubles that threaten James's readers are not in the area of God's provision. God's grace *is* more than sufficient. But James's concern lies in the willingness of his readers to **humble** themselves (Jas. 4:6) in the presence of this sufficient grace.

Humility, then, is our part in this grand scheme of God to solve the dilemma of the human heart. The Greek word James used here for **humble** refers to those who are "lowly" or "of poor circumstances." Given the ongoing problems between the haves and have-nots in this letter, James may have chosen this word deliberately. It is the same word used in 1:9 to refer to the brother "in humble circumstances."

The ability to respond positively and powerfully to God's grace has nothing to do with one's standing among men, but has everything to do with the way one perceives his or her standing before God. This is the truth Jesus laid as the foundation of the Sermon on the Mount in Matthew: "Blessed are the poor in spirit, for theirs is the kingdom of heaven" (Matt. 5:3). Those who truly know their standing before God are the ones who are the beneficiaries of the Kingdom. Standing in God's presence, knowing your brokenness before Him and your utter inability to mend that brokenness is critical to becoming a candidate for receiving amazing grace.

The key is humility—not some self-deprecating whine designed to fool God and thus procure one's desires—but the realistic self-assessment that proceeds from true wisdom (see James 3:13). John Wesley was fond of defining humility as a "proper assessment of self." It will take just such a proper assessment of self to make a person a viable candidate for receiving the abundant provision of God's grace. James explains how this is done.

In a relatively short epistle filled with commands and exhortations, the next four verses comprise the key imperatives of James's mind. Unless these exhortations are obeyed, all others will ultimately count for naught. What sets these particular imperatives apart is that they are aimed at the problem of the heart: double-mindedness, as James puts it. Therefore, understanding what he asks of his readers in 4:7-10 is critical to understanding the entire letter. Initially, these verses are best looked at in their entirety (we will break them down later): **Submit yourselves, then, to God. Resist the devil, and he will flee from you. Come near to God and he will come near to you. Wash your hands, you sinners, and purify your hearts, you double-minded. Grieve, mourn and wail. Change your laughter to mourning and your joy to gloom. Humble yourselves before the Lord, and he will lift you up.** With these words James effectively takes his "home run swing." Unless his readers are willing to take these exhortations seriously, the rest of James's counsel in this epistle will ultimately prove to be "too little, too late."

Consider James's counsel: **Submit yourselves, then, to God.** These first words of exhortation strike at the essence of discipleship. Surrender, submission, "the death to self" represents the first tangible step to be taken in the pursuit of true religion. James's appeal for submission is based directly on what he has already said relative to the problem of divided affections and God's provision of sufficient grace.

The Greek word for **submit** can be rendered, "be subject to." It is a word that does not allow for the kind of halfhearted commitments that have brought about the problems James addresses in his letter. Luke used this word to describe the submission of Jesus to His parents: "Then he went down to Nazareth with them and was obedient to them" (Luke 2:51a). The idea of obedience connected to this word serves James's purposes well (see James 1:22). It is also the word the disciples of Jesus used to describe their triumphant missionary journey: "The seventy-two returned with joy and said, 'Lord, even the demons submit to us in your name'" (Luke 10:17). No one can doubt what level of submission the disciples were talking about here. It is certainly well beyond the level of commitment or submission that accompanies the typical "conversion" of many churchgoers!

Interestingly, Paul employed this same word, in writing to the Romans, to describe why the sinful mind is hostile to God: "It does not submit to God's law, nor can it do so" (Rom. 8:7b). James earlier spoke of that enmity (Jas. 4:4). Now he offers the antidote to such alienation from God—submitting ourselves to God.

No amount of religious sounding talk or pious professions of faith can substitute for the absolutely necessary act of *surrendering ourselves to God*. That has been a cornerstone of the gospel and the heart of the Wesleyan message from the beginning. Apart from such submission of our hearts to God, the overwhelming sufficiency of His grace is frustrated in terms of its ultimate purpose. As part of the theological tradition that believes in the reality of freedom of the will—the ability to choose and determine our destiny with God—the importance of James's words here should never be lost on us.

That movement of submission to God also implies a movement away from the forces of evil. James adds, **Resist the devil, and he will flee from you** (4:7b). The Greek word for **resist** is formed from the same root word that James cites in verse 6, where he tells us that God "opposes" or "resists" the proud. In the same way that God has nothing to do with those who are filled with pride in His presence, so too, we are to have nothing to do with the person and purposes of the Evil One.

And James tells us that the Devil does not respond well to such treatment. In fact, he flees. **Flee** comes from the same Greek word used in Matthew 26:56 to describe the disciples' scattering after Jesus' arrest in the Garden of Gethsemane. It is the word John used to describe the actions of the hired hand in contrast to those of the Good Shepherd: "The hired hand is not the shepherd who owns the sheep. So when he sees the wolf coming, he abandons the sheep and runs away" (John 10:12). When we resist, the Devil flees—he runs away. This is one reason why James was so insistent in chapter 1 that temptation must not be blamed on God. It can be overcome successfully, and the secret of such success is resistance.

Given the epidemic level of interest in Satan and demonology over the past few years, these words of James are worth pondering. Much of the popular literature on the topic portrays the Devil in anything but biblical terms. The Bible consistently portrays the Devil as a dangerous adversary who ought to be respected as a menacing foe, but not feared by the authentic child of God. However, much of the popular literature presents him as a foe thoroughly in control of this earth, who can pillage and inhabit the life of any and every one in a moment's weakness.

Instead of showing him to be the consummate liar and ultimately defeated foe of our victorious Christ, these writings depict him as a kind of eternal ruler of the realm of darkness that is almost equal to the realm of the kingdom of God. James and the rest of the New Testament writers would find this thinking curious indeed. And beyond their dismay at our failure to read the Bible clearly, we suspect that they would easily see much of the popularity of these views as smokescreens. The rush to blame the Devil for all that ails us is often little more than one last effort by the embattled sinful heart to refrain from surrendering completely to God. The words are crystal clear: **Resist the devil, and he will flee from you** (Jas. 4:7b).

In addition to our submission to God, James urges our intimacy with God: **Come near to God and He will come near to you** (4:8a). Note the symmetry of James's thinking: If we resist the Devil, he flees; if we draw near (submit) to God, He draws near to us. Our movement toward God is greeted by a corresponding movement of God toward us! Amazing as it seems, God desires intimacy with us. He wants to be near to us. But He must be a pursued lover. The word James uses here speaks literally of proximity—physical closeness. The problem of the detached heart and detached affections is that they cause us to be detached from God as well. But the good news is that there is something we can do about that detachment from God. This problem is something over which we have a say, and the solution is to come near.

It's not hard to imagine some of James's Jewish-Christian readers shuddering at the prospects of drawing near to God. Jewish history is filled with instances of people fleeing in terror from the presence of God, like at Mt. Sinai, for example. But James has presented in his epistle the God who is the Father of the Lord Jesus Christ, and that Christian conception makes all the difference in the world. Anyone who looks at the person of Christ must see One who invites us—not repels us or terrifies us. This is the necessary opposite to the friendship of the world which creates distance between God and us. We can be as close to God as we choose—the decision is ours. Distance and alienation are not meant to be part of the normal Christian life, and James tells us that we can choose the opposite. But choose we must.

As the well-known story goes, an old man and his wife of many years drove silently down the highway. He sat against one door behind the steering wheel, and his wife sat against the door on the other side. The old man's wife broke the silence by observing that she longed for those courting days when she used to sit so close beside him that they could carry on a conversation without lifting their voices. Having spoken her piece, she sighed and stared out the window. Finally, her husband—a man of few words—simply asked in response to her wishful thinking, "Who moved?"

Whenever God gets separated from His people, it is invariably a case of the people moving away from Him. In Genesis, we read that when God went to the Garden of Eden to walk with Adam in the cool of day, He discovered the fact of human sinfulness in the searching question, "Where are you?" (Gen. 3:9). Adam's attempt to hide himself from God and from intimacy with God has been the foremost expression of human disobedience. And distance—alienation from God—is the consequence of disobedience. That's why James stresses obedience so in this epistle. To people whose affections for other things have clouded their intimacy with God and who have noted God's absence, James plainly asks the question, "Who moved?" Their desires have created distance and awkwardness where God longs for intimate fellowship and mutual devotion.

But no one can come to God as he or she is. For this God is holy. He is absolutely without sin, and nothing sinful can even be in His presence, to say nothing of being in intimate fellowship with Him—thus James's next words of admonition: **Wash your hands, you sinners, and purify your hearts, you double-minded** (Jas. 4:8b). At first glance, two separate acts are urged here—one external, one internal. This appears to be saying that the conditions for drawing near to God in submission involve the whole person, inside and out. But tempting and true as that thought is, in actuality the exhortation to wash one's hands is almost parallel to the exhortation to purify one's heart.

Throughout the New Testament, the same Greek word James uses here for **wash** ("cleanse" [KJV]) speaks of something far beyond what mere human effort can accomplish. In the Gospels, this is the word that is consistently used to describe Jesus' cleansing of the lepers. Cleansing from leprosy is a strong biblical metaphor for cleansing from the ravages of sin. In the book of Acts, Peter used the same Greek word to describe the work of God in the lives of the Gentiles at the house of Cornelius: "He made no distinction between us and them, for he purified their hearts by faith" (Acts 15:9). Paul used this word to urge the Corinthians on to holiness: "Since we have these promises, dear friends, let us purify ourselves from everything that contaminates body and spirit, perfecting holiness out of reverence for God" (2 Cor. 7:1). Paul told the Ephesians of this kind of cleansing which Christ effects in the church, making her holy: ". . . cleansing her by the washing with water through the word" (Eph. 5:26). Finally, given James's emphasis on the necessity of cleansing in order to draw near to God, this word is used in the book of Hebrews to speak of that very reality: "How much more, then, will the blood of Christ, who through the eternal Spirit offered himself unblemished to God, cleanse our consciences from acts that lead to death, so that we may serve the living God!" (Heb. 9:14).

When all of the above is compared with the phrase **purify your hearts** (Jas. 4:8), it appears that this is an example of the kind of "parallelism" (the repetition of similar ideas using different words) that is common in Jewish poetry. James isn't asking for two separate acts, but one. He lays it out in parallel form to emphasize the point so that no one will miss it. And as if to make sure this is the case, he adds the identifying mark of *those who need to do this:* **you double-minded** (4:8).

The Greek word for **purify** is from the root word for "holy," so there is no doubt as to the intention behind this singleness of heart. The purpose of having clean hands and a purified heart is so we can enjoy the fellowship of God's presence in a way that the two-souled man never can. Having a holy heart that enjoys intimacy with a holy God is the ultimate answer to humankind's greatest problem. This is true religion—the faith that James calls all of his readers, and all of us, to embrace.

The words James uses here bring the letter's climactic general exhortations into sharp focus. There must be a thorough cleaning up of lives on the outside, paralleled by a purifying, single-minded reordering of the devotion of the heart on the inside. The combination of external and internal aspects of life reflects the writings of the prophets—from the Old Testament all the way down to John the Baptist.

In particular, the first chapter of Isaiah could be the model here, for in that chapter the prophet railed against Israel's empty religious practices (see James 1:26-27; 2:14-26). Interestingly, Isaiah used terms very similar to the concerns James raises as evidence of the double-minded heart. For example, Isaiah says,

> When you spread out your hands in prayer, I will hide my eyes from you; even if you offer many prayers, I will not listen. Your hands are full of blood; wash and make yourselves clean. Take your evil deeds out of my sight! Stop doing wrong, learn to do right! Seek justice, encourage the oppressed. Defend the cause of the fatherless, plead the case of the widow [see James 1:27]. "Come now, let us reason together," says the LORD. "Though your sins are like scarlet, they shall be as white as snow; though they are red as crimson, they shall be like wool. If you are willing and obedient, you will eat the best from the land; but if you resist and rebel, you will be devoured by the sword" (Isa. 1:15-20).

Isaiah's message to Israel was that empty religion would incur only judgment. Genuine repentance followed by real obedience and righteousness are what God desires. These are James's concerns as well, showing how pervasive the siren call of "virtual religion" has always been.

Jesus also focused on the inner cleansing of the heart, chiding the Pharisees in Matthew's gospel for neglecting it in favor of "outward" cleanliness: "Woe to you, teachers of the law and Pharisees, you hypocrites! You clean the outside of the cup and dish, but inside they are full of greed and self-indulgence. Blind Pharisee! First clean the inside of the cup and dish, and then the outside also will be clean" (Matt. 23:25-26). Jesus' inability to draw near to the religious leaders of His day was epitomized by their inability to grasp the significance of inward cleansing as opposed to empty religious rituals. Perhaps this is why James has been so hard on those who profess to be religious while remaining aloof in their submission to God. Perhaps he remembers all too well the fate of those stubborn, unyielding religious professionals who rejected their own Messiah.

But while James's words have demonstrated the necessity for action—for the willing involvement of the readers in this process—the truth is that this cleansing is something God alone can do. All the lepers who ever came to Jesus for cleansing had to will themselves to come. But once they were before the Master, it was out of their hands. Jesus alone could make them clean.

Having submitted ourselves to God, what then? James's final words in critical exhortation bring us back to God's sufficient grace and the attitude of heart necessary to receive such grace: **Grieve, mourn and wail. Change your laughter to mourning and your joy to gloom. Humble yourselves before the Lord, and he will lift you up** (Jas. 4:9-10). Essentially, this is the posture of repentance and the attitude of humility. It is the posture that must be adopted if one is to receive the grace God has promised (see 4:6). These are the descriptive words of classic Jewish repentance—the willingness to present oneself before God as utterly helpless and broken. To **grieve** is literally "to be wretched, to realize one's own misery." This is the poverty of spirit Jesus spoke of in Matthew 5:3: "Blessed are the poor in the spirit, for theirs is the kingdom of heaven."

Grief is to be accompanied by mourning and weeping. The words **mourn and wail** (Jas. 4:9) also show up in Luke's version of the Sermon on the Mount. And the context in Luke is interesting, given James's use of **laughter** in 4:9 also: "Looking at his disciples, he said: 'Blessed are you who are poor, for yours is the kingdom of God. Blessed are you who hunger now, for you will be satisfied. Blessed are you who weep now, for you will laugh [see Matthew 5:4]. . . . Woe to you who laugh now, for you will mourn and weep'" (Luke 6:20-21, 25b).

Once again, James employs emphasis, or parallelism, to make his point. The combination of the terms **grieve, mourn and wail** (Jas. 4:9) leave no doubt as to the brokenness of heart that is required to submit fully to God's grace. This threefold call to humble repentance is followed by yet another exhortation to sorrow: **Change your laughter to mourning and your joy to gloom.** James is not some killjoy prophet of gloom and doom—he is an absolute realist. Christians ought always to maintain a repentant spirit. The Christian life is a life of repentance, regardless of what the "health and wealth" preachers say.

Walking in close fellowship with God means walking the way of brokenness before Him. How else could we possibly live in intimate fellowship with a holy God? That is precisely John's promise in his first epistle: "If we claim to have fellowship with him yet walk in the darkness, we lie and do not live by the truth. But if we walk in the light, as he is in the light, we have fellowship with one another, and the blood of Jesus, his Son, purifies us from all sin. If we claim to be without sin, we deceive ourselves and the truth is not in us. If we confess our sins, he is faithful and just and will forgive us our sins and purify us from all unrighteousness" (1 John 1:6-9).

We are confessing this life of humble repentance every time we pray the words of the Lord's Prayer: "Forgive us our debts, as we also have forgiven our debtors" (Matt. 6:12). Unfortunately, the life of repentance and brokenness before God is not a popular approach to religion in modern culture, and therefore we can understand the shallowness of much of North American Christianity. The season of Lent (the six Sundays prior to Easter that elevate the need for repentance) is the most disliked season in the Christian year. We would much rather celebrate than come before God broken by our sinfulness and cry out to Him for the grace that He only bestows upon the humble. But the curse of double-minded religion never can be replaced by the blessedness of true religion until the place of authentic repentance is found.[2] This is the promise with which James ends: **Humble yourselves before the Lord, and he will lift you up** (Jas. 4:10).

Given James's passion for true religion as opposed to double-minded religion, it is clear that these first ten verses of chapter 4 represent the climactic moment of the letter. No amount of good intentions or religious discipline can overcome a problem of the heart. That is the truth that underlies the entire new covenant.[3] Giving ourselves totally, unreservedly, and continually into the hands of this grace-giving God is the bottom line distinctive of historic Wesleyanism as well. Wesley and his followers after him have heard James loudly and clearly in echoing his call for full surrender to God's marvelous grace.

James 4 has demonstrated graphically the dangers of the divided heart within the Christian community. The presence of halfhearted believers in the church is bound to produce the very types of problems that James catalogs in his short letter. That's why the message of the call to authentic holiness of life must never, ever be apologized for or neglected. It is the essence of true religion. Having one's life (hands) cleansed and heart purified (unified, as opposed to divided), and thus enjoying intimacy with God, is at the center of the message Christ brought to earth.

John Wesley and James looked at the believing community, and their hearts beat with a similar passion (see introduction). We can live in intimate fellowship with the holy God of Scripture. Wesley was a self-described "optimist of grace," and surely James was as well, on the basis of what he writes here. There is no place where sin has gone where God's grace cannot reach. There is no human condition beyond God's gracious provision when we come before Him broken and humble. This unified, integrated, wholeness of constant intimacy with God is the absolute goal of true religion. This is where the problems confronting the church must ultimately find their resolution.

ADDITIONAL NOTES ON DESIRE

At two key points in this short epistle, James makes reference to the role of desire in a manner that merits a closer look. First, in chapter 1, verses 13 through 15, on the subject of temptation James wrote, "When tempted, no one should say, 'God is tempting me.' For God cannot be tempted by evil, nor does he tempt anyone; but each one is tempted when, by his own evil desire, he is dragged away and enticed. Then, after desire has conceived, it gives birth to sin; and sin, when it is full-grown, gives birth to death." Second, in chapter 4, James began the chapter by asking the critical question, **What causes fights and quarrels among you?** and then answering it with the judgment, **Don't they come from your desires that battle within you?** (4:1).

In verse 5 of the same chapter, arguing that friendship with the world constitutes enmity with God, James asked, **Or do you think Scripture says without reason that the spirit he caused to live in us envies intensely?** This appeal to the Old Testament in verse 5 is followed by the key verses of the epistle, verses 6 through 8: **But he gives us more grace. That is why Scripture says: "God opposes the proud but gives grace to the humble." Submit yourselves, then, to God. Resist the devil, and he will flee from you. Come near to God and he will come near to you. Wash your hands, you sinners, and purify your hearts, you double-minded.**

The relationship between the way James speaks of desire and the Jewish concept of "yetser" is what makes these verses noteworthy. *Yetser* is a Hebrew word that typically refers to desire, longing or inclination. It comes from a Hebrew root meaning "to form inwardly" or "to fashion." In Jewish thinking, every human person is born with a yetser, and the way that desire or inclination is shaped determines a person's spiritual destiny. Shaping the inclinations—the yetser—toward God and His ways is choosing the way of wisdom and peace. Allowing the inclinations to be formed according to sinful desire is choosing the way of destruction and death.

The single most revealing use of the term in the Old Testament is likely in Genesis, which gives God's reason for the destruction of mankind by the flood: "Every inclination *[yetser]* of the thoughts of his heart was only evil all the time" (Gen. 6:5b). This suggests that while God has created us with a yetser, it is something that is "formed" or "takes its shape" *from us*—for example, by our thoughts or willful acts. To the rabbis, the yetser is God's creation, but we are responsible for the evil it produces in us. Its activity leads to such sins as sexual lust and indiscretion, anger and greed, and results in what the rabbis termed, significantly, "double-heartedness," surely akin to what James terms "double-mindedness."

The important truth for our purposes is that the desire—the yetser—is clearly the responsibility and liability of the individual person. Many of the Old Testament usages of the word affirm this idea of intention and the human role in forming and shaping our inclinations. Psalm 103:14 demonstrates this in the psalmist's note that God "knows how we are formed *[yetser]*, he remembers that we are dust."

This is the reason behind James's insistence, first of all, that we can't blame God for temptation, because it is the product of *our own desires* gone to seed. The desire that leads one to sin is not sin itself. The impulse by itself can be neutral. The critical point lies in the person's choice to yield to desire. Second, and most importantly, this is what makes the author's contention in James 4—that God "gives greater grace"—so significant. The problem of the inclination has been of our own doing, yet God provides grace to overcome it.

In several instances, the idea of yetser is shown to be at home in the Wisdom writings of the Jewish tradition.[4] (This is especially true of the Wisdom book known as Sirach.[5] Sirach and the Epistle of James have many interesting similarities.) Standing squarely in that Jewish Wisdom tradition himself, James employs this concept to stress the critical truth that God is not the cause of sin, but that desire willfully inclined to evil in humans is.

Further, as James 4:6-8 clearly shows, a person has a choice; he or she can draw near to God and so on. The rabbis taught that the main weapon against the yetser was the Torah, the Law of God.[6] The Wisdom writings emphasize that one can choose to obey the commandments rather than the evil inclination. This is what makes obedience to the Law in James's epistle so significant. He is not arguing from a legalistic conception, but from a Wisdom conception that makes choosing to obey God the only way to defeat the evil inclination.

James spoke of testings in 1:2-4 and 1:12-14. These testings can have one of two results. It can be resisted, in which case the person becomes mature and complete, or it can be yielded to, which results in sin and death. It is the classic contrast of blessing and curse.[7] Even James's concern with the tongue could be related to the desire; the first-century

Jewish philosopher, Philo, spoke of desire (yetser) making its way to the tongue and causing an "infinity of troubles" (see James 3:5-8).[8]

James's exhortations regarding the necessity of being "single-tongued" (see 3:10-11) fit with this relationship of desire to the idea of double-mindedness. For James, the person who truly attains wisdom is the one who remains faithful in times of testing, times when the yetser or desire is liable to take one into sin. James exhorted his readers that rather than being ruled by desire, they instead could be ruled by the implanted Word (see 1:21). Many of the virtues and vices that James emphasizes in his letter are clearly connected to the idea of the inclination or yetser. James's picture of the ideal person, the person who is wise, is the one who observes the Law, who has overcome the yetser. The opposite of that person is the one who is a fool, one who transgresses the Law—the double-minded person who lives under the power of his or her evil inclinations.

What makes all of the above more than an interesting side trip into Jewish theology is the implications it holds for our Wesleyan distinctives. Our tradition has long contended that the real battle for the soul of humankind is not the battle with outward evils, but the battle over the desires of the heart. We have exhorted our people to go beyond *forgiveness* from the penalty of sin to a place in God's grace where there is deliverance from the *power* of sin. The double-minded approach to religion is doomed because it is constantly subjected to the power of the evil desires or inclinations of a heart that is impure. That's why James stresses the abundance of God's grace to do for us what we cannot do for ourselves and encourages us to submit to God. It is then—and only then—that the Devil can, in fact, be resisted.

Submission involves the washing (cleansing) of our hands and the purifying of our double-minded hearts. This state, near to God, is the place where we can truly be doers of the Word. All the spiritual guides of history have stressed consistently that obedience is the basic ingredient to real discipleship—what James might term "true religion." By submitting ourselves completely to God, we allow the inclinations of our hearts to be shaped by the "wisdom that comes from above" and not by the evil desires of the sinful nature.

ENDNOTES

[1]The Gospels include the New Testament books of Matthew, Mark, Luke, and John.

[2]Blessings and curses refer to the response of God to His people in accordance with their obedience to Him (blessings) or their disobedience (curses). In the Old Testament, God's power was invoked through power-laden words (blessings and curses) often spoken in prayer form. Through these blessings or curses, God's people would call upon Him to provide or care for them by affecting them in a positive way or those around them in a positive or negative way. In Judaism (the belief and cultural system of the Jewish people), some blessings were reserved for the priests, but others were a regular part of the synagogue services. Curses were much less prominent and were forbidden. In the New Testament, the ultimate blessing came from God to mankind in Jesus Christ, and blessings accompanied righteousness. Curses accompanied sin.

[3]A covenant is a solemn promise made binding by a pledge or vow, which may be either a verbal formula or a symbolic action. A covenant often referred to a legal obligation in ancient times. In Old Testament terms, the word was often used in describing the relationship between God and His chosen people, in which their sacrifices of blood afforded them His atonement for sin, and in which their fulfillment of a promise to live in obedience to God was rewarded by His blessings. In New Testament terms, this relationship (the new covenant) was now made possible on a personal basis through Jesus Christ and His sacrifice of His own blood.

[4]The Wisdom Literature includes the books of Job, Proverbs, Ecclesiastes, and Song of Songs (Song of Solomon). Also known as the Books of Poetry. These writings are collections of statements of wisdom, often dealing with the great issues of life, such as the problem of suffering, practical ethics and morality, and the meaning of life and love.

[5]The book of Sirach is also called Ecclesiasticus, or the Wisdom of Jesus the Son of Sirach, and was written by Ben Sirach. Sirach is a book in the Apocrypha. The Apocrypha is the fourteen or fifteen books (or parts of books) that were considered by some to have been written during the time between the Old and New Testaments. In the sixteenth century, the Roman Catholic Church made these books part of their Scriptures, but Protestants have never recognized the Apocrypha in any official way. During the development of the modern Protestant Bible, it was determined that these books did not fit the criteria to be included in the Canon. For instance, their apostolic authorship was questioned, as well as their authenticity, accuracy of information recorded, and agreement with the rest of the Scriptures. These books are still found in the Roman Catholic Bible and a few other versions.

[6]Torah is another name for the Pentateuch (the first five books of the Old Testament: Genesis, Exodus, Leviticus, Numbers, and Deuteronomy). The Hebrew word which *Torah* comes from is translated *law* and refers to divine instruction and guidance. The Torah (or Law) was the instructions and directions given to Israel by God.

[7]See endnote 2.

[8]Marcus, Joel, "The Evil Inclination in the Epistle of James," *The Catholic Biblical Quarterly,* vol. 44 (1982), p. 614.

Part Five

MORE BARRIERS TO TRUE RELIGION

James 4:11–5:12

J ames is a realist. He knows that even when people have fully submitted themselves to God's grace, the Christian life is filled with challenges and difficulties. But the mere existence of problems doesn't necessarily imply that people are spiritually deficient. A certain amount of struggle and conflict within the Christian community is normal—that's the way real families are. The problem comes when these issues continue unresolved. Therefore, having put his finger on the greatest problem and suggested God's abundant provision for it, James continues to deal with the challenges of day-to-day life within the church.

THE BARRIER
OF
JUDGING OTHERS

James 4:11-12

Having dealt with the absolute imperative of purifying the double-minded heart, James turns once again to discuss a variety of problems that continue to threaten the fellowship of the communities. Here he has strong words for the problem of judging others: **Brothers, do not slander one another. Anyone who speaks against his brother or judges him speaks against the law and judges it** (Jas. 4:11a). When there is an atmosphere of jealous striving and divided loyalties, a spirit of judgment is likely to be present as well. The New International Version's use of the word **slander** in its translation of the original Greek term is well-chosen because the word literally refers to "speaking against" someone.

Peter used this term twice in his first epistle, showing the true spirit of the word. He counseled his readers to "live such good lives among the pagans that, though they accuse you of doing wrong, they may see your good deeds and glorify God on the day he visits us" (1 Pet. 2:12). Then, he urged his readers to keep "a clear conscience, so that those who speak maliciously against your good behavior in Christ may be ashamed of their slander" (1 Pet. 3:16). These examples demonstrate that it is not idle chatter James is confronting, but talk designed to harm and offend.

The power of words to damage and maim people already has been documented in James 3. Here in chapter 4 James links his argument against such talk directly to the Law.[1] Maliciously judging one's brother or sister is flaunting one's disregard for the Law, a serious charge indeed for Jewish believers. In fact, James employs this same word in saying that anyone who slanders **his brother** (Jas. 4:11) likewise slanders the Law. Speaking maliciously against our brothers and sisters in Christ is speaking maliciously—with intent to do harm—**against the law** of God. James earlier employed this same kind of argument when he declared that breaking one command was tantamount to breaking the entire Law (see 2:10).

The law was the vehicle that taught the Jews how to be close to God—how to live according to His ways. The Law was an institution revered by the Jews. James's linkage of slandering a brother with disrespecting and placing oneself against the Law was certain to gain the attention of his readers.

But there is another possible angle to James's line of reasoning here that ties this problem with slander to the preceding paragraph. Given James's emphasis on drawing "near to God" in 4:8, this sanction against slander is yet another imperative aimed at helping James's readers to live in close kinship with God. This is especially significant in light of Leviticus 19:16, which states, "Do not go about spreading slander among your people. Do not do anything that endangers your neighbor's life. I am the LORD." This is taken from the so-called "holiness code" which teaches the people how to keep themselves pure so that they can stay in close contact with their holy God (see additional notes at the end of chapter 4 of the commentary).

The Psalms give another example of tying the sanction against slander with holy living in a way that seems more than coincidental, given James's concerns in the preceding paragraph. David wrote, "LORD, who may dwell in your sanctuary? Who may live on your holy hill? [Who may live in nearness to you?] He whose walk is blameless and who does what is righteous, who speaks the truth from his heart and has no slander on his tongue, who does his neighbor no wrong and casts no slur on his fellowman" (Ps. 15:1-3).

Clearly, to speak against one's brother is to speak against the Law, for the Law pointedly prohibits such behavior. Such slanderous talk would be evidence of the kind of hearing the Word without obeying it that James has soundly condemned (see James 1:22-25). Slandering one's brother is looking into the mirror and promptly forgetting what you have just seen.

Jesus had particularly hard words for those who slandered others. In the Sermon on the Mount in Matthew, Jesus warned His disciples, "You have heard that it was said to the people long ago, 'Do not murder, and anyone who murders will be subject to judgment.' But I tell you that anyone who is angry with his brother will be subject to judgment. Again, anyone who says to his brother, 'Raca,' is answerable to the Sanhedrin. But anyone who says, 'You fool!' will be in danger of the fire of hell" (Matt. 5:21-22).

Jesus also tied the practice of slander to the problem of an unclean heart. While arguing with the Pharisees over the failure of His disciples to wash their hands according to the traditions of the elders, Jesus made a clear connection in the Gospel of Mark between slander (along with several other issues James also deals with!) and the impurity of the human heart: "What comes out of a man is what makes him 'unclean.' For from within, out of men's hearts, come evil thoughts, sexual immorality, theft, murder, adultery, greed, malice, deceit, lewdness, envy, slander, arrogance and folly. All these evils come from inside and make a man 'unclean'" (Mark 7:20-23). It seems more than coincidental that James follows His call to holiness and cleansing with a treatment of slander—a vivid illustration of uncleanness.

Throughout this letter James has been particularly conscious of the power of words. Here he warns his readers not only of the power of words by themselves, but of their power to place the speaker in the place of judgment: **When you judge the law, you are not keeping it, but sitting in judgment on it. There is only one Lawgiver and Judge, the one who is able to save and destroy. But you—who are you to judge your neighbor?** (Jas. 4:11b-12). There is a major problem with speaking **judgment** on others. Casting oneself into the role of **judge** is attempting to play God. God alone is **Judge**—of this, Scripture is crystal clear (see John 8:50; Acts 17:31; Romans 2:16; 2 Timothy 4:1; Hebrews 10:30).

Sitting in judgment is trying to do what only God is fully capable of doing. Judging **the law** is judging the **Lawgiver** (Jas. 4:11-12). God alone is the one who is able to save and destroy. How could we possibly consider ourselves capable or worthy of such authority? There is a note of disbelief in James's question in 4:12. His words are echoed by Paul in Romans:

> Who are you to judge someone else's servant? To his own master he stands or falls. And he will stand, for the Lord is able to make him stand. . . . You, then, why do you judge your brother? Or why do you look down on your brother? For we will all stand before God's judgment seat. It is written: "As surely as I live," says the Lord, "every knee will bow before me; every tongue will confess to God." So then, each of us will give an account of himself to God. Therefore let us stop passing judgment on one another. Instead, make up your mind not to put any stumbling block or obstacle in your brother's way" (Rom. 14:4, 10-13).

Don't forget James's clear connection of the use of the tongue with true religion (see James 1:26). Given that relationship, this emphasis upon prohibiting slander and judgment against one's **neighbor** (4:12) is most fitting in the aftermath of the climactic emphasis of 4:1-10. Remember also James's practical approach to true religion. It works! It affects the way we live and the way we treat one another. There is no such thing as holiness that shreds other people's lives in judgmental gossip. There is no such thing as holiness that usurps the prerogatives of judgment that are reserved for God alone. In a culture that is increasingly careless—even slanderous—with its words, James's warning needs to be taken very seriously.

This paragraph is a good example of the pastoral concern that James demonstrates throughout his epistle. Anyone in the service of the church understands full well the destructiveness of careless words. The phenomenon of Christians criticizing and judging one another has been a scandal to the witness of the gospel. This deplorable practice of using words to hurt others has been likened by some to the practice of an army that shoots its wounded rather than try to heal them. James understands that no amount of religious talk or even religious deeds will overcome the damage of a judgmental spirit. Every pastor since James has understood this as well. A judgmental, critical spirit is a daunting barrier to authentic Christianity. Such a spirit has no place in true religion.

ENDNOTE

[1]Law refers to either the Levitical Code (all God's rules and regulations), the Ten Commandments, or the Pentateuch (the first five books of the Old Testament: Genesis, Exodus, Leviticus, Numbers, and Deuteronomy). Often capitalized when it means the Pentateuch or the Ten Commandments.

12

THE BARRIER
OF
PRESUMPTION

James 4:13-17

N ow listen, you who say, "Today or tomorrow we will go to this or that city, spend a year there, carry on business and make money." Why, you do not even know what will happen tomorrow (Jas. 4:13-14a). If the problem in the preceding paragraph centered around the sin of trying to play God, the problem here is the problem of ignoring God. This is the sin of presumption. James assumes an indignant tone that says in effect, "Now, listen well. I don't want to have to say this twice!"

The presumptuous air of the scheming businessman is brought out here in the Greek by the presence of four successive verbs in the future tense—literally, "We *will go* into this city, and we *will spend* a year there, and we *will trade,* and we *will make* a profit." Such pretense, in light of the God James has presented in the letter, evokes James's skeptical response. These people who are already counting their profit **do not even know what will happen tomorrow** or how their lives will be affected.

The disparity between the carefully laid plans of men, as opposed to the power of God, brings to mind the opening verses of Psalm 2, where the psalmist described the utter folly of the nations making their plans as if God is no factor: "Why do the nations conspire and the peoples plot in vain? The kings of the earth take their stand and the rulers gather together against the LORD and against his Anointed One. 'Let us break their chains,' they say, 'and throw off their fetters.' The One enthroned in heaven laughs; the LORD scoffs at them" (Ps. 2:1-4). This is the same

God whom James has presented to his readers, thus his indignant reaction to their presumption. Just as the nations conspire and plot in vain, thinking that they have any real say in the matters of history, James reminds his readers that their destinies, realized or not, are totally in God's hands.

In truth, this is what we today might term the sin of *secularity,* of moving God to the margins of our lives where He is not really a factor in our plans anymore. We pay Him lip service, we do our weekly "nod to God" in worship, but out there in the "real world" we really don't need Him. Quite frankly, many of us would prefer that He just stay out of our way. This is a very serious side effect of double-minded religion. God is effectively ignored and relegated to the sidelines of life. We call on Him in times of trouble, grief, and special need, but otherwise we are doing quite nicely, thank you.

The problem with this virtual religion is exactly as James puts it—it's based on a falsehood. Such playing at religion is based on the notion that humans have power over their lives and futures which, in fact, they do not have. We are deluded by our own egos. In spite of all our accomplishments, we have no real control over the morrows of our lives.

The way of faith—real faith—is to put our tomorrows into God's hands. Jesus said in His Sermon on the Mount in Matthew,

> Therefore I tell you, do not worry about your life, what you will eat or drink; or about your body, what you will wear. Is not life more important than food, and the body more important than clothes? So do not worry, saying, "What shall we eat?" or "What shall we drink?" or "What shall we wear?" For the pagans run after all these things, and your heavenly Father knows that you need them. But seek first his kingdom and his righteousness, and all these things will be given to you as well. Therefore do not worry about tomorrow, for tomorrow will worry about itself. Each day has enough trouble of its own (Matt. 6:25, 31-34).

The only possible inference one can draw from Jesus' words when applied to James's aspiring business tycoons is that they are not seeking first the Kingdom.

The problem with this secular approach to life is that it utterly fails to account for the frailty of human life. **What is your life? You are a mist that appears for a little while and then vanishes** (Jas. 4:14b). Instead of being made of the kind of stuff that can rightly make grand plans for the future, James declares that human life is mere **mist**—literally, "vapor." The Greek word used here is the word *atmis,* from which we get our word *atmosphere.* We aren't tangible matter—we are air! The only other usage of this Greek word in the New Testament is in Acts 2:19: "I will show wonders in the heaven above and signs on the earth below, blood and fire and billows of *smoke"* (my emphasis).

The Old Testament counterpart to James's description of the weightiness of human life are the words of Ecclesiastes 1:2: "'Meaningless! Meaningless!' says the Teacher. 'Utterly meaningless! Everything is meaningless.'" Here again, we see James's Wisdom roots showing.[1] Human life is not under human control as we like to claim. Rather it is vanity—mere air—subject to all the forces around it. Life is marked by boundaries; it is not open-ended. We appear for a little while, then disappear. This is the reality of the human condition, rather than the presumptuous bluster that talks as if we have ultimate say over the course of our lives. James's businessmen are reminiscent of the "rich fool" that Jesus spoke about in the Gospel of Luke. There, a man successful in the eyes of the world lost his soul because he failed to take account of the temporary nature of human life (see Luke 12:16-21).

The transitory nature of human life is what makes our need of this God, "who does not change like shifting shadows" (Jas. 1:17), so great and so desperate. Some observers of human behavior have claimed that the denial of death is the single greatest motivating force at work within the human species. A look around our world substantiates the truth of such a claim. The media hammers away at us daily with a barrage of secular messages that assume that life has nothing whatsoever to do with God. We are sold millions of dollars worth of stuff every year aimed at helping us deny the essential mortality of our lives. Whether it's makeup or creams to hide the wrinkles, exercise equipment to slow down gravity, or some medical miracle that manages to keep death at bay just a bit longer, humans don't want to face the reality of James's words here. But the course of real wisdom is humbly living life in terms of God's will and thus embodies true religion. Just as the sin of presumption is a sign of double-minded religion, so too, the complete surrender of one's tomorrows into the trustworthy hands of God is an important sign of authentic faith.

This truth leads James to counsel another way of approaching life: **Instead, you ought to say, "If it is the Lord's will, we will live and do this or that"** (4:15). In complete contrast to secularism, which places man at the center of life, James counsels a return to authentic "theism," where God inhabits His proper place in the center of our lives. Former Houghton College president Stephen Paine was an entering freshman at Wheaton College when he was asked to fill out a questionnaire. One of the questions asked, "What is the goal of your life?" Paine wrote in the space provided these simple words: "To do the will of God." The phrase "God willing" became the credo of Paine's life, which served him well through decades of leadership as Houghton College president. His life— along with the lives of countless other saints who have lived their lives "God willing"—contrasts sharply with the secularized presumption that characterizes the lives of so many of today's "movers and shakers."

James fully intends to contrast here two distinct approaches to life. One moves God to the margins; the other enthrones God at the center and builds life around Him. One operates solely from the vantage point of human history and time, while the other operates from the vantage point of eternity. From James's viewpoint of eternity, mortal human life looks pretty insignificant compared with what awaits the one who does God's will.

As it is, you boast and brag. All such boasting is evil. Anyone, then, who knows the good he ought to do and doesn't do it, sins (Jas. 4:16). The alternative to the "God willing" approach to life is not only folly, it **is evil.** This failure to enthrone God at the center of life constitutes boasting and bragging. The Greek word James used here for "boasting" is the same word John used in his first epistle when he talked about the similar topic of getting distracted from God: "Do not love the world or anything in the world. If anyone loves the world, the love of the Father is not in him. For everything in the world—the cravings of sinful man, the lust of his eyes and the boasting of what he has and does—comes not from the Father but from the world. The world and its desires pass away, but the man who does the will of God lives forever" (1 John 2:15-17).

This boastful approach to life is sin, precisely because James's readers know better! They know that their lives are not going to last forever. They know that eternity awaits them. They know full well— as James has reminded them—that friendship with the world is enmity with God. They know that to disregard God and His ways is anything but true religion.

To persist in our secularistic folly and attempt to live as if God does not matter is evil. It is the evil of presumption that has settled down over the religious landscape of much of North America like a thick, foreboding fog. We are paying a terribly high price to live in the fantasy worlds of our own pretenses. People are dying before their tomorrows can be realized. False "play religion" may seem to be a bargain to our secularized world, but it ends up being eternally costly.

In making this claim of sin resulting from our not doing what we know full well **the good [we] ought to do** (Jas. 4:16), James gives us one of the classic biblical definitions of sin. Knowing the good we ought to do and yet resisting doing it is the height of presumption. And James's words about doing the good we know to do surely applies to all the admonitions of his fourth chapter. If we persist in our double-minded faith and delude ourselves about the nature of life *while knowing better,* we are without excuse.

ENDNOTE

¹The Wisdom Literature includes the books of Job, Proverbs, Ecclesiastes, and Song of Songs (Song of Solomon). Also known as the Books of Poetry. These writings are collections of statements of wisdom, often dealing with the great issues of life, such as the problem of suffering, practical ethics and morality, and the meaning of life and love.

13

THE BARRIER OF MATERIALISM

James 5:1-6

C hapter divisions, and verses for that matter, are not inspired—only the texts themselves. Thus, even though a new chapter of James's writing begins here, his emphasis on "barriers to true religion" continues. In the first part of James 5, the author continues to address specific barriers that were especially troublesome to the Jewish-Christian communities. These are issues he has dealt with before, but here he deals with them in greater depth. The first barrier James revisits reveals his strong sense of identification with the poor.

In addressing himself to the problems that accompany wealth and materialism, James returns to the social themes that caused him such difficulty with certain segments of the people of his day. These opening six verses contain a condemnation of riches, reminiscent of the words of the Old Testament prophets (especially 5:1-3), followed by a very pointed and sobering accusation as to the consequences of such folly in light of the judgment of God.

1. THE FOOLISHNESS OF MATERIALISM 5:1-3

Now listen, you rich people, weep and wail because of the misery that is coming upon you (Jas. 5:1). This new emphasis begins with the same words of 4:13. There James spoke to the presumptuous; here he speaks to the wealthy. The rich are admonished to "weep and cry aloud over the hardships coming upon" them. The language is similar to the repentant posture exhorted in 4:9, indicating that it is repentance James seeks here as well.

The Greek word for **wail** is used only here in the New Testament (Jas. 5:1) and literally means to "howl out loud" or to "shriek." Simple regret is not what is called for, but a passionate, heartfelt remorse. This is called for in light of the **misery**—the "wretchedness" or "calamity"—of what is coming unless such repentance is forthcoming. James is predicting disaster to befall the rich unless they "produce fruit in keeping with repentance," to use John the Baptist's words from Matthew 3:8.

The reason for such impending doom is stated next: **Your wealth has rotted, and moths have eaten your clothes. Your gold and silver are corroded. Their corrosion will testify against you and eat your flesh like fire. You have hoarded wealth in the last days** (Jas. 5:2-3). Hoarding their **wealth** has placed the rich in immediate danger. Their **wealth has rotted** (the Greek means, literally, "putrefied"—again, a word used only in James's epistle). The particular form of the Greek word used here is what is known as the perfect tense—it signifies that something has happened which has ongoing effects. In other words, the rich have put their trust in something that has become putrid and that has long-range implications for them far beyond the mere loss of their possessions. This reality of long-term significance is why such radical repentance is called for by James in verse 1.

Not only has their wealth rotted, but their **clothes** have become moth-eaten (the Greek term to describe this is another used only here in the New Testament), and their **gold and silver**—those most prized "securities"—have **corroded** (the Greek means, literally, "cankered"—a word used only here in the New Testament). James's employment of four rare terms to describe the pathetic state of affairs confronting the rich indicates his determination to make these people understand the seriousness of their predicament. Their readiness to put their trust in what has been corrupted and destroyed now becomes the chief piece of evidence against them in the moment of judgment.

The **corrosion** of their treasures—literally, "the poison of them"—**will testify against** them. In the coming day of judgment, not only will accumulated riches not be of any advantage, but they also will be used as a "witness" against their owners. James says this legacy of greed will lead to a corrupting judgment of their physical bodies in a manner similar to the way their possessions were corrupted.

This stark judgment is rendered because they have **hoarded** or "treasured" **wealth in the last days.** The Greek word employed here is the same word Jesus used in the Gospel of Luke to condemn the "rich fool" who paid more attention to his overflow harvests than to the mortality of his soul: "But God said to him, 'You fool! This very night your life will be demanded from you. Then who will get what you have prepared for yourself?' This is how it will be with anyone who stores up things for himself but is not rich toward God" (Luke 12:20-21).

The similarities between the judgments rendered in both the story by Luke and this verse from James are readily apparent. In each case, temporal concerns were allowed to take precedence over eternal matters. Earlier in James's epistle (see 1:9-11), the author specifically warned the rich not to glory in that which was temporary at best. Here, James tells them what failure to heed those words could cost.

The idea surrounding the last days points to James's overall preoccupation with the theme of judgment in this letter. Like most early Christians, James believed in the almost immediate return of Jesus to this earth. These early Christians knew that when Christ returned, He would come as Judge to bring justice and to punish those who had neglected to care for "the least of these" (see Matthew 25:31-46).

Not until the latter third of the first century did the Christian church begin to consider that the return of Jesus might be delayed for some time. James's passion and alarm should be read in light of this heartfelt conviction. Remember, too, that James's understanding of Jesus' lordship is almost totally vested in the picture of Christ's triumphant return to earth. This is surely good news for the faithful, but the worst of all possible scenarios for those who have lived in disobedience.

Putting our trust in riches rather than in God is a sure sign that true religion is still far from us. The words of James here recall clearly the teachings of Jesus in His Sermon on the Mount in Matthew regarding the focus of our lives: "Do not store up for yourselves treasures on earth, where moth and rust destroy, and where thieves break in and steal. But store up for yourselves treasures in heaven, where moth and rust do not destroy, and where thieves do not break in and steal. For where your treasure is, there your heart will be also" (Matt. 6:19-21). This is echoed by Paul, who wrote to Timothy, "Command those who are rich in this present world not to be arrogant nor to put their hope in wealth, which is so uncertain, but to put their hope in God, who richly provides us with everything for our enjoyment" (1 Tim. 6:17). And again by the unknown author of Hebrews: "Keep your lives free from the love of money and be content with what you have, because God has said, 'Never will I leave you; never will I forsake you'" (Heb. 13:5).

James's Wisdom roots are also evidenced here, for teachings about the dangers of wealth pervaded the Wisdom Literature of the Jews.[1] For example, Proverbs says, "Do not wear yourself out to get rich; have the wisdom to show restraint" (Prov. 23:4).

Although many of us may hardly qualify as rich, these words ought to sober us and lead us to reflect upon the values of our lives. Jesus was right: Where our treasure is, our hearts are also! Our attitude toward money is an almost foolproof measuring stick of our commitment to true religion. The culture around us preaches accumulation and storing up for the "rainy day." Surely financial prudence is not to be disparaged. The problem comes with the subtle temptation to make our accumulated treasures the desire of our hearts. That's double-minded religion, and that's what James says is so dangerous that we ought to "howl and scream" in remorse over it lest we face the judgment of God.

It is a matter of record that the more money people have, the less they give to charity. In fact, all studies indicate that it is the relatively poor who give the largest percentage of their wealth to the church and to other charitable causes. Why is that the case? Because once we begin to give our hearts to our hoarded wealth, it takes control of us until we can focus on nothing else besides its preservation and multiplication. But James reminds us vividly that no matter how careful we are, all such "stuff" is doomed to the corruption destined for all material things.

The early church had a saying that "there are no pockets on a shroud." The modern-day version of that is this observation: "You will never see a hearse pulling a U-Haul!" In other words, you really can't take it with you. Given the eternal perspective of true religion, we ought to focus on the things that truly matter, rather than risk the calamity of judgment that will confront all who fall prey to the love of money.

But there is another aspect to this problem that makes this issue so emotional to James. The charge of "hoarding" wealth was especially galling to him, given the grinding poverty under which so many of the first Christians lived (see introduction). The fact that some people were denied the basic necessities of life while others lived in luxury is more than this elder saint could take. He now turns his attention to the issue of justice.

2. THE INJUSTICE OF MATERIALISM 5:4-6

Look! The wages you failed to pay the workmen who mowed your fields are crying out against you. The cries of the harvesters have reached the ears of the Lord Almighty (Jas. 5:4). It's bad enough that the rich have hoarded their pitiful treasures only to see them corrode and spoil. But the calamity that awaits them in judgment is mostly the result of the injustice that has accompanied their shameless accumulation. The truest sense of the Greek that James uses here in saying they **failed to pay the workmen** literally refers to wages "kept back by fraud." It is the term Paul used in writing to the Corinthians: "Why not rather be wronged? Why not rather be cheated? Instead, you yourselves cheat and do wrong, and you do this to your brothers" (1 Cor. 6:7b-8). James's use of this term is what makes this an issue of justice.

To defraud people of their wages was condemned uniformly throughout the Old Testament. The "holiness code" of Leviticus 19, which James leans heavily upon (see additional notes at the end of chapter 4 of the commentary), contains this specific command: "Do not defraud your neighbor or rob him. Do not hold back the wages of a hired man overnight" (Lev. 19:13). This is repeated in Deuteronomy: "Pay him his wages each day before sunset, because he is poor and is counting on it. Otherwise he may cry to the LORD against you, and you will be guilty of sin" (Deut. 24:15).

The additional word here regarding the possibility of the poor "crying" to the Lord seems to be the basis for James's warning here to the rich. Specifically, the cries of the defrauded workers reach **the ears of the LORD Almighty** (Jas. 5:4), or *Yahweh Sabaoth* in Hebrew. This name for God is typically translated "LORD of Hosts" and refers to the might of God, especially in a military sense. Although this name for God is used some 264 times in the Bible, it is found only here and in Romans 9:29 in the New Testament. James employs it as an additional reference to the stern judgment sure to afflict those who treat the poor with such contempt.

The history of the God of the Bible is one of being especially compassionate toward the poor. Israel's history as a people is firmly based in the story of God's deliverance of the oppressed slaves of Egypt. In the book of Exodus we read, "The LORD said, 'I have indeed seen the misery of my people in Egypt. I have heard them crying out because of their slave drivers, and I am concerned about their suffering'" (Exod. 3:7). James appeals to this picture of Israel's God in order to make himself absolutely clear to the wealthy materialists who exploit the poor to pay for their own extravagant lifestyles. It is here that James assumes an "Amos-like" posture.

Amos was the Old Testament prophet most associated with the cause of justice. Like James, Amos refused to play along with the rich and powerful of his own day. Rather than simply preach judgment against the neighbors of Israel and make himself popular and secure among the "power brokers" of the times, Amos turned his sights squarely upon the sins of the home folk. For example, when the prophet cried out, "Woe to you who are complacent in Zion, and to you who feel secure on Mount Samaria, you notable men of the foremost nation, to whom the people of Israel come!" (Amos 6:1), his message of coming judgment resulting from injustice parallels the words of James.

Already in James 2 the author indicated the kinds of problems that result when the wealthy are favored. Here in chapter 5 he underscores the extreme danger of the materially minded in terms of judgment.

The prophetic-like indictment of the hoarders continues: **You have lived on earth in luxury and self-indulgence. You have fattened yourselves in the day of slaughter. You have condemned and murdered innocent men, who were not opposing you** (Jas. 5:5-6). These people have lived **in luxury** on the earth (the Greek means, literally, "lived daintily"—a term peculiar to James). Whereas the lot of most people has been hard and even cruel, life has been easy for these living in luxury, at great cost to the poor. They have lived in **self-indulgence**—literally, they have "lived riotously." Remember that it was the prodigal son in Jesus' parable who spent his inheritance in "riotous living" (see Luke 15:13 KJV). This refers to the kind of life that takes no thought of the consequences, but simply lives for the moment. James is of the opinion that such an approach to life is a sure ticket to a most severe kind of judgment.

The reference to **the day of slaughter** (Jas. 5:5) appears to come from the words of Jeremiah. The context of these words in the book bearing the prophet's name are a chilling testimony to just how serious James is about this topic. Appealing directly to God's justice, the prophet Jeremiah said, "You are always righteous, O LORD, when I bring a case before you. Yet I would speak with you about your justice: Why does the way of the wicked prosper? Why do all the faithless live at ease? You have planted them, and they have taken root; they grow and bear fruit. You are always on their lips but far from their hearts. Yet you know me, O LORD; you see me and test my thoughts about you. Drag them off like sheep to be butchered! Set them apart for the day of slaughter!" (Jer. 12:1-3). These terrible words of judgment from the Old Testament prophet appear to be somewhere in James's mind as he writes here.

What a sobering thought to consider that our greed and selfishness here on earth can be little more than "fattening" for **the day of slaughter.** How different should our behavior and attitudes be, knowing that choices and decisions in this life will be accounted for in the presence of God the ultimate Judge? These are terribly heavy words that

James speaks here. In fact, these are the kinds of judgments and charges that likely turned the powerful wealthy against James and brought about his martyrdom (see introduction).

The indictment is widened with this charge: **You have condemned and murdered innocent men, who were not opposing you** (Jas. 5:6). Assessing what is specifically meant here is difficult. The Greek word for **condemned** refers to "pronouncing judgment" which has been roundly condemned in the preceding chapter of the epistle (see 4:11-12). Not only is this done in violation of the Law, but it is aimed toward one who is regarded as **innocent**—literally, "righteous."[2] James has already indicated that a life of "righteousness" is exactly what God desires (see 1:20), but now righteousness has been destroyed. Little wonder that God's sense of justice has been sorely violated.

Further, this "righteous" man who has been condemned and murdered was **not opposing** or "resisting" the rich. The Greek word used here is the same word James used in chapter 4 to speak of God's "resisting" the proud and our "resisting" the Devil. Not only does this underscore the innocence of the victim, but the idea of "nonresistance" will serve James's purposes in the next paragraph (see 5:7-11).

It is difficult to know how literally to take this charge. Certainly history is filled with instance after instance of innocent people being condemned and even killed by the flagrant disregard of their rights by the rich and powerful. Whether directly or indirectly, the lives of many innocent people have been adversely affected and even ended by the failure of others to practice basic justice. James wants his readers to know that the God of Scripture is not deaf to the cries of the innocent and the abused. There is a reckoning day coming in which those who have chosen to put all of their hopes in this present world will indeed "weep and wail." The Bible shows that God has a finely tuned sense of hearing for the cries of the oppressed and enslaved.

These are difficult words for many contemporary Western Christians to wrestle with. Most of us may consider ourselves "middle class" or even among the poor, but the fact remains that we enjoy a standard of living far exceeding that of most of the world. How can we justify the luxury and the waste of resources in light of the cries of the hungry and oppressed of the world? One of the most "Wesleyan" features of James's small epistle is the passion with which the author pleads the case of the poor (see introduction). The large-scale failure of the church to temper its lifestyle in order to live more justly would surely grieve the heart of Wesley today. We must use James's words here to ask whether we contemporary sons and daughters of Wesley have effectively sold our "birthright" of Wesley's social holiness for the pottage of materialism. If we have, not only have we sold out our heritage, but James says we may have dark, disappointing days ahead of us.

Justice is an issue with which evangelical Christians have had difficulty getting comfortable. It has often been associated with the more "mainstream" and "liberal" groups and churches. But to know the history of Wesley and the movement that bears his name is to have a deeply held commitment to basic justice that manifests itself clearly in the distribution of goods. There has been an overall failure within the evangelical community to understand and condemn the phenomena of social evil. We must know that, while some form of marketplace capitalism may be the most just system for the production and distribution of goods, given the desperate sinfulness of the human heart (see James 4:1-5) there are numerous opportunities to use such systems for evil purposes.

Wesley was prepared to speak out against the system when it failed the poor. That's part of the Wesleyan heritage. If we are hesitant to speak out against the system, it may be because we have bought into the system that rewards us with an upwardly mobile lifestyle. If so, it also indicates that we have compromised our positions in Wesley and, more importantly, in *true religion* as James describes it. If we do not wish to "rock the boat," it may be because we have grown too comfortable with our treasures which will rot and corrode in testimony against us someday. The evidence of our commitment to true religion in the coming years may well be best demonstrated by our willingness to stand for justice for the forgotten people of the earth. Our failure to do so will cry out against us and lead to the kind of future that James describes here for the materialistically oriented people of his day. Forewarned is forearmed!

ENDNOTES

[1]The Wisdom Literature includes the books of Job, Proverbs, Ecclesiastes, and Song of Songs (Song of Solomon). Also known as the Books of Poetry. These writings are collections of statements of wisdom, often dealing with the great issues of life, such as the problem of suffering, practical ethics and morality, and the meaning of life and love.

[2]Law refers to either the Levitical Code (all God's rules and regulations), the Ten Commandments, or the Pentateuch (the first five books of the Old Testament: Genesis, Exodus, Leviticus, Numbers, and Deuteronomy). Often capitalized when it means the Pentateuch or the Ten Commandments.

14

THE BARRIER OF IMPATIENCE

James 5:7-11

Be patient, then, brothers, until the Lord's coming (Jas. 5:7a). If materialism and its accompanying dangers are a barrier to true religion, so is impatience. Here James turns back to the readers who are more likely to be the victims described above, to address the temptation they might feel when victimized by injustice. Their tendency in such circumstances is to take matters into their own hands.

The unity of the Jewish-Christian community has been a continual concern to James in this letter, and here he speaks to that issue once again. The word **then** links this paragraph with the words of 5:1-6, but the addressees are surely different. In verse 6, James spoke of the lack of "resistance" on the part of the righteous. This seems to be an attempt to relate the righteousness of true religion to the attitude and practice of peacemaking (see 3:17). In the face of such blatant injustice, it would not be difficult to imagine the temptation to rise up and rebel against the wealthy exploiters and take a most satisfying vengeance. But James clearly warns against such actions. Instead, he counsels patience and perseverance in light of God's promised coming as Judge.

The patience James counsels here is specifically patience in the midst of suffering. Interestingly, the Greek word James uses for **patient** (5:7) is the same root word Jesus used in Luke's gospel when He, too, was counseling patience for His followers: "And will not God bring about justice for his chosen ones, who cry out to him day and night? Will he keep putting them off? I tell you, he will see that they get justice, and quickly. However, when the Son of Man comes, will he find faith on the earth?" (Luke 18:7-8). This reference is particularly noteworthy for its reference to the "cries" of those victims of injustice (Jas. 5:4). Beyond that, the question Jesus raised about finding faith on earth upon His return is James's very concern here—namely, that the righteous live and act like righteous people, that they put their faith in God the only Judge (see 4:11-12) and allow **the Lord's coming** to set matters right between them and their oppressors (5:7).

The reason for and the object of their patience is the Lord's coming. This is undoubtedly a reference to the second coming of Jesus which overshadows the thinking of this letter in so many ways. The Greek word for **coming** is the word *parousia*. This word literally means "presence" (see Philippians 1:26; 2:12). It came to be associated with the idea of "coming" or "advent." Specifically, its usage in New Testament times came to refer to the visit of a person of high rank.[1]

The writers of the New Testament adopted this word almost uniformly to refer to the return of Jesus to this earth (see Matthew 24:3, 27, 37, 39). The hope of Jesus' return to the earth as Lord and Judge has been the fondest hope of true believers from James's day to our own. This hope is the source of all Christian patience. It is the reason we can refrain from anger and vengeance, knowing that the only righteous Judge will take care of those matters in His own way and in His own time. This will be the crowning moment of justice in human history.

The essence of Old Testament Jewish hopes in the coming of Messiah to the earth were contained in the desperate longing for justice. Messiah's coming would be a time when the people of God would finally receive the honor that the world had denied them. So, too, the Christian hope is still grounded in the bodily return of Jesus to the earth. Modern people typically scoff at this doctrine—not surprisingly, those who would have the most to lose by such an event—but the practice of true religion necessitates a firm hope in the ultimate triumph of righteousness and justice. While we do not know when this coming will take place, despite the claims of any number of misguided people professing to have "inside" knowledge, we are to wait patiently for it.

The real question for us to wrestle with is the very question Jesus raised: "When the Son of Man comes, will he find faith on the earth?" (Luke 18:8). That has always been the issue for believers in regard to the return of Christ. Not, when will it be? But, will we be recognizable as His people when He gets here? That's the basis of James's exhortation to patience.

See how the farmer waits for the land to yield its valuable crop and how patient he is for the autumn and spring rains. You too, be patient

and stand firm, because the Lord's coming is near (Jas. 5:7b-8). As he has done prior to this, James turns again to nature to illustrate his point. There is no future for the farmer who tries to take matters into his own hands and bring the harvest on at his own bidding. Instead, the wise farmer is one who **waits.** He **waits for the land to yield** what it has promised to yield in its own time. He is **patient** even as he longs for the needed autumn and spring rains. This reference to weather has been suggested by some as further evidence that the Epistle of James was written for people living in Palestine and Syria who depended so much on the rains described here.

Beyond the geographical relevance of the illustration, James may have had in mind the use of this phrase in Deuteronomy 11. There Moses reminded Israel that the Promised Land they were about to enter would be very different from the land of Egypt. Specifically, Egypt was a place where they could sustain themselves, where they could take matters into their own hands and plant gardens and irrigate them with the plentiful waters of the Nile River. Egyptians never had to worry about drought because of the Nile. But the land they were about to enter now was a land where they would need to put their trust fully in God to deliver them: "Then I will send rain on your land in its season, both autumn and spring rains, so that you may gather in your grain, new wine and oil" (Deut. 11:14; see also Jeremiah 5:24).

The point behind James's reference to this would be the need for implicit trust in God in times of trial, rather than taking matters into one's own hands. This also sheds light on the reason why returning to Egypt became the act of faithlessness for the Old Testament Jew. Returning to Egypt was not only going back to bondage, but also represented a rejection of the life of faith. James wanted his readers to understand that taking matters into their own hands would be rejecting the life of trust and faith in God to deliver His people in His own time.

Like the wise farmer, we are counseled here to **be patient and stand firm, because the Lord's coming is near** (Jas. 5:8). This clause can be rendered more literally, "be longsuffering, establishing your hearts because the coming or presence of the Lord has drawn near." The Greek word translated **stand firm** in the New International Version means to "set fast," to "turn resolutely in a certain direction." This is the word used to describe Jesus in Luke 9:51: "As the time approached for him to be taken up to heaven, Jesus resolutely set out for Jerusalem." Paul used the term when writing to the Thessalonians in the same sense that James uses it: "May he strengthen your hearts so that you will be blameless and holy in the presence of our God and Father when our Lord Jesus comes with all his holy ones" (1 Thess. 3:13).

The early church conceived of the second coming of Jesus as a powerful motivator for righteousness (see 1 John 3:3). James does so here. He wants his readers to restrain the impulse to try to make things happen by their own efforts and instead use the coming of Christ as a motivating force in their lives. That has always been the way of real Christianity, true religion. Martin Luther said that Christians should live every day as if Jesus "was crucified yesterday, rose from the dead today, and was coming again tomorrow." That's James's advice for all of us.

James adds an additional piece of advice for the impatient: **Don't grumble against each other, brothers, or you will be judged. The Judge is standing at the door!** (Jas. 5:9). The Greek word which the New International Version translates here as **grumble** can be rendered *murmur,* a word which has a vivid history with the people of Israel (see Exodus 16; Numbers 14–16). The word is typically translated in the New Testament by the English word *groan,* with the idea of "sighing or groaning" because of undesirable circumstances. Here in James 5 it has a more direct application of groaning or complaining against someone.[2] The point James wishes to make is directly related to the experiences of Israel in Old Testament passages. In the wilderness wanderings, when times were tough and trials very real, the people had a way of turning on one another.

Most of us have had the experience of being in less-than-ideal circumstances and, as a result, growing increasingly impatient with those around us. That's what James wants his readers to anticipate and to avoid. These believers are oppressed and sorely tried. The tendency will be for them to grow ever more impatient with one another to the point where the attitudes and goals of true religion will be lost in the fury of open warfare between Christians. Sadly, church history is filled with examples of such things happening, and every local church has learned how quickly "molehills become mountains" when the pressure is on. That's why James counsels patience.

Further, the necessity of refraining from grumbling is presented in the context of the judgment which is to come. Grumbling or murmuring against our brothers and sisters is standing in judgment of them, which has been prohibited throughout this epistle. Beyond the mere prohibition of such attitudes, however, is the liability of our being judged by **the Judge** himself (Jas. 5:9; see Matthew 7:1-2). And, according to James, **the Judge is standing at the door.** Again, this demonstrates the prevailing belief of the early church in the immediate return of Jesus to the earth. In such an atmosphere, the idea of being before the Judge of the Ages any moment was a powerful motivating force.

Even though we have revised our understanding of the Second Coming to accommodate an unknown number of years between the first and second advents of Jesus, we should nevertheless allow the reality of judgment to temper our attitudes and actions toward one another. True religion does not use adverse circumstances, regardless of how difficult or trying, to excuse unloving behavior toward our brothers and sisters in Christ. Part of the meaning of having our "hearts established" is putting away the responses of the flesh and being patient toward one another, even as God has been patient toward us. James proceeds to illustrate this patience.

Brothers, as an example of patience in the face of suffering, take the prophets who spoke in the name of the Lord. As you know, we consider blessed those who have persevered (Jas. 5:10-11a). The prophets are offered by James **as an example**—literally, an exhibit for imitation—of what he means by **patience.** Here are people whose lives were marked by the blessing of being called by God and allowed to speak in His name. Yet all Jews knew that the lives of the prophets were anything but easy. Indeed, the prophets often were subjected to the most trying of circumstances demanding a quality of faithful, steadfast patience as they waited upon God for deliverance. This is what James wants his readers to see.

As he did in chapter 1, James again explodes the myth of so-called "success theology" which equates the ease and luxuries of life with God's blessing. Who can be more blessed than those who are honored to speak, "Thus saith the Lord"? But look at the circumstances of their lives. They were clearly God's people, but their lives were difficult and trying. They had to be patient, trusting fully in God to deliver them.

This call to patience fits into the overall context of the epistle in calling for understanding and steadfastness in the midst of trials (see James 1). Referring directly to 1:12, James reminds his readers that the definition of a blessed person is one who has **persevered** through the tough times (5:11). The Greek word for **persevered** literally means "stayed behind." Luke used this word in his gospel to describe Jesus' "staying behind" in Jerusalem after His parents left to return to Nazareth (2:43). Paul used the word in 1 Corinthians to describe the fortitude of real love (see 13:7).

Perhaps the clearest example of the word's usage here in James 5 is seen in the way the unknown author of Hebrews used it in chapter 12 of that epistle: "Let us fix our eyes on Jesus, the author and perfecter of our faith, who for the joy set before him endured the cross, scorning its shame, and sat down at the right hand of the throne of God. Consider him who endured such opposition from sinful men, so that you will not grow weary and lose heart" (Heb. 12:2-3). The significance of **persevered** (Jas. 5:11) for James is demonstrated here. The application lies in Hebrews 12:7: "Endure hardship as discipline; God is treating you as sons. For what son is not disciplined by his father?"

The Old Testament prophets, and especially Jesus Christ, demonstrated the importance of being able to endure patiently in the hope of a greater goal. James wants his readers never to lose sight of the goal which makes patience in tough times a realistic possibility. Perseverance in such circumstances is a sign of true religion. James and all the biblical writers agree that the blessing of God is not measured by the immediate or by the material. It comes to those who are steadfast to the end. The Deuteronomy 11 passage referred to above speaks of blessing and cursing in stark terms and relates both to the willingness of Israel to persevere through the lean times when it would be tempting not to trust God.[3] The godly examples of the prophets are meant to model the proper response in tough times for all who claim the mantle of true religion.

James offers one further illustration of patience: **You have heard of Job's perseverance and have seen what the Lord finally brought about. The Lord is full of compassion and mercy** (Jas. 5:11b). The saying that so-and-so has "the patience of Job" has become a cliché of sorts. The life and circumstances of Job's adventure with God have become the norm—the measuring stick—by which patience is evaluated. Rightly so, says James.

Job is the ultimate example of one who demonstrates perseverance in the face of trials. Because we know the story so well, we may tend to forget that this was not a pleasant experience for Job. Indeed, it was the most unpleasant of times for this chosen servant of God. Job didn't always respond with perfect patience or understanding. He had some days that were decidedly better than others. He grew discouraged at times, and he said some things he later regretted.

In short, Job was human. But the bottom line for Job and for all of us must be in the way we *finish*. Job finished well. And James specifically calls to the attention of his readers **what the Lord finally brought about.** The Greek word expressing the phrase **finally brought about** is the New International Version's translation of the Greek word *telos*. It means "end" or "purpose." It is the word that the New

Testament uses most often to speak of "perfection." The most important thing that happened to Job in the story of his up-and-down adventure is that those terrible experiences were used to serve God's ends or purposes for Job's life. In short, the times of testing brought forth perseverance which in turn brought forth completion and maturity. Job demonstrated what God means when He speaks of a mature, complete or "perfected" human being (see James 1:4). It is simply someone whose faith is steadfast, no matter what is going on around them. It is a person who in the worst of times is willing to trust God and wait patiently for His loving purposes to win the day.

James reminded his readers of his point earlier in 1:2-4. There we were told that if we will persevere in times of trial, then God will faithfully use those experiences to accomplish His ends and goals in our lives. That's what He did with Job, and that's what He will do with all who put their faith in Him and patiently persevere. Why? Because that's the kind of God He is. He is **full of compassion** (Jas. 5:11). The Greek word behind this phrase, used only here by James, is a compound word that is necessary to communicate adequately the measure of God's care for us. The part of the word that means "compassion" literally refers to inward parts or entrails. This is the word Luke used to describe the fate of Judas in Acts 1:18: "With the reward he got for his wickedness, Judas bought a field; there he fell headlong, his body burst open and all his intestines spilled out." The people of James's day associated deep affection with the inward parts, akin to the way we would speak of loving someone "with all our heart." Obviously, we mean more than a piece of coronary muscle weighing a pound or two.

Now, it's one thing to speak of human beings having such deep feelings, but it's quite another to speak of God in this fashion. The Greeks, who viewed the gods as unemotional and detached from humans, were scandalized by such thinking. But throughout the Bible, the God of Israel is portrayed as a Being who is filled with compassion for His creatures. The ultimate example of God's feelings for humankind are exemplified in the person of Jesus. The shortest verse in the Bible, John 11:35, says simply, "Jesus wept." But those words correctly model the way God relates to His children. That's the view of God that James presented in 1:17-18, and it's the view of God he returns to here.

God is also described as being **full of . . . mercy** (Jas. 5:11). Like compassion, **mercy** is part of the biblical portrait of God which is best demonstrated in the life of Jesus. While James is surely interested in justice for his readers, he is most content to assure them of God's mercy.

All of us should take great comfort in the reality and depths of God's mercy. None of us can afford only to demand justice from a holy God. We should also gratefully receive His offer of mercy.

James has spent a good amount of time and space in this short letter urging patience. We know that the kinds of problems confronting the believers to whom he writes are conducive to impatience. But is impatience really that harmful? James certainly thinks it is, and little has changed in our modern times to dispute his conclusion.

Few attitudes are more harmful to the cultivation of authentic spiritual life than impatience. And impatience is most pervasive when times are tough. The human spirit is not naturally steadfast. We tend to believe in our ability to take matters into our own hands and change things in accordance with our own desires, which are often deceitful and depraved. Further, the trying times of life have a way of making us turn on one another in destructive and evil ways. So the need for patience—for steadfastness—is always near. James encourages us to keep our hopes fixed on the compassionate and merciful Judge who will reward those who persevere with the crown of life (see James 1:12) and who will perfect His purposes for us in the midst of the storm (see 1:2-4).

ENDNOTES

[1]Walter Bauer, *A Greek-English Lexicon of the New Testament and Other Early Christian Literature,* 2nd ed., translated by William F. Arndt and F. Wilbur Gingrich (Chicago: University of Chicago Press, 1979), p. 630.

[2]Ibid., p. 766.

[3]Blessings and curses refer to the response of God to His people in accordance with their obedience to Him (blessings) or their disobedience (curses). In the Old Testament, God's power was invoked through power-laden words (blessings and curses) often spoken in prayer form. Through these blessings or curses, God's people would call upon Him to provide or care for them by affecting them in a positive way or those around them in a positive or negative way. In Judaism (the belief and cultural system of the Jewish people), some blessings were reserved for the priests, but others were a regular part of the synagogue services. Curses were much less prominent and were forbidden. In the New Testament, the ultimate blessing came from God to mankind in Jesus Christ, and blessings accompanied righteousness. Curses accompanied sin.

15

THE BARRIER OF IMPIETY

James 5:12

Above all, my brothers, do not swear—not by heaven or by earth or by anything else. Let your "Yes" be yes, and your "No," no, or you will be condemned (Jas. 5:12). The final barrier to true religion that James speaks of in this letter is the barrier of impiety. Impiety is literally the lack of reverence. Reverence is a feeling of awe; it is the feeling we have when we are conscious of being in God's presence. The lack of reverence is a severe obstacle to true religion.

Impiety can show up in a variety of forms in human behavior and attitudes. The practice of making oaths is the way a lack of reverence for God is manifested in the communities to whom James writes. The background of James's concern is obviously Jesus' words in the Sermon on the Mount in Matthew: "Again, you have heard that it was said to the people long ago, 'Do not break your oath, but keep the oaths you have made to the Lord.' But I tell you, Do not swear at all: either by heaven, for it is God's throne; or by the earth, for it is his footstool; or by Jerusalem, for it is the city of the Great King. And do not swear by your head, for you cannot make even one hair white or black. Simply let your 'Yes' be 'Yes,' and your 'No,' 'No'; anything beyond this comes from the evil one" (Matt. 5:33-37).

Jesus' words, in turn, were based on a couple of Old Testament texts. First, and not surprisingly for James's purposes, from Leviticus comes the command, "Do not swear falsely by my name and so profane the name of your God. I am the LORD" (Lev. 19:12). The third of the commandments recorded in Exodus also stands in the background to both Jesus' and James's concern over this issue: "You shall not misuse the name of the LORD your God, for the LORD will not hold anyone guiltless who misuses his name" (Exod. 20:7). In addition to these two well-known Old Testament texts, the book of Numbers contains a variety of prescriptions about oaths (see Numbers 30). There's more said in the Bible about oaths than about many other better-known issues.

So what's the problem? Is this merely a matter of obscure references to Jewish laws about making oaths? Hardly. Jesus, in the Sermon on the Mount, and now James both cite this as a problem that has to do with telling the truth. The real point behind the Jewish laws regarding oaths had to do with God's desire for His people to be truthful to one another and truthful to Him, since He is the always-present listener to our conversations.

The old saying, "The first casualty of war is the truth," helps us to grasp James's concern here. James is talking to communities that are enduring difficult times and are, in some respects, on the verge of open conflict. The first victim in an atmosphere of mistrust and insecurity is typically truth telling. In such an environment, people become suspicious of each other, and truthfulness can become very slippery.

That's the purpose behind oaths. To convince people who might not believe us otherwise, we underscore our words with oaths like "I swear to God," "Heaven being my witness," or "May the earth swallow me up if I'm not telling the truth." It's an all-too-common practice that we feel is needed when truthfulness is considered too difficult or too inconvenient.

To justify this kind of behavior, the Jews of the first century constructed elaborate formulas for swearing oaths which seemed to keep the "letter" of the Law, while permitting the practice to flourish.[1] For example, Jesus cited the common practice of the day of using oaths, but by swearing by something that had no binding power, the swearer felt free to break his word without having actually sinned. In short, the problem with oath making was that it was a way to sound honest without actually being honest. It was another example of virtual spirituality or false religion.

Not only does this practice undermine the practice of true religion, but it also undermines real community, which is a primary concern of James in this letter. When people utilize the latest linguistic games to avoid being truthful with one another, real community—in any Christian sense—is simply not possible. In an atmosphere already tense with class conflict and judgmental spirits, James worries that oath making merely contributes to the suspicion and mistrust that poisons the fellowship of the believing community.

This epistle's absolute relevance to modern Western culture shows itself yet again at this point. We live in the culture of the "big lie." Words are used deceitfully on purpose. Advertisers bombard us daily with claims that push the limits of credibility and truth. We have come to the place of assuming that our elected leaders routinely lie to us, resulting in our re-creating the atmospheres of Matthew 5:33-37 and James 5:12. We are part of a "community" that pretty much expects to be lied to, so we employ devices that are meant to reassure people that they really can trust us. The employment of oaths is intended to signify an island of truth in a sea of falsehood. James is saying that the presence of such "necessities" as oaths is an indictment upon a community claiming to be followers of the One who claimed simply, "I am the truth" (see John 14:6).

In the Sermon on the Mount, Jesus taught about the kind of community that truly represents the Kingdom He inaugurated on earth. In that kind of community where God is always reverenced—where we act and speak in light of His constant presence among us—oaths become unnecessary. When we live and act as if we live every moment in God's presence, we value our fellow human beings as God's children who thus deserve the truth. Again, oaths become unnecessary. A simple "yes" or "no" will suffice.

Authentic Christianity has been described as a "countercultural" way of life. It's becoming increasingly clear that simple honesty and truth telling run unmistakably counter to modern culture. James's conviction is that the Jewish-Christian communities to whom he writes should be places where words *do* matter and where truth is a way of life, not an exception that has to be noted by the invocation of some special "truth-telling formula." He urges his readers to be the kind of people who simply mean what they say, apart from any dramatic appeal to oaths. Failing to be that kind of people betrays an inability to understand the nature of true religion. It also betrays the fundamental impiety of our lives where we act as if God isn't present when we play the cultural games of "acceptable" dishonesty.

Jesus said that the Temple, Jerusalem and the earth should not be invoked in oaths because they are parts of something that belong to God. Acting otherwise demonstrates a patent lack of reverence. That's why such actions are condemned by the Old Testament Law, by Jesus, and now here by James.

Living as if God were absent is the exact opposite of real religion, which lives in the constant presence of the Creator. Further, buying into the cultural ideas of honesty and truth telling effectively forecloses the possibility of a genuine Christian community. An authentic Christian community is the only community that can navigate successfully through the issues and problems that James has mentioned in this epistle. It is that kind of community that James describes in the final paragraph of the letter.

ENDNOTE

[1]Law refers to either the Levitical Code (all God's rules and regulations), the Ten Commandments, or the Pentateuch (the first five books of the Old Testament: Genesis, Exodus, Leviticus, Numbers, and Deuteronomy). Often capitalized when it means the Pentateuch or the Ten Commandments.

Part Six

THE DISPOSITIONS OF TRUE RELIGION

James 5:13-20

The Epistle of James is written to church people living in community. Beyond any individualistic interpretations of this letter, the concern of James with the vitality of the community must be remembered. Given this concern, it is fitting that James brings his epistle to a close with a beautiful description of what real community is about. In these final verses, James pictures for us the prospects and possibilities of those who together share the quest of true religion.

Throughout this short letter, James has addressed the problems of "part-time" religion. He has chronicled the curse of double-minded faith which effectively barricades the blessing reserved for those who practice true religion. In 5:12, James encouraged his readers to reject the temptation to play at community. He urged them to resist adopting the culturally acceptable approach to truth telling and honesty. In a real community, people's words are enough—yes or no. This was portrayed within the context of impiety, a lack of reverence for God.

The impious life is the life that assumes God hides out in His little heaven and leaves us alone on earth to run our own show. True religion, on the other hand, brings God into every part of human existence. This is the necessary starting point for building an authentic Christian community—the realization of God's constant presence and involvement in our lives. James's final paragraph shows us how this kind of life is led.

James brings his letter to a close by presenting a picture of authentic, wholehearted faith. He speaks here of "dispositions"—attitudes and actions that characterize the genuine Christian community. What we find described here is all too rare in an "image is everything" world. The type of community pictured here is scarce even among the thousands of Christian churches that dot the landscape of much of North America. But there is a reason for that, a reason that hearkens back to the fundamental message of this small but powerful letter. The qualities of life and soul that James describes in these final eight verses are only available to those who have "purified their double-minds" (see 4:8).

James is not trying to discourage his readers or any of us by showing us our shortcomings. Rather he seeks to encourage us with the possibilities of a genuinely wholehearted embrace of true religion. Here is the community of the truly religious.

16

THE DISPOSITION OF AUTHENTIC SPIRITUALITY

James 5:13-16a

The kind of community that lay behind James's concern in 5:12 is really not much of a community at all. It is more of a gathering of individuals. It is the kind of place where people are typically left to their own designs to deal with the ups and downs of life. Thus, oath taking is a necessary part of the game in order to convince people you really mean business.

But that's not the Christian community James portrays here. The intentional transparency of authentic spirituality comes through clearly: **Is any one of you in trouble? He should pray. Is anyone happy? Let him sing songs of praise. Is any one of you sick? He should call the elders of the church to pray over him and anoint him with oil in the name of the Lord. And the prayer offered in faith will make the sick person well; the Lord will raise him up. If he has sinned, he will be forgiven. Therefore confess your sins to each other and pray for each other so that you may be healed** (Jas. 5:13-16a).

Looking at this paragraph in its entirety gives us the advantage of seeing the whole picture. And that's precisely what James means to portray: wholeness. Instead of religious faith being something that a person "uses" when convenient, James wants his readers to know that true religion is an all-encompassing way of life. That's the essence of "wisdom" thinking in the Jewish tradition. The Law was given to help us live in healthy, productive ways.[1] It is intended to touch all aspects of

197

our being. That is why James chooses a variety of human experiences here and connects them to a variety of spiritual realities.

If you are **in trouble** (Jas. 5:13), you are not in it by yourself. You can pray! This recalls James's encouraging of his readers in 1:5 to ask God to provide what they lack in their fight against trials. In fact, the word **trouble** refers to the very kinds of hardships that must be endured through perseverance. This shows James's full-circle return to his opening theme in the final paragraph. Yes, life is difficult, and it can be filled with troubles. But we are not out there on our own. We must cultivate the disposition of prayerfulness in our lives. We must nurture a habit of mind and soul, the practice of taking everything in our lives into the presence of this giving God (see 1:17-18). Prayer is as natural as breathing in the practice of true religion.

If you are **happy,** then **praise** God and sing (5:13)! Life is meant to be an act of worship. This is a recognition of all those gifts God gives to us (see 1:17-18). Actually, this use of the word **happy** is directly related to the preceding reference to **trouble.** The word **happy**—being cheerful—has the idea of being encouraged in the midst of hardship. Besides James's usage here, the original Greek word is found only three other times in the New Testament, all in Acts 27. That is the story of Paul's shipwreck where Paul twice encouraged the crew to "keep up [their] courage" (Acts 27:22, 25) because God had assured Paul that they would survive. Then, in verse 36, Luke recorded that the crew was encouraged by seeing Paul eat, so they began to eat as well. Thus, to be happy is not necessarily related to everything going your way, but it is to experience joy in the midst of difficulty. This is a disposition that makes worship something extremely sacred in the eyes of God.

This is another linkage to James 1 and the admonition to "consider it pure joy" (Jas. 1:2) when we encounter trials of various kinds. Experiencing victory and triumph in times of trial is all the more reason to look to God, this time in grateful worship. The word the New International Version translates here as the phrase, **Let him sing songs of praise** (5:13), is the Greek word that gives us the term *Psalms.* Psalms was the hymnal of Israel, so it's not surprising that in times of victory and triumph James encourages his readers, steeped in the religion of Israel, to turn to their national source of celebration.

The essence of true Christian worship comes through clearly here as we see people in the midst of life's experiences—some good, some bad—admonished to pause in order to include God in those experiences. In troubling times, real believers seek after God in prayer as the compassionate and merciful Father who gives what is lacking to all who seek in authentic faith. In times of victory and triumph, God is properly celebrated as the Giver of every good gift. He is recognized as the One who is part of every element of our lives and present with us through it all.

Rather than presenting worship as some "feel-good" meeting where everyone is trying to forget about the rest of their lives, James says we should pursue just the opposite. We should aim for an authenticity in our worship that dares to place the context of our entire lives in the broader context of God's love and grace. The one who can do that has reason to be cheerful, no matter what is happening at the moment. What a taste of realism authentic Christian worship is! It is people experiencing all the possibilities of human life, coming together to place those experiences in the larger context of true religion. That's authentic spirituality. And that disposition of real worship characterizes the people of God.

James continues in 5:14 by saying, in essence, "If anyone is sick, he is not alone." The reality of authentic Christian community makes such concerns community concerns. In such moments, they **should call the elders** (Greek: *Presbuteros,* from whence comes our English word *Presbyterian*) **to pray over him and anoint him with oil.** Oil has long been the symbol of the presence of the Holy Spirit. To anoint a sick person with oil is to acknowledge the presence of God and His willingness to be a part of this circumstance of human life.

Actually, the word **sick,** though well attested in the New Testament, can also be rendered *weak.* If that word were employed here, it would broaden the concern back to the issue of chapter 1 of the epistle, regarding the ones who fear their ability to persevere through temptation. But though this does appear to be an alternative way of looking at the verse, it has been associated historically with the possibility of healing prayer.

The interesting feature of this exhortation to call for the elders of the church to anoint and pray for the sick, James says, is that having anointed **in the name of the Lord . . . the prayer offered in faith** will heal the sick and **raise him up.** Further, if sin is involved, James says it **will be forgiven** (5:14b-15). This recalls the story in Mark 2:1-12 where the paralyzed man was lowered through the roof and was healed by Jesus after He pronounced the man forgiven of his sins.

One of the first things that strikes us from Mark's story is how it answers the question of "whose faith" is at issue in healing a sick person. It would seem from Mark's story that it was a combination of the faith of the paralytic man himself and his helpful friends. If that was the case, then James is saying that the faith of the sick person in calling the elders in the first place, combined with the faith of the praying elders themselves, is what brings healing. Remember James's warning in 1:6-8 about asking for something out of doubt? (Those men who carried the paralytic to Jesus represent the kind of combination of "faith and deeds" that James celebrates in chapter 2! That's putting into practice what you believe.)

The second feature that is striking from the Mark 2 story, in applying it here, is the way physical healing is combined with spiritual healing or forgiveness. In Mark's story, Jesus forgave the sins of the paralytic man before He healed him. The religious leaders were offended by Jesus' pronouncement of forgiveness. It was in response to their reaction to His granting of forgiveness that Jesus healed the man to show His authority to forgive sin, which He said is much harder than mere physical healing.

If James has this story in mind here, he is stressing the essentially redemptive nature of Christian spirituality. While healing is certainly a possibility, not everyone is likely to be healed. Failing to be healed is not eternally significant. But failing to be forgiven is. James's desire to link physical and spiritual healing is in the best tradition of vital Christianity. The ultimate issue with which praying elders ought to be concerned has to do with forgiveness.

This leads to his summarizing statement in this paragraph: Therefore, on the basis of this all encompassing spiritual approach to life, **confess your sins to each other and pray for each other so that you may be healed** (Jas. 5:16a). Life in a genuine Christian community is life lived apart from pretense. It assumes honesty and truthfulness, and as we shall see below, it assumes authentic love for one another. In that kind of environment, healing can be accomplished because much of the healing process involves confession, or "coming clean."

To **confess** is literally, "to say the same thing." Thus, to confess our sins would be "to say the same thing" about our sins that God would say about them. Needless to say, this is why genuine confession is so rare. We would much rather put our own "spin" on our sins. But John assured us in his first epistle that when we adopt a posture of genuine confession, healing is the consequence: "If we confess our sins, he is faithful and just and will forgive us our sins and purify us from all unrighteousness" (1 John 1:9). Note the emphasis of John on purifying from unrighteousness. It has also been James's interest throughout the letter.

This verse is another indication of the affirmation that Wesley would have for James's epistle. Wesley's "bands"—small groups of believers who met regularly to share their lives with one another—practiced "confession." In these sessions, there would be strict accountability for the sins in one's life, not for the purpose of judgment, but for the purpose of prayerful support, encouragement and, most of all, healing forgiveness. Wesley knew that this was a key to growing deep in the Lord. He and his followers have practiced it throughout the years. It is heartening to see this kind of small group accountability becoming an ever-growing part of the spiritual exercises of many modern Christians.

The relationship between one's physical health and spiritual well-being is becoming clearer all the time. How many sick people in our world could be healed if they knew they could be forgiven? How much of the physical pain in our world is rooted in spiritual causes? James's admonition here to holistic spirituality in the context of real community is a key component to the practice of true religion.

One truth that easily could be overlooked here is the emphasis on the church as a healing community. James's concern throughout this letter is to preserve the health and vitality of the Christian community—the church. Among other reasons for wanting to do so is that the health of individual Christians depends directly upon the health of the Christian community. For those of us who have grown up in the Protestant West, which emphasizes individualism, that is a difficult concept to grasp. But James's words here about healing demonstrate that it is in community that the healing grace of God operates most effectively.

This ought to give us pause as we watch any number of high-profile "healers" going from city to city, setting up their ministries and calling people to come and be healed. James and the other New Testament writers would be absolutely aghast at such practices. Their view would be that if you want to be healed, you should go to the church where people know you—know you well. In fact, you should gather with people who know you so well that you can confess your faults to them, so that not only physical healing is possible, but spiritual healing as well. High-powered individuals claiming to have the healing power of God apart from the community of faith would be considered an oddity, if not an outright heresy.

The church, the body of Christ, functioning together in love and honest accountability, becomes a powerful place of authentic healing of every sort. That's the kind of community James wants his readers to embody. That's the kind of community that can deal effectively with the trials of human life.

The disposition of spirituality that emerges here is a welcome respite from the modern tendency to neatly compartmentalize our spiritual lives into one section marked "Sundays Only!" That is precisely the kind of "religion" that James has been arguing against throughout his letter. When religion has a little room all to itself, its real purpose—that of affecting all of life—is thwarted. The way of wisdom—the way of true religion—is to live all of life in the presence of God. One of the identifying dispositions of true religion is the ability and the willingness to practice the entirety of life within the reality of God's redeeming presence, and to do so with others who share that disposition of heart and soul.

ENDNOTE

¹Law refers to either the Levitical Code (all God's rules and regulations), the Ten Commandments, or the Pentateuch (the first five books of the Old Testament: Genesis, Exodus, Leviticus, Numbers, and Deuteronomy). Often capitalized when it means the Pentateuch or the Ten Commandments.

17

THE DISPOSITION OF RIGHTEOUS PRAYER

James 5:16b-18

The prayer of a righteous man is powerful and effective. Elijah was a man just like us. He prayed earnestly that it would not rain, and it did not rain on the land for three and a half years. Again he prayed, and the heavens gave rain, and the earth produced its crops** (Jas. 5:16b-18). Another disposition that characterizes the community which faithfully practices true religion is that of **effective** prayerfulness. Notice how James directly links **prayer** that is **powerful and effective** to being **righteous.** Righteousness is the fruit of true religion and God's purpose in our lives (see 1:20). Therefore, James wants his readers to grasp the necessary link between righteousness and the effectiveness of their prayers.

The final phrase of 5:16 literally reads, "A petition of a righteous man being made effective is very strong." That literal rendering enables us to sense James's point. For one thing, the word "petition" singles out one aspect of prayer, namely making requests of God. To ask God for things is to believe He can give them, but James argues that petitions accompanied by righteousness are all the more effective. In other words, a righteous life is the key to an effective prayer life.

The Greek word James used to express the idea of the prayer "being made effective" is the word Paul employed when reminding the Philippians that "it is God who *works* in you to will and to *act* according to his good purpose" (Phil. 2:13, my emphasis). God always acts with effectiveness; His purposes in acting are realized. Paul's use of the word clearly shows the idea of "effective working," which is what James seeks to convey. The particular form of the word in the Greek also underscores James's intention to link righteousness with the effect of the petition itself.[1] So, in keeping with his overall emphasis upon the need for true religion permeating every aspect of our lives, James argues here that the effectiveness of our prayers depends upon the kind of wholehearted commitment that results in righteousness.

James's choice of the example of Elijah shows us how significant righteousness is in making our prayers powerful and effective. First, note James's emphasis that **Elijah was a man just like us** (Jas. 5:17a). In one sense this is difficult to believe, for Elijah was one of the more colorful characters of the Old Testament. He was considered the model Jewish prophet, and all the Jewish-Christians in the communities to whom James wrote would know his story well. The episode from Elijah's life that is best remembered is the incident on Mt. Carmel where the contest was held pitting Elijah against the prophets of Baal (see 1 Kings 18). Elijah was presented as one who sought after righteousness and thus was powerful and effective in his prayers.

Given James's intent to show the necessary correlation between effective praying and righteousness, Elijah serves as the perfect model. For one thing, Elijah's righteousness was beyond question. This is what makes him stand out so in the narratives of 1 Kings. One of James's key themes has been to connect faith and life, walk and talk, and so on. Being what you claim to be is the proof of one's faith. It is because Elijah walked closely to God that his prayers were effective. James wants his readers to grasp the potential for prayer, but just as important, he wants them to understand the need for a righteous life to realize that kind of potential. Because Elijah was **just like us,** there is no reason that such effectiveness in prayer could not be duplicated by the Christians reading James's epistle.

James's story from Mt. Carmel also proves that powerful prayer changes things. The background of the story in 1 Kings plays right into James's purposes here. The immediate problem leading to this contest was a drought—brought on by prayer to teach Ahab a lesson. The people of Israel, instead of turning to God for help in the drought, increasingly turned to the pagan god, Baal. Baal was a storm god. He was supposed to be effective in solving the problems of drought. The contest on Mt. Carmel showed how much more effective prayer to the true God was than calling upon Baal. Remember, James wants his readers to prayerfully trust God to deliver them from their problems, rather than turn to the pagan ideas of false religion that surround them.

In the 1 Kings story, Elijah (along with the rest of Israel) watched as God responded directly to his prayers on the mountain that day. As James reminds us, it was *prayer* to God, not Baal, that solved the problem. And the answer came down from heaven (see James 1:17-18; 3:17), which is where the real answers to our problems will originate as well. To claim that **Elijah was a man just like us** (Jas. 5:17a) is to say, then, that all of us can be encouraged that God will respond to our prayers in appropriately similar ways. Why try to take matters into our own hands when God is so willing to grant the petitions of a righteous person?

But the key to such effectiveness remains righteousness, which includes asking or praying in the will of God. Elijah's ministry was characterized by absolute obedience to God. He did what he did in the 1 Kings story as a result of hearing God's word to him. Elijah did not act presumptuously on his own, making his own plans (see James 4:13-17). Because Elijah acted in accordance with the will of God, he saw dramatic results in his life and ministry, and especially in response to his prayers.

James wants his readers to make the connection between obeying God and then asking in prayer for those things which are in accordance with the will of God. They must never suppose that they can ask with selfish motives and be effective and powerful in their prayers (see 4:2-3). Just as Elijah's prophetic success is based on obedience to God, so the prayers of the people will be fruitful in accordance with their righteousness— their ability to live and pray in God's will.

It is absolutely necessary to maintain the kind of close relationship with God where we know what God wants, because effectiveness in prayer is based upon seeking *God's* desires rather than our own. Elijah demonstrates the possibilities of prayer when one walks close to God in righteous obedience. James seeks to encourage an active kind of righteousness in the lives of his readers, particularly as it relates to their prayers. For it is the righteous person who truly knows God's will and, as a result, can pray powerfully and effectively. The real prayer of faith which is able to raise the sick and bring about the forgiveness of sin is the prayer offered in accordance with God's will by the people walking close to Him.

James's emphasis on righteous prayer is a window into understanding both the prayerlessness and the powerlessness of our day. We have observed many who have generally given up on prayer because they have decided either that it doesn't work or that they can meet their own needs more efficiently. James spoke to some of these issues in his fourth chapter. But, more likely, the prayerlessness of our times is a result of divorcing righteousness from prayer. The halfhearted prayers of halfhearted people hardly qualify as the kinds of prayers James commends here. The shallowness of our lives and faith commitments has caught up with us to the point that we are experiencing large-scale power failures in terms of our prayers.

It has been James's intent from the beginning of his letter to stress the necessity of having one's heart properly attuned to God before we expect God to answer our prayers (see James 1:5-8). The problem with much of the prayers in the modern church is not a problem with God. The problem is with those who pray. If we choose to live according to our own desires, while expecting God to give us answers to our haphazard prayers, we are bound to be disappointed.

The character or disposition of true religion is that of righteous prayer. Righteous prayer is prayer that flows naturally and powerfully out of the depth of one's relationship with God. Knowing God, we know His will, and, knowing His will, we pray in His name. That kind of prayer is effective and powerful. The alternative is the barren and prayerless spirituality that characterizes so much of modern Christendom.

There is one other possible reason why James employs the example of Elijah here. It has to do with his overall emphasis on solving the problem of double-mindedness. Elijah's ministry came at a point in Israel's history where double-minded religion had won the day. In fact, the real purpose behind the contest on Mt. Carmel was to win the people over from their flirtations with the pagan god, Baal. This was at the heart of Elijah's challenge to the people of Israel who observed the contest that day: "So Ahab sent word throughout all Israel and assembled the prophets on Mount Carmel. Elijah went before the people and said, 'How long will you waver between two opinions? If the LORD is God, follow him; but if Baal is God, follow him.' But the people said nothing" (1 Kings 18:20-21).

Here is double-mindedness in the Old Testament. The episode on Mt. Carmel, including Elijah's example of powerful, effective and righteous prayer, was meant to enable Israel to stop their wavering between God and Baal. That James appeals to this well-known incident to make his point about the need for righteousness (and total commitment to God) in prayer seems too obvious to be coincidental.

The connection is strengthened when we remember the meaning of Elijah's name. This prophet's name literally means "my God is Jah" (from "Yahweh," the Hebrew name for God). Not only does Elijah provide the perfect example of righteous prayer, but he serves—by virtue of his name—as the opposite of double-minded religion. Whatever else they could say about Elijah, with a name like that, no one could say he wasn't clearly committed.

What would happen if our commitment to God was as obvious to those around us as was Elijah's? Would not the whole atmosphere of our lives radically change? Would not our prayers become powerful and effective? Would not the petty little problems that plague us and divide us disappear into insignificance in light of the reality of knowing God? This kind of up-front, total commitment is the disposition of true religion—a disposition that makes prayer a weapon of redemptive change in a world desperate for righteousness.

ENDNOTE

[1] The word here is *energoumene*, a participle in the middle voice. To speak in the middle voice is to show action that is dependent upon something other than the one acting. In this case, it means that the prayer is effective because of its being prayed by a righteous man—it is "made effective" by the presence of righteousness.